The President as Interpreter-in-Chief

CHATHAM HOUSE STUDIES IN POLITICAL THINKING
SERIES EDITOR: George J. Graham, Jr.
Vanderbilt University

THE PRESIDENT AS INTERPRETER-IN-CHIEF

Mary E. Stuckey

University of Mississippi

Chatham House Publishers, Inc.
Chatham, New Jersey

THE PRESIDENT AS INTERPRETER-IN-CHIEF

Chatham House Publishers, Inc.
Box One, Chatham, New Jersey 07928

Publisher: Edward Artinian
Production supervisor: Chris Kelaher
Cover design: Antler & Baldwin Design Group, Inc.
Composition: Bang, Motley, Olufsen
Printing and binding: Courier Companies, Inc.

Library of Congress Cataloging-in-Publication Data

Stuckey, Mary E.
    The President as interpreter-in-chief / Mary E. Stuckey
        p.   cm.
    Includes bibliographical references and index.
    ISBN 0-934540-92-6
    1. United States—Politics and government—1945– 2. United States—Politics and government–1933–1945. 3. Rhetoric—Political aspects—United States—History—20th century. 4. Presidents—United States—History—20th century. I. Title.
E743.S83   1991
353.03′5—dc20   91-13427
                                                   CIP

Manufactured in the United States of America
      10 9 8 7 6 5 4 3 2 1

To the memory of Bill Davisson,
who liked fairy tales

To laugh often and love much;

To win the respect of intelligent persons and the affection of children;

To earn the approbation of honest citizens and endure the betrayal of false friends;

To appreciate beauty;

To find the best in others;

To give of one's self;

To leave the world a bit better, whether by a healthy child, a garden patch, or a redeemed social condition;

To have played and laughed with enthusiasm and sung with exultation;

To know even one life has breathed easier because you have lived—that is success.

— *Ralph Waldo Emerson*

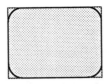

Contents

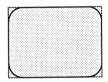

Acknowledgments

ALL AUTHORS owe a tremendous debt to many people. This is particularly true in my case, where people from different disciplines have given me the benefit of their encouragement, advice, and support. Whatever faults remain are solely due to my stubborn insistence and are completely my responsibility.

First and foremost, I would like to thank Robert E. Denton, Jr., for his time, help, and advice. Kathleen Kendall, Craig A. Smith, and Justin Gustainis all sent many helpful and interesting ideas in my direction. George Graham, series editor at Chatham House, furnished insightful (and expeditious) commentary. Thomas Cronin provided encouragement and helpful comments. The students in my presidency class and American government seminars provided insight and enough questions to keep me always honest. I thank them.

I spent the fall of 1990 as a National Endowment for the Humanities fellow at the Project on the Rhetoric of Inquiry (POROI), the University of Iowa. Not only did this allow me to devote my time and energy to completing this project but I also gained immeasurably from the criticism and advice of the other scholars. They gave me the benefit of their advice, criticism, and support. Many thanks are due to these POROI scholars for their kindness, their generosity, and their scholarly acumen: Fred Antczak, Francis A. Beer, G.R. Boynton, Kenneth Cmiel, Marianne Constable, Robert Harriman, William Lewis, John Nelson, and Ira Strauber. Special thanks to John Nelson and Katy Neckerman for administrating the workshop.

Projects such as this depend on the support of family and friends. Susan Prieto, Jennifer Hall Beese, Joseph Dolan, Karen Dolan, Mike Ferry, Laurie Rhodebeck, and Melanie Trexler provided all the support any one could ask for, and then some. To my parents, I owe a special debt of gratitude. Once again, I thank them for their encouragement, support, and pride in me.

At Chatham House, my thanks to Chris Kelaher for all his hard work and to Edward Artinian for his guidance and support.

This book is dedicated to the memory of William I. Davisson, who touched the lives of many students, scholars, and colleagues in ways that will never be forgotten. Thank you, Bill.

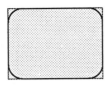

Introduction: The President as
Interpreter-in-Chief

THE PRESIDENT has become the nation's chief storyteller, its interpreter-in-chief. He[1] tells us stories about ourselves, and in so doing he
tells us what sort of people we are, how we are constituted as a community. We take from him not only our policies but our national self-iden-
tity.

The president's talk has become the central focus of our political attention, and he talks to us mainly through the medium of television.
American presidents, like all political actors, live in and adapt to complex
political environments. Television is an increasingly important part of
those environments. As the nation has increased in size and complexity, as
the franchise and our notions of what and who constitute the American
polity have changed and expanded, and as traditional linkages between the
leaders and the led have eroded, public and persuasive features of the presidency have gained in relative importance to more traditional and explicitly constitutional functions. The argument of this book is that the medium of communication, interacting with historical and social pressures,
influences presidential decisions about what to say and how to say it.

The presidency is a fluid institution. At any point in time the office
is a combination of constitutional mandate, established practice, and the
personal style and preferences of the current occupant. Not all presidents
exhibit all the changes discussed in this book all the time. Personal pro-
clivities and preferences affect how each president adapts to the evolving
institution. Presidents respond to the legacies of their predecessors (lega-

cies that are subject to changing interpretations), to prevailing political problems and possibilities, and to their understanding of the "final" judgments of history. Increasingly, a large part of the prevailing political problems and possibilities involves television.

How past presidents used the communication media constrain their successors in the office. Presidents prior to Franklin Delano Roosevelt had a wide degree of latitude in deciding whether or not to maintain a high public profile; since FDR, that choice has diminished. Presidents can no longer choose whether to engage in public leadership, only what form that leadership will take. As presidents increasingly emphasize the ceremonial aspects of the office, its deliberative possibilities have eroded. This in turn limits the presidents' rhetorical options and opportunities.

Initially, presidential images were transmitted through a variety of media and were the distillation of a variety of factors: past reputation, party affiliation, previous offices held, and so forth. As television comes to dominate other forms of political communication, the images it projects become the dominant images of the president and presidential candidates. Franklin Roosevelt and Harry Truman seem more complex, more dynamic than current presidents because our images of them were more varied, our sources of information more rich. As television images dominate, presidential images flatten, become simplified.

The American mass media, and the news reporters that represent them, are the most visible and constant link between the leaders and the led. Most Americans receive most of their political information, develop most of their relationships with political actors, through the media. Television has supplanted print and radio as the primary source of information about politics, and presidents increasingly rely on television to communicate with the American people. This change in the medium of communication brings with it important changes in the president's environment and contributes to changes in perceptions and conduct of the office of the presidency.

These changes can be seen most clearly through a close analysis of presidential speech. By beginning with the administration of Franklin Roosevelt, we can observe the changes in the media and in the conduct of presidential speech as they unfold and develop over time. As the television cameras intrude ever more deeply into the presidency, the fact of television becomes an ever more critical element in the complex environment surrounding the presidency. Television does not simply mean that presidents talk more. It also means that they talk differently. This has consequences for both the presidency as an institution and the American polity in which that institution is embedded. This book presents an analysis of those differences and seeks to discover how presidential communication has changed with the inception of the modern presidency and its interaction with the modern mass media, especially television. This analysis is based on the belief that the medium through which a president communicates affects the nature of the communication and that understanding television's relationship to presidential communication is a vital component in our understanding of the current presidency.

The dominance of television as a forum for presidential communication has meant changing the strategies involved with creating, maintaining, and directing public support. Presidents who communicate over television tend to adopt strategies that lead to diffuse support for the person who is president, rather than specific support for the policies espoused by a president. This does not mean that there was ever a golden age of presidential communication when presidents communicated in a sane, rational way solely about policy proposals (it is not even my purpose to inquire whether and how such communication might or might not be desirable), but I do suggest that the balance has shifted away from the substance of policy making and toward generalized support.

Something valuable has been lost in making this shift. In deemphasizing the president's deliberative role in favor of the ceremonial role, our notions of community, of what it means to be a member of a polity, have been eroded, and cheapened, have become less authentic because our beliefs are increasingly divorced from our practices. Our political life has suffered from the degradation of our political language. As presidential interpretations have shifted from the long argumentative and premise-laden discourses of earlier years to the visually privileged assertive discourse that characterizes modern televised communication, the American polity is prompted to lose sight of its origins, its philosophical grounding, and its self-understanding.[2] Presidents continue to celebrate our national identity through ceremony; they increasingly fail to apply it publicly through deliberative rhetoric. This failure undermines the public understanding of our national ethos.

Presidents alone are not responsible for this impoverishment. Nor is television technology. The interaction of the two, with the consent and often the enthusiastic support of the American public, has helped to create a situation in which certain kinds of communication are privileged above others. Few presidents are fools. Most of them are fully cognizant of and capable of adapting to specific strategic imperatives. Communicating with the American public through television has become one of those imperatives. The ways in which presidents and presidential candidates currently adapt to that imperative has led to an impoverishment of our political language and a corresponding impoverishment of our political understanding.

Presidential Speech as a Category for Study

Scholars in the field of communication studies have long been interested in presidential speech and presidential speech making.[3] The interest of political scientists is of more recent vintage.[4] Using a variety of methods and approaches, these scholars have found that presidents not only talk more but that they increasingly emphasize ceremonial occasions and eschew policy discussion in favor of symbolic appeals and stances (sometimes even transforming the latter into the former).[5] This is particularly clear in a campaign environment.[6]

The authors of the Constitution feared precisely these aspects of the presidency and sought to curb the public, and potentially demagogic, features of the office. As the electorate expanded, beginning in the early nineteenth century, and as Progressive reforms opened the political process to that expanded electorate, the public became an increasingly important part of presidential calculations. Presidential communication was no longer restricted to a relatively small group of homogeneous elites. Presidential audiences grew and diversified.

At the same time, presidential responsibilities also grew and diversified. As the office became more central to the governing process and the public imagination, scholars and presidents developed and articulated new understandings of presidential power. Richard Neustadt, for instance, began a shift away from formal, functional, and constitutional understandings of the presidency toward an informal model of bargaining and persuasion.[7] But the broad focus remained on the president's relationship with other governing elites.

This understanding of the presidency was supplemented, in the 1980s, by a new scholarly focus on the president's relationship with the public. Jeffrey K. Tulis and Samuel Kernell offer both descriptive and evaluative analyses of the increased presidential focus on public support rather than elite consensus.[8] For them, the deliberative processes of the presidency are being eroded,[9] and policies are serving the president's rhetorical needs.[10] The strategies involved with strengthening public support for the individual who is currently president lead to a weakening of the institution of the presidency. When the president depends upon public support, his rhetoric will be designed to maintain that support.

4

Introduction

Presidents communicate to the mass public more than ever before. In addition, they increasingly engage in this communication through television, which in turn alters the form and the content of presidential communication.

Televised Communication

One of television's most important effects is the creation of a "dramatised society":

> For the first time a majority of the population has regular and constant access to drama, beyond occasion or season. But what is really new—so new I think it is difficult to see its significance—is that it is not just a matter of audiences for particular plays. It is that drama, in quite new ways, is built into the rhythms of everyday life.[11]

As the world "out there" becomes more complex, more unknowable, we increasingly resort to dramatic forms—storytelling—to make that world intelligible. Humans have always relied on stories to render the world meaningful,[12] but television, in rendering drama so pervasively, places extraordinary emphasis on the person of the storyteller in a way that is not merely an expansion of the previous role.

The president has become a presenter; public argument has been largely supplanted by public assertion. This change is a matter of kind as well as degree, and is related to changes in society as well as technology.

"Television is very much a poor man's medium: the interest-poor, the education-poor, and the information-poor."[13] Given that "television gives considerably more attention to politics than most viewers feel they need or want,"[14] politicians know that behaving in ways that increase their dramatic impact will help keep audiences interested and more supportive. They must feed into the dramatic demands audiences are accustomed to having fulfilled through television drama. Solutions must be found quickly, presented dramatically, and fulfilled completely.[15]

One result of the new technology in the age of information is what Sidney Blumenthal calls the "permanent campaign."[16] This is a new kind of politics in which "issues, polls, and media are not neatly separate categories. They are unified by a strategic imperative ... the elements of the permanent campaign are not tangential to politics: they are the political process itself."[17]

The history of presidential campaign rhetoric is full of examples of evasiveness, vagueness, and symbol mongering. Governing rhetoric, in contrast, the speech associated with presidents while in office, has been characterized by the absence of these elements and a concentration on the deliberative mode. The combination of increased polling and the strategies associated with television, which have led to the permanent campaign, have also led to a blurring of the distinctions between campaign rhetoric and governing rhetoric. With the decline of party structure, discipline, and workers, television commercials and media appearances not only serve to mobilize voters but also to govern the nation once the election is over.

In other words, presidents can no longer rely on traditional means of garnering and maintaining public support. The political parties are weak, and the formal institutional links between the leaders and the governed have largely broken down. As Congress increasingly ceded power and responsibility to the president, the office came to dominate the federal government. Congress can act less responsibly now than in the past because Congress is, in fact, less responsible for policy than in the past. The president is now responsible for developing national policy.[18]

The president is also responsible for communicating the content and implications of policy. In an increasingly media-dominated society, the communication process affects both the institutions that develop policy and the policies developed by those institutions.[19]

With radio, the door opened for a more personalized brand of political leadership. The president could be present in the homes of the electorate, his voice part of the family circle. He became an intimate. Television heightens this intimacy, bringing the president's face as well as his voice into the living room, and reducing the formal distance between speaker and audience. Because presidential communication increasingly means televised communication, presidents have had to adapt their message and style to fit the medium.

This means that political language forms, which "perform a crucial function by creating shared meanings, perceptions, and reassurances among mass publics,"[20] are now being consciously and consistently manufactured for audience effect rather than for policy content or out of personal character.

The bulk of most political discourse is centered on the engineering of consensus; a process that involves rationality and fact-finding, but frequently defines a superior point of view. It is primarily a process that works by using existing beliefs and attitudes to build agreements.[21]

6

The existence of television as the major conduit of political communication means that this process of consensus building will involve less and less "rationality and fact-finding," and more and more manipulation of "existing beliefs and attitudes." Which leads to the possibility that the kind of consensus under construction is less viable, less stable, and less meaningful than would otherwise be the case. This is particularly significant in the case of presidential speech. As an increasingly rhetorical office, the presidency can profitably be studied from a rhetorical perspective.

Rhetorical criticism analyzes public discourse in an endeavor to understand the public meaning of shared symbols, for a society develops an understanding of itself by negotiating the meaning of such symbols.[22] In this negotiating process, some voices speak more loudly, more clearly, than others. In the United States, one of these voices belongs to the president.

When a disaster occurs, a war is declared, or a major event of any kind happens, we rely on television to present and interpret that event for us. Television, which tends to both simplify and personify complex issues, privileges the presidential voice and exacerbates presidential interpretive dominance. In so doing, television has influenced the altered place of the president within the American political system and has affected both the form and the content of presidential speech. By beginning this analysis with the inception of the modern presidency and the development of personalized, mass politics that occurred simultaneously with the institutional growth of the office, this book provides an exegesis of those changes from a rhetorical perspective. By examining the form and content of presidential speech and argumentation patterns, we can arrive at a more thorough understanding of the changes in the persuasive opportunities available to the president and the consequences of those changes for our political life.

Conclusion

The strategies involved with "going public" affect our politics. These strategies are of relatively recent vintage, and they are, as yet, imperfectly understood. Clearly, presidents are talking more. It is not clear, however, that they are thinking more lucidly about what they are saying. Kathleen Hall Jamieson believes that "the disposition toward eloquence" is no longer cultivated[23] and that our political rhetoric and political understanding have suffered as a result. Language, like democratic politics, involves negotiation of meaning. Presidents, by virtue of their institutional position, have a privileged position in the negotiating process. Television, which highlights the presidential voice, further privileges this position. Televised presidential communication has fallen into habits and adopted strategies that undermine the negotiatory process and thus undermine our national self-understanding. By systematically studying the rhetoric of modern presidents and the relationships between that rhetoric and the media through which they were communicated, we can further the process of understanding the state of our present political language and political life.

The study explores carefully all the public speeches of Presidents Franklin Roosevelt through Ronald Reagan and approximately the first two years of George Bush's administration. All their public speeches, remarks, press conferences, and news briefings are included. Historical and contemporary accounts are also used. All the material is public. Private conversations and interactions are relevant only to the extent that they affect the public stance, image, and communication of the president.

Chapter 1, "Political Rhetoric in the Premodern United States," discusses the early history of American public speech and how it formed a base for the speech of the modern presidents. The chapter divides American history into five eras and focuses on the style of speech, political culture, and technology associated with that speech in each era. The eras include the colonial period, when political communication was oral and confined to small groups; the revolutionary period, when political communication was both oral and written as a response to the growth and diversity of the community; Jacksonian America, when the expansion of the franchise led to an increase in the quantity of political communication as well as a heightening of emotional appeals; the Civil War era, when the great issues under discussion allowed for powerful and sweeping rhetoric; the postwar period, which saw the commercialization of political speech as oratory became public speaking; and the early twentieth century, when the president became the focus of our national politics, and the rhetorical presidency was born.

Chapter 2, "The Development of Mass-Mediated Politics: Franklin D. Roosevelt and Harry S. Truman," describes the beginning of mass-mediated and personalistic politics, and the successes and failures associated with that beginning. Special attention is paid to Truman as Roosevelt's rhetorical successor.

Chapter 3, "The Birth of Televised Politics: Dwight D. Eisenhower and John F. Kennedy," details the rise of television politics and the predominance of personality as opposed to character in our national politics. These presidents reveal how the old style of politics fared given a new medium of political communication. During this period, specific policies became subordinated to the image that a candidate or officeholder projected; television provided a unique and as yet incompletely understood way of communicating politics.

Chapter 4, "Television and Personality: Lyndon B. Johnson and Richard M. Nixon," describes how politicians began to understand the power of the new media and began to exploit it, and both Johnson and Nixon ended by feeling exploited by the television medium, as the presidency lost the distinction between the public and the private spheres. This era reflects a new emphasis on image management and information control, and details the benefits and problems presidents encounter through the new medium.

Chapter 5, "The Issue of Control: Gerald R. Ford and Jimmy Carter," analyzes the weaknesses of their approach to media politics. The importance of thematic control of the national agenda is paramount. Neither Ford nor Carter was able to use television successfully, although there is evidence that both were very conscious of its power and the importance of images. The reasons for this failure are discussed.

Chapter 6, "Mastering Televised Politics: Ronald Wilson Reagan and George Herbert Walker Bush," describes how the old style of politics was replaced by a style befitting the television medium. The politics of support describe the dominant form of campaigning and governing in the present period.

Chapter 7, "(Almost) 'Everything Old Is New' Again: The Consequences of Television Politics," offers a summary of the arguments and prescriptions for the future of American presidential speech and American political language.

1

Political Rhetoric in the Premodern United States

Public Speech and Public Politics

From the earliest colonial beginnings, public speech has been an important part of politics and culture in the United States. But although continuously important, the precise role, meaning, and influence of public rhetoric over our national politics has changed over time. In part, changes in public rhetoric resulted from changes in the political culture of the United States, and in part, the changes were occasioned by changes in the technologies associated with communication. Presidential campaigning and governance relate to, and depend upon, societal organization and technology.[1] As these changes have taken place, the role of the president in the political system has also changed. The president's function has moved from being one of administration to one of legitimation as the spoken word comes to dominate written text and as electioneering and governing move ever closer together. This changing role has increasingly constrained the president's rhetorical opportunities. A tactic that once seemed to open new opportunities for presidential leadership has contributed to an environment that, by making more demands on the office, has left the president with fewer options.

These changes are associated here with specific eras in the history of the United States. The colonial period, revolutionary era, Jacksonian America, Civil War period, postwar period, and early twentieth century all have distinctive political cultures, styles of rhetoric, and technologies for communicating that rhetoric.

Rhetoric in the Colonial Period

During the colonial period, rhetoric was primarily spoken and thus was intended to be listened to, rather than read. "From the beginning, the American colonist was distinguished from his fellows by the fluency and the nature of his public speaking and by the extent of his listening."[2] Much of this rhetoric came in the form of sermons. Puritan preachers, widely regarded as teachers by their parishioners,[3] were expected to preach two sermons on Sundays, another on Thursdays, and address the congregation on all religious and civic ceremonial days. Sermons were important to American cultural development, for they combined theological topics with practical applications.[4] The colonists understood speech to be both persuasive and redemptive. Through speech, the community could discover the truth and act on it; the discovering and the acting were both essential ingredients of the formula. From the seventeenth century onward, speech in America was a means to an end, not an end in itself.

For the Puritans, public address was a self-conscious means to communality, a way for the people of a community to draw together and reach a common understanding of their goals and identity. The sermons of the Mathers and other colonial preachers reveal a preoccupation with the task of transmitting the word of God into a community on earth and the importance of the people themselves retaining the faith necessary to make such a task realizable.

These Puritan sermons, brought from the old world into the new, provided "a ritual designed to join social criticism to spiritual renewal, public to private identity, the shifting 'signs of the times' to traditional metaphors, themes, and symbols."[5] In other words, as the Puritan communal identity changed and developed, the jeremiad changed and adapted to both influence and reflect that change.

The jeremiad, as the primary reflection of Puritan political rhetoric, functioned to reaffirm the community's faith in their errand, set out communal norms, provide detail and condemnation of the community's failure adequately to live up to those norms, and provide a "prophetic vision that unveils the promises, announces the good things to come, and explains away the gap between fact and ideal."[6] All of this was a way of defining and redefining the Puritan community and the mission of the "city on a hill" from which the Puritans derived their understanding of themselves.

The most important colonial preacher was undoubtedly John Cotton, who "shaped and defended Congregationalism and supported a transitional form of theocracy."[7] Cotton sought the middle ground during the theological debates of second-generation Puritan Americans and attempted to define "general prescriptions and rationales for the Puritan community's way of life."[8] Relying on concrete metaphors and images from nature and the family, Cotton strove to preserve the original themes and practices of Puritanism in the face of mounting diversity.

That diversity was at least partially fomented by preachers such as Jonathan Edwards and George Whitefield, two Calvinists who played key roles in the spiritual revivalism of the Great Awakening. Edwards believed that spiritual enlightenment came through the senses. He thus adopted a preaching style that appealed to those senses, using emotional appeals and theatrical techniques in defense of the Great Awakening. Although he ultimately failed in his ambition to bring "an increasingly secular people back to pure Calvinism through his preaching and writing,"[9] he contributed much in the way of oratorical technique.

George Whitefield, another eighteenth-century Puritan preacher, also contributed to the new style of rhetoric. He understood that the old religion of the rationalist Puritans left many people's emotional needs unsatisfied, and he attempted to redefine a religion that could satisfy both rationalist theological claims and "the need felt by great numbers of people to reinvigorate Protestantism through a more popular, more affecting, and more individualized mode of worship."[10] A master propagandist, Whitefield preached more than five hundred sermons across the country, and some reports list his audiences as numbering in the thousands.[11] His was the first attempt to reach a mass audience, and he was remarkably successful in terms of popular appeal.

The Puritans understood leadership to be both religious and secular, and sought to reduce the barriers between the world of God and the corporeal world. They accomplished this, in large measure, by envisioning America as "the child of prophecy and promise."[12] Puritan leaders were responsible for conveying the desires of God to his people on earth, and for instructing them in the ways they must live in order to bring about the Apocalypse. Challenges to the authority of the Puritan leadership, such as those offered by Anne Hutchinson and Roger Williams, were thus also perceived as challenges to the entire Puritan errand. These challenges were resolved in the only way possible consistent with Puritan doctrines of community and mission—dissenters were banished. Freedom of speech and expression was of limited use in establishing God's word on earth.

The technology available to the colonists was limited, and it is not surprising that their rhetoric was primarily oral. Indeed, not until the early decades of the eighteenth century did the local printing presses challenge the domination of public address as the disseminator of information and the agent of persuasion. And even in the years immediately preceding the Declaration of Independence, much of the widely circulated printed matter had its origin or instigation in the pulpit or in town meeting.[13]

Because the rhetoric of the time was oral, it was appropriate only for a small, relatively homogeneous population. A speaker's influence was contained to those who could hear his voice, and given the political structure of the time, with its notion of hierarchical leadership, there was not much room for discussion and debate over conflicting ideas. Dissenters either left of their own free will or were exiled. In time, however, the grip that the theocracy held on the political structure of the New England colonies loosened as they increased communication between themselves and the other colonies, particularly between Massachusetts and Virginia. Free speech and the right to dissent became important elements in the colonists' thinking and helped form the basis for the American Revolution.

Rhetoric during the Revolutionary Period

The study of revolutionary rhetoric presents some problems because much of what has come down to us is the product of eighteenth-century recollections rather than the original texts. Nevertheless, some rhetoric was recorded and preserved, primarily patriotic orations and revolutionary sermons.[14] The authors of these speeches—and of all revolutionary rhetoric —were quite conscious of "being involved in a battle of ideas and principles";[15] their oratory exploited many forms of argumentation, ranging from the deliberative style that characterized *The Federalist Papers* to the wildly ad hominem invective of Tom Paine. This diversity of forms reflected their diverse audiences. Revolutionary rhetors addressed both the mass audience (primarily orally) and a smaller, more elite audience (primarily through pamphlets and private letters).

Addressing the mass audience was geared toward justifying the revolution and creating support for the leaders of that revolution and the government they founded:

> In a sense, the revolution was talked into being—not only by the harangues of Sam Adams and Patrick Henry, but, long before, in the sermons that asserted the equality of all men in the sight of God;

in the town meetings where delegates dared to challenge the prerogatives of the Royal Governor; and in homes and taverns where families and friends conversed about problems that they themselves had to solve in their own way.[16]

From what we know about the public speech of the founders, much of their rhetoric was confined to pamphlets, private and semiprivate correspondence,[17] speeches in the local legislatures and law courts, and later, in the Continental Congress. After the revolution, the arena of public speech continued to include pamphlets and the floor of Congress. The spoken word remained the primary means for reaching the broad mass of the public.

Persuasive evidence exists of widespread susceptibility to spoken eloquence. Town meetings, special days of prayer, fasting, and thanksgiving, ceremonial occasions like those commemorating the Boston Massacre and the signing of the Declaration of Independence provided frequent opportunities for public address; and if we may trust eyewitness reports, packed houses and enthusiastic audiences were the rule.[18]

Rhetoric is always created with the audience in mind. Sam Adams and Patrick Henry were, of course, the two most noted orators of the day, and they have well-deserved reputations as "rabble-rousers." By contrast, George Washington maintained a low public profile. He spoke rarely and then only on ceremonial occasions and in muted tones.

John Adams, who succeeded Washington, was also a reluctant public speaker. The only speeches recorded during his presidency are the annual addresses required by the Constitution, and "even as president, Adams preferred writing correspondence to giving speeches."[19] Partly this may have been a result of his shyness, partly of his feelings on the appropriateness of presidential public speech, and partly a reflection on his lack of oratorical ability. Whatever the case, his reputation as a public speaker is not a high one.

Strangely enough, the same can be said for Thomas Jefferson, whose written prose would lead one to conclude that he was an orator of no mean ability. On the contrary, Jefferson is said to have been "one of the least effective public speakers to hold the nation's highest office."[20] While he was well known for his "dispassionate reason and cool logic,"[21] these are not characteristics that move an audience or earn one a reputation for eloquence. The fiery oratory of Patrick Henry was more well known and more widely listened to than the "sober reasoning and solid argumentation,"[22] that characterized Jefferson's public speech. Indeed, Jefferson thought so little of his oral persuasive abilities that he discontinued the practice of reading his annual addresses to Congress personally and had them delivered by someone else, a practice that continued until Woodrow Wilson. Clearly, Jefferson's prose was better read than heard.

The same might be said for James Madison, who "rated rather poorly as a platform orator in the traditional executive public speaking situation, but his temperament, training, and technical mastery of reasoned debate made him one of the more effective communicators in the history of American deliberative assemblies."[23] Madison, like Washington, Adams, and Jefferson, lacked the personal style and flamboyance of a Patrick Henry or Samuel Adams, yet Madison defeated Henry in the ratifying debates in Virginia, and he, not Henry or Adams, was elected to the presidency.

All of which reveals an interesting trend among the first presidents—none of them was an able speaker. This is reflective of the low premium the founders placed on popular rhetoric and the "popular arts." Clearly, reasoned argument and personal virtue were more important to the early presidents—and to the men who elected them—than the ability to turn an epigram or inflame an audience. In fact, the oratorical power of an Adams or Henry would likely have been considered dangerous in a chief executive. While all these men considered oratory and persuasion important elements in democratic politics, it was not the function of the president to engage in this oratory or persuasion. The president was above the public side of politics. For him to engage in public politics would have been equivalent to demagoguery; rabble-rousing was not among the virtues that the founders ascribed to a successful president.

This deemphasis on public speaking does not mean that the early presidents were blind to the emotional side of politics. Even at this early stage, presidents engaged in some small degree of "public image-making," particularly regarding their wealth and social status.[24] Revolutionary-era presidents were also both conscious of and oriented toward the preservation of their public images. George Washington, for example, "like most other eighteenth century gentlemen ... was acutely aware of his public persona, and he took care to write and speak so as to create a favorable view of his motives, character, and achievements."[25] Part of this care involved the extensive use of ghost-writers, which Washington used during both the revolution and his presidency.[26]

Even though the early presidents were conscious of their public images, this does not imply that they engaged in the kind of activity associated with "going public."[27] Quite the contrary, a low profile was integral to the public images of the early presidents, who were expected to be above the political fray and not to engage too blatantly in the world of partisan politics. This was, of course, more true of George Washington than of any other president, but it is true that for all the early presidents, public speech and public speaking were kept to a minimum.

In addition, the founders had a specific understanding of leadership that would have been abrogated by assigning a larger role to public speech. As James Ceaser points out, "the founders sought to devise a system that would prevent electoral contests that turned on the use of the 'popular arts,' meaning issue arousal and the emphasis on those aspects of character that played to popular passions for an attractive or interesting leader."[28]

While Jefferson favored an executive that was somewhat closer to the "immediate opinions of the people,"[29] he was also afraid of "unregulated popular leadership."[30] The founders were profoundly suspicious of popular leadership as a means of soliciting power and sought to establish a forum of leadership that depended on character rather than personality. This is, of course, entirely dependent on a polity that is small enough to allow an individual's character to be well known. Congress was seen as the arena in which issues were most appropriately fought out, and speeches at small gatherings of like-minded people remained the rule.

But, in time, the United States became simply too large and too diverse for such address to be feasible, and although it took some time for printing presses to supersede the spoken word, supersede they did. With a transition from oral to written rhetoric came also a change in the style of rhetoric.

Rhetoric in Jacksonian America

The effect of the growth in the territory and population of the United States was clearly felt during the Jacksonian era.[31] Reaching such a broad and diverse population required extensive use of the technologies available for mass communication: The partisan press flourished, as did party rallies. The Lyceum and Chautauqua movements began during this period, as did mass politics, bringing with it a whole new conception of popular leadership. Andrew Jackson took full advantage of the available means of communication and ensured himself broad access to the electorate, if not broad appeal to them. Along with the other changes Jacksonianism brought a similar change in the popular understanding of leadership.

Martin Van Buren, the Little Magician, institutionalized the party system in the United States and hoped to control the excesses of popular leadership through adherence to strong parties, where presidential aspirants (and all political candidates) would be unable to appeal to popular passions because of the necessity of adherence to the principles of one of the political parties.[32] The president, in this schema, continued to maintain a relatively low public profile; his written texts were widely disseminated, but he spoke rarely. The president was still seen as above the political fray, and there was little to be gained in undermining the status of the office by engaging in political brawls when the partisan press could do that for him. In addition, political entertainment and excitement were readily obtainable at the mass rallies, where political celebrities would quote and defend the president who could remain comfortably at home and not engage in any personal vilification. The unseemly side of politics was best left to others.

Note that "unseemly" here does not refer to assuming a partisan political stance. In this age of strong parties, such partisanship was expected, and certainly Jackson himself was not shy about engaging his opponents. But it is important to note that he did so through the written word, not in public appearances. The president's person was viewed publicly primarily on ceremonial occasions, for he represented the nation, and to undermine that would undermine his own position as president. Presidents were still widely considered more as administrators than legitimators; their "speaking" was not only confined to the written word but also to subjects that came under their legitimate purview. For a president to speak on matters that did not relate directly to his administrative function was for a president to speak inappropriately and risk his legitimacy.

"Fun-loving, hard-drinking, quick to accept a bet, Henry Clay was a hail-fellow, delightful man whom everyone enjoyed and respected."[33] Clay attained prominence for his role in the Missouri Compromise and the nullification crisis as an exponent of compromise and Union. Known as the Great Pacifier, Clay's rhetoric was simple, direct, and clear. He used simple metaphors, designed to improve clarity without adding the obfuscating flamboyance so common at the time.[34] One is left with the impression that the issues Clay discussed and the passion with which he discussed them, rather than the mechanics of speech, impressed his audiences.

The same cannot be said of the other famous speaker of the period,

Daniel Webster, who took rhetorical elegance to new heights.[35] Known for his success at forensic rhetoric, Webster also excelled at ceremonial address, and in his famous "Reply to Hayne," he attained national stature as an orator. His eulogy for Adams and Jefferson, delivered on 2 August 1826, was so moving that "many said afterwards they felt Adams' presence in the hall."[36]

Both Webster and Clay, however, not only spoke well; they spoke about issues of great moment. As part of a continuation of the revolutionary tradition, presidents were, by inclination and custom, discouraged from taking an active oral part in these debates. Presidential communication was primarily written, and this written discourse, such as Jackson's statements on the Bank,* were of crucial importance. While admittedly Jackson "strengthened the presidency, redefined its role, and profoundly altered its relationship to the people,"[37] these changes would not become apparent until the Civil War presidency of Abraham Lincoln. No other president of the Jacksonian era had Jackson's relationship with the people.

This does not mean that the masses were left out of the debates of the time. Commercial lecturing in America began by way of an article by a New England manufacturer, Josiah Holbrook, published in the *American Journal of Education,* in October 1826, suggesting the establishment in every community of a Lyceum in which educational lectures might be presented. Part informational and part entertainment, the Lyceum lectures grew in popularity until by 1835 there were three thousand of them across the nation.[38] Audiences flocked to hear the renowned speakers of the day, and reputations were often made on the Chautauqua circuit. Important issues were discussed, and debate flourished. One of the most popular speakers was Sojourner Truth, the ex-slave turned orator, a black woman who drew much attention from the abolition movement.[39]

This is not to say that the Lyceum lectures were always enlightening and carried out on an elevated intellectual plane. Not at all. "Basically,

---

* Jacksonian democracy crystalized in its opposition to the Bank of the United States, headed by Nicholas Biddle and supported by Henry Clay. For Jackson, the Bank of the United States symbolized consolidated national power, constitutional impiety, aristocratic power, social inequality, and economic instability. Clay pushed for an extension of the Bank of the United States charter; it was passed by Congress, vetoed by Jackson. That veto message remains one of the most powerful and important summations of the meaning of Jacksonianism. See Marvin Meyers, *The Jacksonian Persuasion: Politics and Belief,* rev. ed. (Palo Alto: Stanford University Press, 1960).

the bill of fare offered to the Chautauqua audience was remarkably like that provided in the *Reader's Digest* magazine: an ultra-respectable 'home, heaven, and mother,' moral tone spiced with adventurous sensationalism and at least the appearance of great daring in the airing of liberal ideas."[40]

While the Chautauquas helped expose a largely middle-class audience to many of the important ideas of the time, there is no question that much of the important oratory took place on the floor of Congress. Henry Clay and Daniel Webster began discussions of the meaning of Union, and the Great Compromise was hammered out in public debate.

It was debate that differed markedly from earlier times, however, as sectional rivalry increased personal animosity, and vilification and violence were not uncommon. One analyst describes the period as "the new age of demagogy that was ushered in with Jackson's election," and chronicles how "rich and well-to-do candidates for the presidency (and lesser offices) began shamelessly to plead poverty and humble origins, under the evident conviction that voters would respond favorably to men of such background."[41]

The more electioneering rhetoric intruded into the halls of Congress, the less room there was for deliberative rhetoric. The same dynamic came to affect the presidency.

Rhetoric during the Civil War Era

Abraham Lincoln moved further than any other president toward the legitimating function of the presidency, for he took it as his duty to interpret the events surrounding the Civil War as reflective of the moral life of the nation. In so doing, he established the presidency as the locus of national identity. The president's voice was not the only authoritative voice, however. It is significant that of the well-known oratorical figures of the period, only Abraham Lincoln was elected president. During this period in the history of the United States, as in the Jacksonian period, Congress was considered the appropriate forum for the discussion of important issues, and the noted speakers of the day were largely from that body. Andrew Johnson chose to ignore this in the 1866 congressional campaign and succeeded only in establishing himself as a clear target for his political opponents. Public speaking was deemed more appropriate to congressmen than to presidents.

William Yancey, an Alabaman, was one of the chief antebellum "fire eaters" and one of the most important oratorical figures of the pre–Civil War South, whose "greatest achievement was the popularizing of Cal-

houn's tenets."[42] Part of the power of Yancey's oratory came from his belief that all the issues facing the United States could be understood in sectional terms. From this conviction he elaborated a self-consistent and
emotionally evocative theme, and it fueled his argumentation and was the
basis for "a rhetoric of unbending defiance."[43] Yancey's political stance
against the preservation of the Union did not stop him from touring the
North in support of the southern candidate for the presidency in the election of 1860, where he won acclaim for his humor and ethical appeals.[44]
His audience appeal notwithstanding, Yancey was considered too radical
to be entrusted with elective office, but he is the best remembered "orator
for secession."

On the opposite extreme of the slavery issue stood Charles Sumner.
A prominent social reformer and abolitionist, Sumner was elected to the
U.S. Senate for the first time in 1851.[45] Sumner made his reputation in
the Senate as an outspoken opponent of slavery. He spoke out against the
Fugitive Slave Act in 1851, but his most famous speech was entitled "The
Crime Against Kansas" and was given over a period of two days in 1856.
The speech contained unrestrained vilification of the South and personal
attacks on several prominent southern senators. One southerner, taking
offense, beat Sumner unconscious. The beating, even more than the
speech, aroused northern ire against the "barbarism of slaveholders."[46]

It is worth noting that Sumner's speech not only lasted for two days
but that people were willing to listen to him for that long. Given that
kind of time and that kind of attention, the rhetors of the period were free
to elaborate their philosophy at length, support it with a wealth of historical detail, and embellish it with any number of grand gestures. They had a
degree of rhetorical freedom that our contemporary televised speakers
might well envy.

The best-known orators of the period are those men who fought to
sustain the moderate course. Partly, of course, this reflects the inevitability
of the victors writing history. But partly it shows the quality of speech
produced by Stephen A. Douglas and Abraham Lincoln. As in the Jacksonian period, the emphasis is on speakers other than the president; his
voice, which must represent all the people, became, in many ways, more
muted as the Civil War approached, and it became unclear just what "the
people" could agree to stand for. Smaller publics, smaller audiences, in
contrast, could be easily—and appropriately—represented by any number
of less inclusive speakers, such as congressmen, senators, and candidates
for elective office.

Stephen Douglas, a long-time advocate of territorial expansion and a defender of the principles of self-government, was elected to the Senate from Illinois for the first time in 1846.[47] The Little Giant favored the Mexican-American War and played a key role in the Compromise of 1850. He attained national prominence when he introduced the Kansas-Nebraska Bill of 1854, basing his arguments on the principle of popular sovereignty.[48]

Douglas is, of course, best known for his participation in the debates with Abraham Lincoln during the 1852 senatorial race. While Lincoln won in the popular vote and garnered national prominence as a result of the debates, Douglas won enough legislative districts to return him to the Senate.[49] The issues discussed in the debates, however, undermined Douglas's ability to appeal to a national audience as "it was increasingly necessary . . . to reconcile popular sovereignty with positive protection of slavery for southern audiences and yet to reduce the moral callousness it conveyed to Northerners."[50] Douglas's vehement support of popular sovereignty reassured neither side.

Trained in the rough-and-tumble of stump speaking in the West, "Douglas used generous doses of personal attack, ridicule and reductio ad absurdum in discussing his opponents' views."[51] These tactics left little uncertainty about what Douglas opposed; precisely what he stood for was generally more difficult to determine.

That cannot be said to the same degree of his debating opponent, Abraham Lincoln. While not highly regarded by his contemporaries as a speaker, Lincoln, with his folksy metaphors and natural images, his parables and his economy of phrase, may well be the finest orator in an age known for its oratory.[52] Indeed, Lincoln is credited with bringing about a major change in American oratory, since "he established a trend toward brevity and simplicity in public oratory."[53]

He first received national attention for his debates with Douglas, which remain "Lincoln's most publicized political speaking; they were not his best, but they were his most dramatic."[54] With his ungainly appearance and unpleasant voice, Lincoln was at a disadvantage as a speaker. Nevertheless, he campaigned extensively for the Senate and for the presidential nomination.

After his nomination, however, Lincoln greatly reduced his public appearances, since he was now a sitting president and endowed with the dignity of that office, not a mere presidential aspirant. He spoke little as president, and his reputation for eloquence is based almost entirely on his inaugural addresses and the Gettysburg Address.[55] When Lincoln did speak, he differed stylistically from most of his contemporaries:

The orators of Lincoln's day, many of whom became almost folk heroes of their communities, attracted admirers by their elocutionary perfection: classical allusions, sweeping metaphors, rich, rotund voices, and grandiloquent manner. Not so with Lincoln; he did not strive to emulate these oratorical greats. He presented himself as a common man.[56]

Lincoln used this image as a "common man" combined with biblical clarity of expression to attain and keep popular support. This was necessary because of the upsurge in campaigning and the "popular arts" during the years immediately prior to the Civil War. The expansion of the railroads made national tours more feasible; the importance and sectional nature of the disputes made them more necessary. Emotions ran high, and rhetoric that created and sustained emotional responses was highlighted. Lincoln's audience was less bifurcated than that of the early presidents. He talked less to an elite on the one hand and the mass on the other. Instead, his audience was more of a middling sort. His rhetoric had to capture that middle ground to be persuasive.[57]

This period is marked by a shift in the historical positions of Congress and the presidency vis-à-vis one another. As Lincoln accrued more power for the presidency, he also shifted the public understanding of what the presidency should be and what it should mean. As Lincoln used his position as president to define the nature of Union, he also took a step toward emphasizing the legitimating possibilities of the presidency and away from a strict adherence to understanding the office as a predominantly administrative entity.

Rhetoric in Post–Civil War America

The dominant issues during this period were Reconstruction, race relations, and money. Money dominated the agenda. The heroes of the Civil War were replaced in the public imagination with the men of Wall Street, and "the best men" were increasingly forsaking the "dirty" world of politics for the lucrative one of business. "The principal preoccupation of the nation was the accumulation of wealth; the contribution of the politician was to maintain a favorable climate for undisturbed moneymaking, not to engage in the agitation of unpleasant social issues."[58]

The issues of Union and the meaning of our national identity were no longer the main focus of public life; they had been replaced by "interests," or competing views of how to ensure economic prosperity within an unfettered capitalist framework.[59] Along with the denigration of public life came a denigration of public speech. That denigration was aided by the increased commercialization of the lecture circuit. The high educational and religious ideals of the Chautauqua movement "succumbed to the temptation to woo financial success through increasing popularization."[60] This commercialization of public speech changed the character of public rhetoric in the United States:

> The professionalism of public speaking converted it (on the commercial platform) into a means of earning a living. Such speaking came to be judged basically in terms of whether an audience would pay to listen; and whether they would want the speaker back. A predominant skill became that of giving the people what they wanted to hear.[61]

The prevalence of newspapers largely replaced the floor of Congress as the proper forum for the discussion of ideas. It is not surprising, then, that the most admired speakers of the period were not politicians at all, but activists and writers. Of these, Ralph Waldo Emerson was the best known. While present generations know him from his written work, to his contemporaries Emerson was best known as a public speaker.[62] Most people learned about what he said by reading about him in the press.

This was probably good news for Emerson, as he was widely known as a poor speaker: "Neither a soul-winner nor a rabble-rouser, Emerson was not even adept at communicating the substance of his thought in an entirely coherent fashion."[63] What Emerson did do was project a certain persona—one that flattered the audience as well as reassuring them. Emerson was the "representative democratic man,"[64] and he was able to stand before audiences as one of them—all people could be like Emerson, for he was no more special than any of them. This is a powerful appeal to a people who have recently undergone a war and are still undergoing the depersonalizing effects of mass industrialization.

These audiences were given similar reinforcement by another famous lecturer, Mark Twain. Twain recognized that audiences wanted to leave a lecture feeling that they had learned something, and he designed his folksy, commonsensical humor toward that end.[65] A forerunner of humorists like Will Rogers, Twain used his vernacular perspective to poke fun at the pomposities and overblown rhetoric of many of the Lyceum lecturers. Once rhetorical devices are pointed out for what they are and subjected to ridicule, their appeal and effectiveness are greatly reduced.

Twain and others like him helped simplify and shorten political speeches and hastened the decline of long arguments as a fundamental part of speech making in the United States. But creating good rhetoric without the traditional forms and structures is no easy task, and the rhetoric of this period reveals the awkwardness of adapting to a new form of speech.

Presidents were not immune from the perils of this new style of rhetoric. The speeches of these presidents are colorless, terse, and without vision. None of the presidents of this era earned reputations for their oratorical skill. This lack of oratorical ability is not the sole responsibility of the presidents in question. One analyst believes that "the sorry state of American political oratory was directly traceable to the sorry state of American politics."[66] Others thought it was more directly attributable to the increasing prevalence of newspapers, and "yellow" or sensational journalism was thought by many to degrade both its subjects and its audiences.

Rhetoric during the Early Twentieth Century

This period showed a disgust with the "money grubbing" ways of the previous period, and as the problems of unbridled industrialism became too obvious to ignore, a group of reformers rose to prominence and inaugurated a new period of mass politics in the United States. The period is dominated by Theodore Roosevelt, William Jennings Bryan, and Woodrow Wilson. It is worth noting that in contrast to earlier periods, when presidents were not known for their oratorical ability, two of the three best-known speakers during this period attained that prominence as presidents. As adept as each of these men was with words, the times had changed, and audiences were no longer interested in speeches lasting days and that traced the history of Western civilization by way of making a point about the industrial United States. Speeches were both shorter and more colloquial than previously, and as "oratory became public speaking," inspirational messages were replaced by informational ones.[67] In addition, slogans became increasingly important as the period wore on and the "make it snappy" spirit of the 1920s took hold.[68]

Theodore Roosevelt believed that the executive had broad powers and the responsibility to use them. He also knew that exercising those powers without the consent of the people was a risky endeavor. Which is why he understood the presidency as a "bully pulpit," a place where the president could exercise his moral leadership. He was remarkably successful at this leadership: "As governor, no less than as president, he met bitter opposition by the conservative leaders of his own party; and as governor hardly less than as president, he mobilized public opinion so dramatically that he forced one legislative breakthrough after another."[69]

It is important to recognize, however, that Roosevelt, while he

> was the first president to successfully appeal "over the heads" of Congress, he did so in a way that preserved and did not preempt, Congress' deliberative capabilities and responsibilities.... Roosevelt did not speak directly to the people on the eve of crucial votes, as is sometimes the case in our time, nor did he attack congressmen during the debate. For him, there was a marked contrast between campaign speeches, where such attacks were justified and a pleasure, and governing, where they were not.[70]

Even as the presidency assumed a more legitimating than strictly administrative role, electioneering was still kept largely separate from issues of governance. The president was rhetorically more limited in this respect than was the presidential candidate. The candidate had something to prove: She is competent, or he is tough. The president had nothing to prove, but the polity to represent. These are still seen as separate activities requiring separate tactics and adaptations. Both, however, by this time, rested on the creation and maintenance of public, not merely elite, support. Where the early presidents had led through example and policy, the presidents following Roosevelt would increasingly rely on the arts of persuasion.

Woodrow Wilson, although detested by Roosevelt, learned much about moral suasion from him. Wilson's presidency, important because of its position in relation to so many changes in the international role of the United States, is also unique in its relation to American presidential rhetoric. Two events were particularly crucial to Wilson's transformation of presidential rhetoric and presidential leadership: World War I and the battle over the ratification of the postwar treaty and the League of Nations.

Because of Wilson's strong moral rhetoric in his portrayal of the war as one that would "make the world safe for democracy," "the war became a crusade, and the American people supported it with the enthusiasm and self-sacrifice of crusaders."[71] This reflected both the moral tenor of the times and Wilson's understanding of leadership as "associated with guidance rather than rule. He believed that oratory is the strong bond that both arouses the followers and holds the leader to a tight rein."[72] For Wilson, the president's task is to illumine the way; the followers' task is to ensure that the light they follow is not held by a false prophet. And both

Congress and the people as a whole supported Wilson and the war effort in a remarkably united and noncontentious fashion.

The fight over the treaty ratification and the League of Nations was somewhat more problematic. In defense of the League, Wilson made an unprecedented national speaking tour. He traveled over eight thousand miles in three weeks and delivered some thirty-seven speeches.[73] The fight over the League, while in many ways a personal struggle between Wilson and Senator Henry Cabot Lodge,[74] was carried out in the most public of ways, which would not have been politically or personally acceptable to presidents of an earlier age.[75]

Wilson's defense of the League "was beset with difficulties. In 1919 there was no radio to carry the president's voice to millions of listeners. His appeal was limited to those within the range of his voice and to those who read friendly or unfriendly press reports."[76] Although it must be remembered that this was no small number, the ceaseless exertion required in a national tour nearly killed Wilson. While this was not the first time a president had stumped the country looking for support (Andrew Johnson, for instance, made a similar tour in 1866), it is notable that this tactic failed, at least in part, because of the concern caused by the president's unexpected entry into the popular forum. Presidents, by custom and by tradition, relied on the written word or on the spoken word as reported in the press. Wilson and Roosevelt had much to do with changing that tradition, but they both paid a political price for their efforts in persuasion.

Wilson's impact on the presidency of the United States has been summarized by Neils Thorsen:

> On the one hand, the president was the chief executive, and in Wilson's view, the natural head of efficient and responsible government. On the other hand, the presidency was destined to become the primary symbol of American national power as Americans moved consciously toward becoming "a single community." . . . Wilson clearly favored the legitimating function over the executive, administrative function.[77]

Rhetoric under the Wilson administration reflected this preference, as he spoke to the people instead of writing to Congress, as had been the fashion before him.[78] In addition, building on the legacy of Theodore Roosevelt, Wilson used a "visionary rhetoric" that articulated a view of the future and sought to propel the people toward that vision.[79] Wilson and Roosevelt provided a view of the world and of the presidency that was profoundly to influence the rhetoric of the presidents who followed them.

Summary and Conclusions

From the earliest colonial beginnings, the tenor and quality of politics in the United States have been reflected in the tenor and quality of our national public rhetoric. During the colonial period, rhetoric was predominantly confined to the pulpit and was viewed as a means of teaching and uniting many small communities. By the end of the revolutionary period, written rhetoric dominated as an effort was made to reach a broader and more diverse audience.

The first major change in American public rhetoric is associated with the mass politics and appeals of the Jacksonian era and the "new age of demagoguery." The president still had not assumed a speaking role; his voice was heard through the press and surrogates. The partisan press is a key feature of this period. Rhetoric was both written and oral as the Lyceum and Chautauqua movements gained momentum and popularity.

During the Civil War, the debates over slavery and Union were waged in the Chautauquas and on the floor of Congress as well as on the campaign trail, which had become an increasingly popular means of reaching the common people. Orators of the caliber of Henry Clay, Daniel Webster, and Abraham Lincoln dominated both public speaking and public politics.

In the post–Civil War era, politics was replaced by business as the preeminent profession in the United States, and political rhetoric began a slide that would result, by the twentieth century, in "public speaking." The age of eloquence was ended, and public speech, which in the United States had always had a profoundly pragmatic orientation, became informational, terse, and utilitarian. By this time, however, the president has begun to speak publicly, and his speech is more inspirational, more focused on the office as a "bully pulpit" than has been the case before.

Eloquence enjoyed a resurgence under the reforming presidents of the early twentieth century, for

> if popular rhetoric was proscribed in the nineteenth century because it could manifest demagoguery, impede deliberation, and subvert the routines of republican governance, it could be defended by showing itself necessary to contend with these very same political difficulties. Appealing to the founders' general arguments while abandoning

some of their concrete practices, Roosevelt's presidency constituted a middle way between the statecraft of the preceding century and the rhetorical presidency that was to come.[80]

The coming of the rhetorical presidency was hastened by Wilson's adaptation and extension of the tactics and practices used by Theodore Roosevelt. And as Wilson chose his strategies, so did the presidents who came after him, until "the legitimating function" almost completely eclipsed the administrative function. The stark contrast between George Washington's strictly administrative role and Wilson's legitimating role is clear and powerful. As the legitimating function begins to dominate, the spoken word takes precedence over the written, and the distinctions between electioneering and governance become increasingly blurred. A discussion of the dynamics of this process and the contributions of the modern presidents to it constitute the rest of this book.

2

The Development of Mass-Mediated Politics: Franklin D. Roosevelt and Harry S. Truman

The presidency is preeminently a place of moral leadership.
— *FDR*

My job is to convince people to do what they should have the sense to do in the first place. — *HST*

The Presidency Goes Public

Mass-mediated and personalistic politics originated with Franklin Roosevelt and were institutionalized by Harry Truman. Their rhetoric is characterized by appeals to nationalism and internationalism, appeals that carry with them the implication that the president will be the center of American life and American government. Roosevelt's and Truman's public speeches also used vitriolic rhetoric when dealing with opponents, who are characterized as "moneychangers" or "selfish"; those opponents are outdated and cannot keep step with the new challenges America faces and the new role in the world America must assume.

These two presidents brought the United States into a position of world power. Echoing Woodrow Wilson, Roosevelt and Truman based the American claim to power on superior moral character supported by superior military arms. They also recognized the power inherent in self-interest. American involvement in World War II was necessary to save the free world and secure American self-interest, just as the Korean conflict was necessary to prevent a third world war and preserve American security.

Neither Roosevelt nor Truman sought political power for predominantly personal reasons, and both recognized the division between the institution of the presidency and the individual who was president. They were capable—eminently capable—of lambasting their opponents in clear and blunt terms. But politicking rarely overlapped governing, and their ability to govern was not hampered by the lack of a clear policy program. Both Roosevelt and Truman used the radio to supplement other tactics of governance and communication. For Roosevelt, public and personalized leadership tactics provided opportunities; the constraints imposed by these opportunities become increasingly evident with Truman's presidency.

"By comparison with Franklin Roosevelt, 'all previous presidents were Trappists who didn't even talk to themselves.' "[1] As Roosevelt's successor, Harry Truman was expected to continue this public presidential persona. Although Truman's style differed greatly from that of Roosevelt, the two presidents were very similar in their relation to and use of the communication media of the time. They did not enjoy the same success with radio: Roosevelt mastered its use; Truman was always rough and uncomfortable with the medium, and relied on personal appearances and interviews instead. But both used rhetoric explicitly designed for radio, and the widespread use of radio dominated the style and kinds of appeals used by both men.

Radio and Franklin D. Roosevelt

Summarizing the presidency, the presidential rhetoric, or both, of any president is a difficult task. Summarizing the public character and speech of Franklin Delano Roosevelt is particularly difficult. Roosevelt is still a source of controversy and debate; one thing scholars agree on is that he was a complicated and often contradictory man. Certain themes stand out, however. Among these themes are FDR as the consummate user of the media, including the radio, newsreels, and the press; the particular style that made his use of the various media so effective; and the particular substance of his appeals, which made a lasting impression on the ideals and organization of governmental institutions in the United States.

The Public Papers and Addresses[2] available to us contrast sharply with those of recent presidents because of the predominance of material addressed to Congress and the relative lack of material addressed to the public at large. Most of FDR's communication directed at Congress is in the form of requests for legislation.[3] An overwhelming amount of the speeches addressed to the public are given during election years. Roosevelt did not govern publicly except on specific occasions and with regard to specific issues. In addition, the number of purely ceremonial speeches is limited; Roosevelt was more likely to turn a ceremonial occasion (the dedication of a dam, for example) into an occasion for the discussion of policy issues than to turn discussion of a policy issue into a ceremonial occasion. Most of his purely ceremonial rhetoric involved foreign dignitaries or unusual events.[4]

Roosevelt's speeches are, on average, much longer than the speeches presidents give today. His "Fireside Chats" average seven pages, and his "Informal, Extemporaneous Remarks" average four pages. Roosevelt's speech patterns are more informational than entertaining, familiar, or "chatty." His speeches develop arguments, often relying on a summary of the history of his administration (in matters relating to campaigns or New Deal policies in particular) or the history of the issue at hand (particularly regarding war policy).

His leadership style included a sense of "vigor . . . and a leadership of frankness too. Appealing features of the Rooseveltian personality were his candor and his humility."[5] Roosevelt conveyed all these characteristics through the medium of radio by stressing the emotional side of generalities and other "political gimmicks"[6] and by coupling action with active rhetoric.[7] This is important because while Roosevelt was clearly aware of the symbolic dimension of his actions and would often explicitly discuss some action as a symbol of a point he was trying to make, the actions were policy oriented as well as symbolic. In other words, the point Roosevelt wished to illustrate came first, and dominated. The illustration came later, and depended on the policy.

Nearly all scholars agree that "the Roosevelt presidency was distinguished by the variety of ways in which speech making was effectively employed. Speeches were used to inform, to persuade, to motivate, and to inspire."[8] Using the media as he did gave FDR several advantages, all associated with "the rhetorical presidency." His Fireside Chats, for example, were used to maintain and enhance presidential power by persuading the people to move Congress,[9] and his press conferences enabled him to control the flow of information, manage the news, and use the press as a scapegoat in times of trouble.[10]

Because he was so keenly tuned to the advantages of his relationship with the press, FDR held an enormous number of press conferences. He met with the press on an average of twice a week.[11] He can therefore be credited with institutionalizing the "symbiotic relationship between the White House and the media."[12] The relationship has since been described as "a bad marriage. They cannot live without each other, nor can they live without hostility . . . it is conflict within a shared system."[13] At this point, however, the "marriage" appeared reasonably healthy. Roosevelt's press conferences were predominantly friendly in tone, respectful, and well regulated. The content was wide ranging, organized informationally, and his conversations with the press were open and convivial. This was possible because the press conferences were private, closed to the public, and, by custom, the president controlled what got quoted and when.

The off-the-record nature of these early press conferences is particularly important, for it gave Roosevelt time. Time to find out what issues were important to the press, how they were framing the issue, and how best to counter or control the eventual publication of a given story. It also gave him time to make decisions and change decisions that had already been made. This is a luxury that has been increasingly lost to more recent presidents.

While Roosevelt's relations with the press were friendly in private, there was also a certain amount of conflict. He publicly characterized the press as unswervingly opposed to him, and rarely mentioned the press except to criticize it. This reinforced his public strategy and helped mitigate the effects of some of the criticism that appeared in the press from time to time. It should also be noted that evidence indicates that the press was not noticeably hostile to Roosevelt, either in news, columns, or editorials, and that Roosevelt was surely aware of that fact.[14]

As Halford Ryan points out, "the scapegoat technique" was very popular with FDR,[15] and addressing his opposition in pejorative terms was one of his favorite tactics: "But the most vociferous opponents of reform in this small minority were actuated not by any conscientious apprehension about further recovery, but by a realization that their own economic control and power, which they had enjoyed during the so-called boom era, were being destroyed."[16]

Interestingly, except for his frequent strictures against the press,[17] Roosevelt usually kept such pejorative references for use against campaign opponents and the Germans, Japanese, and Italians during the war:[18] "Today the whole world is divided between human slavery and human freedom—between pagan brutality and the Christian ideal."[19] Like Theodore Roosevelt, Franklin knew and understood the difference between campaign rhetoric and that of governance.[20] Also like Theodore, Franklin Roosevelt excelled at vituperative campaign oratory: "Many among us have made obeisance to Mammon. . . . To return to higher standards we must abandon the false prophets and seek new leaders of our own choosing."[21] And while he left no doubt about how he felt regarding opponents to his policies in general and the New Deal in particular, FDR did not engage in rhetoric designed to undermine the legitimacy of his opposition. He thought they were wrong, but he seldom indicated that that they were unpatriotic (the wartime experience is a limited exception to this rule).[22]

In addition to his use of the print media, Roosevelt was aware of the limitations and potential of radio. During the 1944 campaign, for example, Governor Thomas E. Dewey bought time immediately after one of Roosevelt's radio talks in order to capitalize on Roosevelt's audience. Roosevelt finished his speech five minutes early, leaving dead time between his talk and Dewey's scheduled appearance. The audience turned en masse to other stations.[23]

Roosevelt's style was uniquely suited to radio. "To President Roosevelt, the microphone personified a single American listener. Unlike most politicians, FDR never forgot that radio listening was done by individuals and family groups, not by hordes who filled auditoriums."[24] Roosevelt's ability to understand the intimacy of the new mass medium gave people the feeling that he understood them as individuals, a feeling that is increasingly important during times of crisis. "The public was moved by the ingenuity with which the Democratic candidate managed to weave together theories and facts, and color them with genuine emotional fervor. This man, they felt, knew how the crisis hit them."[25] Further, "he sought the people; he made the people the object of his regard; he wooed them that he might lead them."[26]

And in wooing them, Roosevelt excelled at addressing the emotions of his audience. The emotions he addressed most often were fear, courage, and optimism. Fear is one of the dominant themes of FDR's rhetoric, and the phrase for which he is most often remembered is "the only thing we have to fear is fear itself." What is less remembered, but just as important to an understanding of the Roosevelt rhetoric, is that he followed that clause with a characterization of fear and the appropriate response to it: "nameless, unreasoning, and unjustified terror which paralyzes needed efforts to convert retreat into advance."[27]

For Roosevelt, fear is an obstacle to overcome. It is important, however, that he takes the time to describe fear and the causes for it. This description pulls the audience in and helps them feel that their concerns are understood and shared by the president. Only if he understands the cause of the fear can he help the audience overcome it. At this he excelled. Roosevelt's most vituperative strictures were reserved for those who, in his words, "spread the gospel of fear"[28] and did not see the need for prompt and decisive action on the part of the federal government.

Moreover, for Roosevelt, the way to overcome fear is through action. Action allows FDR to portray a courageous image, and through action he conveyed the optimism and buoyancy that were so important during times of national crises. Roosevelt reveled in the possibilities for action. In accepting the Democratic nomination for the presidency in 1932, Roosevelt defied tradition and flew to Chicago to accept the nomination in person. He capitalized on the symbolism inherent in such a flight at such a time:

> The appearance before a national convention of its nominee for President, to be formally notified of his selection, is unprecedented and unusual, but these are unprecedented and unusual times. . . . My friends, let this be a symbol of my intention to be honest and to avoid all hypocrisy or sham, to avoid all silly shutting of the eyes to the truth in this campaign.[29]

This was a tactic FDR used frequently: He insisted that the gravity of a situation be faced, admitted to, and then overcome. For FDR, challenges were important to the life of a person, and to the life of a people. Through facing and overcoming obstacles, individuals and nations realize and fulfill their potential strength. He says, "The tasks that we face in the reordering of economic life are great. They call for courage, for determination, and for what you have abundantly out here, the hardihood of the pioneer."[30]

The metaphor of the pioneer and the theme of American history are prominent in Rooseveltian rhetoric. He was fond of harking back to the days of Jefferson and Jackson and of remembering the challenges and obstacles faced by the early Republic:

> I am happy to stand here tonight and declare to you that the real issue before the United States is the right of the average man and woman to lead a finer, a better, and a happier life. And that was the same issue, more than a hundred years ago, that confronted Andrew Jackson.[31]

During both the Great Depression and the early days of World War II, FDR often recalled Washington at Valley Forge and Lincoln at Gettysburg, noting that "generation after generation, America has battled for the general policy of freedom."[32] All presidents, of course, call up images of past leadership and attempt to tie themselves symbolically to those leaders. But few presidents have led during times of extraordinary crises—crises that made the parallels Roosevelt was drawing more powerful.

It is important to note that Roosevelt, while he advocated vigorous and decisive action throughout his tenure, was not (at least not rhetorically) in favor of random action. For Roosevelt, action was planned. Planning—along with the ability to adjust plans—was a key theme during much of the Roosevelt administration. "Legislation [is] not ... just a collection of haphazard schemes, but rather the orderly component parts of a connected and logical whole."[33] He often claimed that "the administration and the Congress are not proceeding in any haphazard fashion in this task of government."[34] This was particularly important more for the likelihood of such an appeal creating reassurance than for any truth that may or may not lie behind the words. Roosevelt certainly had ideas; that he had specific and detailed plans is less likely. But the people believed that he had plans, that he had the crisis under control. And this was important because of the short-term support it gave Roosevelt and because of the long-term effects this belief had for the institution of the presidency.

As the public came to believe that Roosevelt could lead them out of the depression, and as he led them through World War II, people became accustomed to looking toward Washington. Nationalism, one of Roosevelt's main themes (discussed below) came to mean presidential government. And presidents who were to follow Roosevelt found a world of high, often unrealistically inflated expectations of presidential potentialities.

Roosevelt was able to acquire and inflate these expectations both because of the crisis situation when he was elected and because the medium of the radio allowed him to develop a personal—almost an intimate—relationship with the mass public, something no president before Roosevelt had the technology to accomplish.[35] The development of this relationship became something all presidents after Roosevelt assumed the obligation to attempt. This is a specific type of leadership, and one that is essentially new with Roosevelt. Other presidents conducted image politics and engaged in mass appeals to the public. But the quality of instant access and the sheer scale on which FDR was able to design and present such appeals engendered a new style of leadership. Presidents through Roosevelt were able to choose whether they would engage in mass appeals, and such appeals were generally confined to election years. No president after Roosevelt had such a choice: Presidential leadership became, by definition, public leadership.

And while Roosevelt reaped many benefits from this style of leadership, it also put a certain amount of pressure on him to perform up to expectations. One of Roosevelt's dominant themes, therefore, was his stress on the need for continual support from the people for his policies and his personal brand of leadership. Once a president's leadership depends on mass approval, maintaining that approval becomes a priority.

One way that Roosevelt sought to maintain support was through the two-pronged tactic of enumerating past accomplishments and stressing the need for future improvements. Statements like, "but, in addition to our immediate task, we must still look to the larger issue" were not uncommon.[36] He could also be very specific about the consequences of failing to support the president: "We have invited battle. . . . We have earned the hatred of entrenched greed. . . . They seek the restoration of their selfish power."[37] In other words, Roosevelt stood for the forces of democracy and social justice against the forces of unbridled capitalism and "economic tyranny."

This is not to imply that Roosevelt was, or thought of himself as, a socialist. Despite the fact that his opposition tried hard, and not entirely without justification, to tar Roosevelt with the brush of socialism, it is clear that Roosevelt's intended reforms of the system were designed more to save than to drastically alter it.[38]

FDR saw the presidency as "preeminently a place of moral leadership," and he did exert such leadership, derived from his personal sense of values. "Vague though it was, this set of moral rules embraced one idea in particular that was of cardinal importance to Roosevelt and to his country. This was the idea of responsibility for the well-being of one's fellow-man."[39]

The theme of social justice and service to one's fellow man are prominent throughout FDR's rhetoric. Roosevelt thought in human terms, and he spoke in human terms: "What do the people of America want more than anything else? To my mind, they want two things: work, with all the moral and spiritual values that go with it; and with work, a reasonable measure of security—security for themselves and for their wives and children."[40] He also understood the people's need to be understood by the president, and fulfilled that need: "I have come, not primarily to speak, but rather, to hear; not to teach, but to learn. I want to hear of your problems, to understand them and to consider them as they bear on the larger scene of national interest."[41]

Roosevelt did not use this tactic merely as a campaign gimmick, although it surely paid off in terms of votes and public support. FDR also advocated social justice and public service, and he put his policy money where his campaign mouth was. In addition to his constant castigation of the "moneychangers in the temple," he stressed the importance of people aiding one another. In an address at the graduation ceremonies of the U.S. Naval Academy, for example, he said:

> You have an advantage over many other young men, not alone in having survived the tests requisite to your receiving your diplomas, but especially in that you have learned discipline, responsibility, industry, and loyalty—the very elements upon which, in every walk of life, every worth-while success is founded.... Nevertheless, when you make a close examination of any profession, you will find very few successful men, or for that matter women, who do not take into consideration the effect of their individual efforts on humanity as a whole.[42]

The above quote not only reveals Roosevelt's insistence on the importance of service, it also reveals that he so far understood the American conscience as to realize that Americans do not expect social service and sacrifice to arise spontaneously and for no reward. Roosevelt tied service to self-interest; one becomes successful by recognizing humanity as a whole, one prospers by serving:

> Let us well remember that every child and indeed every person who is restored to useful citizenship is an asset to the country and is enabled to pull his own weight in the boat. In the long run, by helping this work we are contributing not to charity, but to the building up of a sound nation.[43]

In addition to his insistence on social justice, FDR was equally insistent on overcoming sectionalism and parochialism and inaugurating an age of nationalism in the United States. "The political and philosophical theses of FDR's New Deal rhetoric were that the president and the Congress had the legal power and the political obligation to address a national Depression at the national level with national legislation."[44] Nationalism and its related theme of interdependence were major aspects of the Roosevelt rhetoric. They were made viable by the fact of radio, for national appeals to localized audiences are difficult to make. But on radio, paradoxically, people listen in intimate settings while being conscious that this is a shared intimacy; people in other, equally intimate situations are also listening to the same broadcast. Through the medium of radio, politicians were able to address a national audience. Because of the medium of radio, citizens were able to experience being part of a nation, unified by the presidential voice.

Roosevelt's appeals were directed toward heightening this experience. He often referred to the need to let sectionalist, particularist animosities go, to realize our national (sometimes international) interdependence and to think and act nationally. He said that "there are two enemies of national unity—sectionalism and class—and if the spirit of sectionalism or the spirit of class is allowed to grow strong, or to prevail, that would be the end of national unity and the end of patriotism."[45] It was the duty of the president to prevent the growth of either the spirit of sectionalism or the spirit of class. Roosevelt insisted that "leadership has meaning only as it brings about cooperation."[46] This cooperation was to exist between the federal and state governments,[47] between individual businessmen,[48] among members of different religious groups,[49] and among branches of government.[50] Roosevelt was a powerful advocate for the development of what he called "an American point of view."[51]

A powerful component of this point of view was the bipartisan nature of Roosevelt's appeals. Even on the occasions of Jefferson and Jackson Day dinners, normally a time for Democrats to get the partisan spirit flowing for the year to come, Roosevelt always stressed the need to appeal to an audience that transcended party boundaries. This is not to imply that FDR was incapable or uninterested in acting in a partisan fashion. Most emphatically not. It is to state, however, that he was an astute enough politician to broaden his appeal by broadening his audience. That this appeal paid off in terms of increasing nationalism and the national profile and role of the president was an additional—and perhaps not wholly unintended—consequence.

The theme of interdependence was used in international issues as well, and Roosevelt is rightly recognized as one of the first presidents to understand the interrelationships among nations. This recognition provided the rhetorical impetus behind the Good Neighbor Policy, as well as lending rhetorical strength to Roosevelt's conduct of foreign policy in general and World War II in particular.

This simply furthered the process of increasing nationalism and increasing reliance on the president as the source of inspiration, legislation, and national morale. It is with Roosevelt, and through Roosevelt's use of radio, that the president began to take on the role of national agenda setter. It is with Roosevelt, and through Roosevelt's use of radio, that the president was charged with defining, articulating, and focusing the national character and the national mission. These tasks were never onerous or problematic for Roosevelt; he had, after 1936, a national majority. More important, he had one national crisis after another, and in times of crisis, the presidential power to take decisive action and have that action approved is greatly enhanced.

It is important to note that Roosevelt believed in social justice, in the importance of service, and he not only spoke in human terms, he usually acted in humanitarian fashion. Roosevelt not only spoke of "translating principles into human terms," he worked toward ensuring that "the object of the government is the welfare of the people."[52] He used his rhetoric, his personality, and his political acuity to advance certain policy aims, and that rhetoric, without those aims, would have been hollow and ineffective, for it would have lacked the conviction and the passion that were clear aspects of the Roosevelt style.

In sum, Roosevelt's rhetorical strength depended on his ability to reach a national audience with a powerful, unifying message. The message would not have been as powerful without the fact of the Great Depression. The national appeal would not have been viable without a truly national medium. Roosevelt both understood and used radio well. His successor lacked Roosevelt's commanding presence, resonant voice, and facility for eloquence. What Truman did have was the technology of a new medium and the political savvy of the old. The ways in which he used these attributes place him well within the Rooseveltian tradition.

Harry S. Truman: Old Politics and New Technology

Most scholars and contemporary observers begin by noting the differences between Truman and Roosevelt: differences of style, of ability, of philosophy, of result.[53] These differences should not be overlooked, but they should not be allowed to overshadow the points of similarity. Truman and Roosevelt attempted to do the same things: provide a certain measure of social justice, improve the quality of life for less prosperous Americans, maintain good relations with our allies, and preserve the New Deal coalition in the face of national change. This last was to prove the most difficult. Roosevelt could do it until 1944 on the strength of his personality and promises of future largesse. Truman was faced with the task lacking Roosevelt's personality and unsure of being able to deliver on his promises because of congressional hostility. But his appeals are remarkably Rooseveltian in character, if not in style.

In fact, Truman, more than Roosevelt, may be responsible for institutionalizing some aspects of the modern presidency. For while Roosevelt did many things associated with the modern presidency, such as hold regular press conferences, Truman may have been able to reverse those procedures, and they would have become Rooseveltian idiosyncrasies. In continuing many of Roosevelt's innovations, Truman institutionalized them and made them aspects of the office, rather than of the individual who occupied it.[54]

The stylistic differences between Truman and Roosevelt are immense and important. While FDR was known for his eloquence, "Harry Truman was too blunt to be called eloquent."[55] At the same time, he, like Roosevelt, was relaxed and confident in dealing with the press, and he maintained pleasant relations with individual reporters even while he lambasted the media for bias. Truman maintained Roosevelt's rules governing press conferences and thus also maintained Roosevelt's control over the press. He also kept up the Rooseveltian tradition of complimenting reporters while criticizing columnists and editors.

> It is the duty of the editors of those great publications to see that the news is the truth, the whole truth, and nothing but the truth. And these great ones do just that. But we do have among us some publications which do not care very much for the truth in the news, and sometimes make propaganda out of it, and then write editorials about it. But an editorial written on misrepresentation in the news is just as bad as the foundation on which it rests.[56]

Truman was honest and straightforward as well as blunt, which also distinguishes him from his predecessor. Where FDR loved the game and "enjoyed juggling friends and potential enemies,"[57] Truman lacked FDR's subtlety and preferred to deal straight from the shoulder (or shoot straight from the hip, depending on your feelings about Truman). This caused no few problems for Truman because he also lacked FDR's diplomatic skills; he could not (or would not) refuse to answer questions posed by the press and often let them place words in his mouth (the Korean "police action" is the most famous example). While we all might hope for a president who, like Truman, apparently has an "utter lack of guile,"[58] there are also disadvantages to speaking so bluntly. Truman's willingness to answer questions and his penchant for short, sharp answers often created the impression that he lacked patience and depth of understanding, and contributed to less-than-ideal press relations.[59]

Truman lacked FDR's finesse, and he also lacked his ego. Truman was a humble man, and, as far as his ability as an orator over radio went, there was good reason for that humility. The diction required to communicate well over the radio differs from that associated with live speaking. Truman excelled at the latter, but was never fully comfortable with the former. "From the start, it was clear that Harry Truman had a speaking problem. He spoke much too fast, almost to the point of being unintelligible, and with a flat Missouri accent."[60] A radio sound man was once overheard remarking, "He ain't no Roosevelt."[61]

This difference in oratorical ability was also apparent in the word choices made by the two presidents. Roosevelt had the gift of the apt phrase, the powerful metaphor. Truman spoke straight from the heart, and what came out was pure corn, obnoxious to members of the "Brain Trust," but appealing to the mass, and, after so many years of FDR, somewhat refreshing.[62] It is interesting to note that Truman, in his public discourse, is insistent on portraying himself as distinct from FDR in this regard. Truman was open to the point of bluntness, and blunt to the point of tactlessness; traits that lent him an all but unassailable image of honesty. One could believe Truman because he appeared to lack subtlety. Truman's rhetorical choices bolstered an overall image of honest dealing and forthright action, as Roosevelt's rhetorical choices bolstered his image as courageous and canny.

Despite these differences in style, there are clear similarities in content and approach. The similarities between the two presidents are strongest in Truman's first years in office, and many of them are occasioned by the necessity of providing continuity. Truman's first speech as president, designed to provide continuity and at the same time demonstrate that Truman was in command, relies on the power of recalling the dead president and uniting and acting in his name. Truman says, "Our departed leader never looked backward. He looked forward and moved forward. That is what he would want us to do. That is what America will do."[63]

This promise of continuity was problematic. The question of "what Roosevelt would do if he were alive," while perhaps interesting, was no real guide for the new president, for despite his rhetorical emphasis on planning, FDR was better at improvising than planning, and his specific plans for the future were uncertain at best.[64] By invoking Roosevelt's name, Truman gained a foundation for his own ideas, a justification for his policies. Unfortunately for Truman, it also gave his critics, particularly those who had been close to FDR, a convenient hook to hang their ideas on, and a ready justification for their criticisms. Mentions of FDR gradually faded away, except for use on ceremonial occasions, as Truman began to adapt to his new role, as the Fair Deal took over from the New Deal.[65] Truman increasingly insisted that he supported New Deal policies because of personal belief rather than because of political position. This theme became more prominent as Truman sought to define his own political identity as distinct from, but not in opposition to, Roosevelt.

This is a difficult problem of definition, and one that has plagued all presidents who have succeeded men of their own party. They inherit a legacy that they must not betray, but at the same time they cannot afford to be seen as a lackey to their predecessor. In Truman's case, this was a particular problem: His reputation in the Senate was clouded by his close connections to the Missouri political machine. Clearly he did not want to retain the presidency as merely a "Roosevelt man."

Truman managed this problem by referring to ideals, and making comments like "Franklin D. Roosevelt gave his life while trying to perpetuate these high ideals."[66] First, Truman would define ideals, then refer to FDR, then advocate a specific policy in Roosevelt's name. By the end of the talk, however, Roosevelt was dropped, and the policy was clearly Truman's.[67] This allowed Truman to capitalize on his relationship with Roosevelt, to legitimate both his position as president and his specific policy, and at the same time to begin establishing an identity of his own.

But that identity never strayed too far from the New Deal fold. The symbolic issues that Truman relied most heavily on during his administration were the questions of nationalism and internationalism. Truman did not have the difficulty Roosevelt did on the nationalism issue. Roosevelt's appeals and the world war had essentially settled the issue, and the South was a "solid" member of the Democratic coalition. At least it was until 1948, when Truman split the Democratic party and hastened the breakup of the New Deal coalition by forcing the issue of race.

By Truman's day, sectionalism was not really a problem. Nationalism was more a question of who got to be included in the postwar economy. Given the difficulties and economic dislocation involved with the transition to a peacetime economy, this was not easily resolved. Blacks were demanding a greater role in national politics, and Truman felt a deep responsibility to allow them that role.[68] Truman believed deeply in the values of democracy, and, for him, those values had to be applied to all American citizens. If nothing else, it was a necessary prerequisite for the maintenance of American moral superiority over the Soviet Union. He said, for example, that "in this country, democracy is not a slogan—nor is it a propaganda smokescreen. It is a practice, a way of doing things."[69]

And Truman had both the integrity and the courage to apply this belief to civil rights at home as well as Soviet abuses abroad. He believed that "talent and genius have no boundaries of race, or nationality, or creed," and he made no bones about saying so or advocating policies to reduce the "boundaries of race."[70]

On the internationalism issue, Truman, like FDR before him, often insisted that the United States must "learn to live with the world as a whole, and not by itself,"[71] and urged international cooperation instead of traditional American isolationism. This theme is, of course, most prominent during discussions of the United Nations. Internationalism, as opposed to isolationism, was much more a real issue for Roosevelt than it was for Truman, however, for FDR had to fight isolationism to involve the United States in the world war. Truman had no such difficulty. By the time he succeeded to the office, the United States was fully involved internationally, and no serious objections were raised to American participation in the United Nations.

Truman used the issue of internationalism for two different purposes: as a way of building support for the Korean war and other policies associated with the cold war, and as a weapon against his opposition in Congress. In the first case, Truman often used the issue of isolation to build support for the Korean conflict and his other cold-war policies. This was much more pronounced in Truman's second term, and it involved asking his audience to make a choice: One was either against communist aggression, and therefore allied with Truman, or one was an isolationist of the sort that approved the appeasement that led to World War II. "The United States was faced with a clear choice, which was debated up and down our land.... You know the outcome of that debate. The overwhelming choice of the American people was—and is—against the dangerous futility of isolationism and for full cooperation with other nations toward peace and freedom."[72]

Truman also used the threat of isolationism as a way of casting his congressional opponents as dinosaurs, out of touch with the modern world, and therefore not to be taken seriously. In making this argument, Truman often began with a remembrance of Pearl Harbor and/or Munich and then moved to a threat that, to Truman, was just as real, just as serious: "The crisis we face tonight is caused by a group of men within our own country who place their private interests above the welfare of the nation."[73] There are clear echoes of Roosevelt's strictures on "moneychangers" in this language, and it achieved the same ends. Middle- and lower-class Americans are given a clear enemy, and at the same time they are given a champion against that enemy. Truman may have lacked Roosevelt's inspirational qualities, but he could "give 'em hell" and thus satisfy the longing many Americans had for clear-cut issues and obvious choices in the ambiguous postwar world.

This use of clear choices is one reason for the success of Truman's remarkable presidential campaign of 1948. "If ever a successful campaign was patched together with scissors and paste and sheer bravado, it was that incredible effort of 1948 when Harry Truman upset not only his Republican rivals but the massed forces of the nation's press, public opinion polls, and political experts, including his handlers and seconds."[74] He managed this remarkable victory primarily through the use of two related tactics: the whistle-stop tour and vituperative rhetoric against the 80th Congress.

The whistle-stop tour of 1948 was the last of its kind in American politics. The whistle-stop provided Truman with an opportunity to engage in old-style politicking—the kind he knew best. Truman may not have adapted well to radio, but he could deliver a quick speech with lots of punch to a crowd of small-town farmers and merchants. These were people Truman understood. He could speak their language, plow a straight furrow, and realize the significance of federal refusal to purchase storage bins. Moreover, Truman understood the power of this identification and capitalized on it incessantly. He called the 80th Congress into session on "Turnip Day" and gleefully exclaimed, "They pretend to sympathize with the farmers, but they've never even heard of Turnip Day!"

The effect of this kind of speech was bolstered by Truman's personal presence. FDR had not been a physical presence; his intimate relationship with the public was electronically created. Dewey's campaign also deemphasized the personal presence of the candidate. Harry Truman, though, was right there, in the trenches, joyfully savoring the give-and-take of campaigning with hecklers and supporters alike.

By 1952, airplanes and television had largely replaced the rear-platform remarks Truman was noted for, and had eliminated the kind of rhetoric Truman excelled at—a rhetoric that depended upon physical presence, a sense of localism, and the ability to use exceptionally forthright language. None of these traits are politically feasible over nationally viewed television. But in 1948 "there was no need to get into elaborate discussions of foreign or domestic policy. There simply wasn't time. So he could tell the crowd what he thought of the Eightieth Congress in the plainest, bluntest terms."[75] And tell them he did.

The Republicans are committed to a program that benefits special interests, the powers of big business and monopoly. The only people who have prosperity under the Republicans are those who live on the fat profits made by exploiting the workers, farmers, and the common, everyday citizen. . . . The Republican leadership wouldn't give the American people the kind of housing they need because the rich real estate lobby opposed it. . . . The Republican party has always been dominated by the forces of reaction. . . . Do you believe in a government that puts people ahead of property, that thinks that the little fellow has just as many rights as the big fellow? All right—then you better vote the Democratic ticket.[76]

As enjoyable and amusing as this kind of rhetoric is, there is a problem with it. If the presidency is a "place of moral leadership," and one of the tasks of presidential leadership is to educate, then this style of rhetoric falls far short of the ideal. In giving people clear enemies and clear choices, Truman (and Roosevelt) also gave them a misleading understanding of the complexities of the world. The classic example of this is Truman's cold-war rhetoric, which contributed to Americans' fear of Russia and may have strengthened the burgeoning "Red Scare" in this country,[77] because "to obtain authority for what he considered necessary measures against Soviet expansionism, he appealed to anti-communism at home. To be in a position to take a tough stance against the dangers of communism abroad, he took a tough stance against domestic communism."[78]

This rhetoric could be harsh indeed. Truman's second term is full of threatening rhetoric and accusations of "Soviet aggression." He stressed that the United States wanted only peace, but in the face of the communist threat, "our foreign policy is not a political issue. It is a matter of life and death. It is a matter of the future of mankind."[79] This threat is no mere matter of Korea, either: The Soviet Union "wants to control all Asia from the Kremlin."[80]

Truman's stance, plus Senator Joseph McCarthy's skillful use of the mass media, gave McCarthy enormous power—a power unintended and strongly opposed by the president. This, more than anything else, points to the dangers of "public politics." For "going public" as a strategy is available to all politicians, not just to the president. Granted, the president has more resources and greater facility at public politics than any other political actor, but any single charismatic national leader can use the mass media as well as the president, and in ways that can actively harm the president's image. Another example of this dynamic is General Douglas MacArthur's speech before Congress, which was carried on national television. Television gave Truman's enemies and opponents a national forum even as it gave the president a national audience. Truman faced, as Roosevelt never had to, the dangers and pitfalls inherent in public politics. This is less an indication of Truman's weakness than it is of Roosevelt's strength. No one was as adept at radio use as Roosevelt. Many people, however, were as able to use television as Truman. Roosevelt and radio grew up together; Truman used radio, and appeals designed for radio. But it was Dwight D. Eisenhower who brought the art of television politics into the mainstream of American politics. Truman excelled in a different rhetorical situation, the stump speech. As this form of presidential communication became increasingly deemphasized, the rhetorical and communicative options open to presidents and presidential candidates diminished.

One of the things that is essential to an FDR style of mass leadership in the age of radio—Truman's age—is the need for presidential leadership also to be predominantly inspirational leadership. Many scholars and observers fault Truman for failing at this particular brand of leadership:

> Harry Truman did not have the capacity—the magnetism, charm, charisma, or whatever that ineluctable quality is—for strong personal leadership. He was liked, he was admired, he evoked steadfast loyalty in many, but he could not inspire. People gave him their hands, but not their hearts. He could make them laugh, but he could not make them cry. He was a plain man with honesty and guts (give-'em-hell-Harry), but you couldn't picture him in gleaming armor astride a white horse.[81]

One wonders how much of a misfortune this was. For the founders, for example, Truman's inability to inspire a national audience would hardly have been a problem. They were much too concerned about the possibility of demagoguery to yearn for a president on a white horse. But in the age of mass-mediated politics that Roosevelt inaugurated with his own personal style, personal inspirational ability became a key factor in American evaluations of presidents and presidential candidates, placing a new constraint on occupants of, and aspirants to, the presidency.

Truman's inability to inspire on a personal level led him to rely heavily on the inspiration inherent in the office of the presidency. He always believed that the cheering and supportive crowds were there for the presidency and not for the man who was president, and worried deeply about the "power of the presidency to hurt."[82] This led him to rely heavily on the ceremonial aspects of the office, and Truman greatly expanded the visibility of the office. Although this was a natural outgrowth and logical extension of the way in which FDR had handled the office, Truman's conduct provoked considerable criticism from Roosevelt insiders:

> With Harry Truman in the White House, the list of presidential appointments had become a geography lesson ... the Strawberry Queen from Alabama, a cowboy in a big sombrero, a Chamber of Commerce secretary from Indiana, the Minister from Liberia paying a courtesy call. ... At the end of his first year in office, Mr. Truman had done several things. He had lost whatever influence he had once had over Congress. He had split organized labor and confused the liberals. And he had had his picture taken doing more things than any other man in the White House.[83]

This list of activities is hardly surprising to an observer of the modern presidency. But it was worthy of notice in 1947 precisely because of the fact that presidents prior to Truman did not engage in such activities on the scale that Truman did. But faced with the obligation to engage in public leadership, and lacking Roosevelt's facility with the radio, Truman stressed personal appeals, and these appeals had the same effect on the "customers" as the rhetoric of the whistle-stop had on the electorate. Presidential ceremonies, in this sense, are Fireside Chats carried on by other means.

It is also interesting that Truman refers to the strawberry queens, cowboys, secretaries, and ministers as "customers." Partly this may reflect Truman's previous incarnation as a haberdasher. But more than that, it is an indication of his awareness that he, as president, is selling something. That something is his leadership. This is a democratic way of looking at things, for a democratic leader needs public approval—or at the least, public acceptance—in order to lead. It is also an indication of the kind of presidency that emerged under Truman and Roosevelt and that had its roots back with Theodore Roosevelt and Woodrow Wilson.

FDR was able to accomplish much of what he did because of the unusual circumstances during his tenure in office. No one, by 1932, doubted the severity of the national crisis. After Pearl Harbor, no one doubted the importance of U.S. involvement in the war. In using similar appeals, in the late 1940s and early 1950s, Truman was faced with the difficulty of convincing people that there was a crisis. His constant insistence on the dangers of communism point to weakness rather than strength: If the danger was generally accepted, it would not have to be stressed. Truman is forced to resort to such apprehensive rhetoric as "this attack [on South Korea] has made it clear, beyond all doubt, that the international Communist movement is willing to use armed invasion to conquer independent nations.... This is a direct challenge to the efforts of the free nations to build the kind of world in which men can live in peace."[84] Truman's speeches were apt to begin with appeals to fear: "Our homes, our Nation, all the things we believe in, are in great danger. This danger has been created by the rulers of the Soviet Union."[85]

While Truman appealed to fear, as Roosevelt did, he did not overcome it as well. The rhetoric was there, but rhetoric does not operate in isolation. Other factors are involved as well, and Truman simply lacked Roosevelt's ethos. Americans were not necessarily willing to trust in Truman to lead them out of the danger. So Truman ended by creating and appealing to fear without assuaging it.

Another problem with this is that crisis-style rhetoric when there is no generally agreed-upon crisis is not likely to be taken seriously and will create more problems than it solves. For Roosevelt, the nature of the depression and World War II as crises made presidential leadership important and benign. For Truman, the lack of such clear-cut crisis made the same appeals seem pompous and unwarranted. In his speech justifying the seizure of the steel mills during the steelworkers' strike of 1952, for instance, Truman claimed that "these are not normal times. These are times of crisis.... Our national security and our chances for peace depend on our defense production. Our defense production depends on steel."[86] It is significant that neither the American people nor the U.S. Supreme Court agreed with this argument. Both groups decided that the crisis was not as grave as Truman pictured it and responded accordingly. Here, Truman overreached himself, as FDR had in his attempt to pack the Supreme Court. Given a crisis, Americans are willing to relinquish power to an activist executive. But they remain uncomfortable with this relinquishment and are quick to repudiate an incautious president.

What this means is that for presidents to lead in the way that Roosevelt and Truman attempted to lead, for these kinds of appeals for the president as a benevolent national leader to be effective, certain conditions must be met. The president must be able to create and maintain the ethos of a national leader. For Roosevelt, this was accomplished through the device of the Fireside Chat; for Truman, through the kind of stump oratory that characterized his 1948 whistle-stop campaign. Truman used Rooseveltian appeals. But he did not have Roosevelt's ethos or Rooseveltian crises. Instead of the Great Depression, he had a postwar recession. Instead of the Supreme Court fight, he had the 80th Congress. Instead of World War II and Hitler, Truman had Korea and "Uncle Joe" Stalin. Of all of them, the only one that proved truly effective for Truman was his campaign against the Republicans of the "do-nothing" 80th Congress. This kind of dynamic is to prove true for more presidents than Truman, and such campaigning rhetoric will increasingly dominate presidential speech making.

In sum, Truman was, in many ways, an apt successor to Roosevelt. He shared the general philosophy of the New Deal and used many of the appeals designed by Roosevelt. These appeals were effective over radio; Truman was not. He took the same language Roosevelt adapted for radio on the road and onto the rear platform of the presidential train. They worked there because such speeches were short and punchy; they aroused emotion quickly and painted pictures vividly. Such language would rapidly be outdated, however, as television became the dominant channel of political communication in the United States.

Conclusions

After the Eisenhower inauguration, at a luncheon given for the former president, Truman turned pensive. " 'Two hours ago,' he mused, 'I could have said five words and been quoted in fifteen minutes in every capital of the world. Now I could talk for two hours and nobody would give a damn.' "[87] Truman meant this as a testimony to the power of democracy: that the transition had been both smooth and absolute. But it is also a reflection on the nature of the office. The world war and the growth of the mass media had combined to make the office of the presidency the most powerful—and the most visible—in the world. The question whether that power can be maintained in the environment of high visibility is one that did not yet trouble the American national scene. The problems with the new strategies of "going public" were barely visible: Truman's troubles with Senator McCarthy and General MacArthur were seen as problems created by his own personal weaknesses, not as problems brought about by the potentialities of the new media and the demands that media and the American public placed on the presidency.

The new media were not yet totally dominant. Even given the popularity of radio, personal speech making was still a prevalent mode of political communication, as the 1948 campaign proved. People still wanted to see their candidates in person, and the candidate who ignored that wish did so at his peril. Television would change this: Voters would be able to see the candidates without leaving their living rooms, and American politics would be irreversibly altered.

Issues would no longer dominate political speeches, as they did during this era. The speeches of both Truman and Roosevelt were long, used developmental arguments, and, more often than not, provided a history of the issue under discussion. Both presidents also relied on vivid descriptions and evocative emotional phrases. In Roosevelt, this inspired. In Truman, it comforted some and repelled others. But in both cases, it provided a link between the issues under discussion and the individual concerns of the audience. This is principled rhetoric, for while it used the techniques of persuasion, and sometimes involved ethically dubious appeals to the exclusion of real education of the electorate, these appeals were not used in isolation. They were connected to issues, and they were designed to win public approval of and support for specific policy proposals. With the advent of television, the connection between persuasive appeal and policy substance would gradually weaken. The details of this process are discussed in the following chapters.

3

The Birth of Televised Politics:
Dwight D. Eisenhower and
John F. Kennedy

Now I think, speaking roughly, by leadership we mean the art of getting someone else to do something that you want done because he wants to do it, not because your position of power can compel him to do it, or your position of authority. — *DDE*

The presidency needs someone creative and dynamic. The President alone must make the decisions. The President cannot share power, cannot delegate. He alone is chief of state. — *JFK*

The Potential of Televised Politics

This period marks the beginning of televised politics. The old style of politics has not been replaced by the new style, but the new style is augmenting the old. The public, aided by television, is beginning to turn more and more to the president, whose voice is becoming privileged above other voices in the national government. Both Dwight Eisenhower and John Kennedy were adept at the use of television, and television supported both of them in their bids for election and during their time in office. Their rhetoric is essentially based in television, but it is not designed only for television; the print media are still very strong, and much of the country continues to rely primarily on radio. Despite the political gulf between Eisenhower and Kennedy, the two presidents stand together in terms of the influence of television on the institution of the presidency. Their rhetoric illustrates both their political differences and their rhetorical similarities.

Both Eisenhower and Kennedy replaced sitting presidents of the opposing party. This gave them the conditions under which they were able to provide alternatives to the prior administration, and to do so in stirring and ideological terms. Change is more dramatic than stability; the rhetoric of both men reflects this: Eisenhower had a Great Crusade, Kennedy a New Frontier. Yet this talk of change led people to expect change, a dynamic that created both opportunity and challenge for both presidents.

Eisenhower used the media to project images that calmed and de-emphasized emotion, which allowed him room to maneuver. Kennedy used the same media to arouse and channel popular emotion to provide justification for his actions. Both men used television as a tool for leadership. They were not afraid of it, nor were they dominated by its imperatives. They were affected by those imperatives, however. It shows in their shortened sentence structure (true even of Eisenhower's somewhat convoluted grammar), their tightening of argument, and above all, in their reliance on the existence of pictures to evoke emotion. Gone are the vivid descriptions of a scene or of a situation. They have been replaced by photographs of those scenes or situations. Where FDR had to ask his listeners to have a world map with them as they listened to his discussion of World War II, Kennedy could gesture to the map behind him as he discussed Cuba. This affected the style, tenor, and possibilities of presidential speech.

Dwight D. Eisenhower and the Politics of Nonpartisanship

Eisenhower, modern research tells us, is one of the most misunderstood presidents in U.S. history. Professional politicians of his own time consistently undervalued him, the intelligentsia ridiculed him, and the press reviled him. And all indications are that he wanted it that way.[1] Eisenhower's approach to leadership was to undersell himself as much, and as often, as possible. He often began speeches by remarking, "I must say that my imagination was not quite up to the task of deciding what I could say to you on a Sunday that was worth taking your time for";[2] or "I can't think of any really good reason to give you for absorbing this much of your time this afternoon."[3]

This humility had some clear advantages, but it also carried risks. Among the advantages are the refreshing nature of honesty: Few of us really like long speeches, and most of us are convinced that they are a waste of our time. It is nice to know that an occasional speaker is aware of and sympathetic to that fact. It gives the audience an immediate and sympathetic bond with the speaker. In addition, this approach helped bolster Eisenhower's claim to be nonpolitical. Everyone knows that professional politicians love to get up and talk about nothing for hours. Eisenhower is different: he speaks only when he has something to say, and even then he is more likely to speak briefly.

But humility can be a risky strategy. A president who continually undersells himself is likely to be underbought by the American public. Eisenhower at least partially reduced this risk by referring, often obliquely, to his past military experience. His status as a general, a commander, and a hero is thus subtly brought into play, and any temptation to undervalue the president is somewhat abated. He would say, for example, that "from personal experience, in war and peace, I have come to recognize your dedication to truth and to the welfare of your country."[4] This bolsters Eisenhower's image by referring to his heroic past. It also supports him because he assumes the role of judge: Eisenhower is able to recognize others' dedication to truth and country because of his personal and intimate relationship with that truth and that country.

This appeal to his heroic image did not entirely mitigate the possibility that the electorate would undervalue the president because Eisenhower relied on two contradictory appeals in constructing his national ethos: He was heroic and at the same time he was the humble man of the people. One cannot conceive of the eighteenth-century electorate announcing that they liked George (or John or Tom or Jim); yet the slogan most often associated with the 1950s is undoubtedly "I like Ike."

The closer presidents try to get to the people, the more common bonds they attempt to establish with the electorate, the more they risk. The distance the founders established between the leaders and the led is a protective distance. Familiarity may not necessarily breed contempt, but it does not do much to discourage it. Television actively encourages familiarity and even intimacy. When presidents, using television, shorten that protective distance, they open the door to familiarity. Eisenhower clearly gained in the short term because of this strategy—Eisenhower's popularity was high throughout his tenure in office. In the long run, President Eisenhower may have been weakened, for popularity is not respect, not is it power; and the institution of the presidency was certainly changed, for the success of Eisenhower's strategy left a legacy few later presidents would ignore.

In the short term, however, Eisenhower was one of the most popular presidents of this century. He attained and maintained this personal popularity without the benefit of a strong political party, an accomplishment that would have been impossible without the mass media. Before Eisenhower, unpopular individuals could be elected because of their ties to a popular party or to a popular party platform. As Eisenhower discovered, and candidates since Eisenhower have realized, strong candidates need television more than they need parties. Richard H. Rovere summarizes this discovery: "Truman's party put Truman in power; Eisenhower put Eisenhower's party into power."[5]

What is particularly interesting about this is that Eisenhower put and kept his party in power by deliberately and consistently eschewing partisan rhetoric. Eisenhower may have deliberately underplayed partisan politics because he realized that it would not be an effective strategy for a member of a minority party,[6] or he may have done so because of his stress on "the need to promote the Administration's public relationships as though they were selling a product,"[7] and he realized that divisiveness was not a good marketing device. Whatever his reasoning, Eisenhower's public speech is dominated by two tactics: It is never negative, and it is never divisive or partisan.

One of the single most agreed upon elements of the Eisenhower presidency is his steadfast refusal to use negative appeals. This is related to his respect for the dignity of his office, his understanding of the Constitution,[8] and his ability to use a positive approach as part of an overall political strategy, placing himself as statesman above the petty concerns of other, "mere" politicians.[9] Whatever the rationale behind it, it is clear that Eisenhower both disliked and distrusted negative campaigning and preferred, whenever possible, to appeal to the positive.[10] In a speech at West Point, he said, for example:

> We are trained to deal in facts. To be truthful. To present our case as forcefully, as eloquently, as our talents may permit.... In the life that you find outside the Armed Services there seems to be a prevalent notion that if you call enough names, if you hammer enough desks, that you are a great leader. Happily, the Academy has never subscribed to any such false belief.[11]

This does not mean that Eisenhower was blind to the political benefits attached to negative campaigning. He was clearly aware of them. He was also clearly aware that a large part of his personal political appeal stemmed from his own status as a man above the political fray. He once remarked to an aide that "this is what I mean to people—sense and honesty and fairness and a decent amount of progress. I don't think people want to be listening to Roosevelt, sounding as if he were one of the Apostles."[12] Besides, Eisenhower had no real need to be negative himself—Richard Nixon filled that role admirably during campaigns and while Eisenhower was in the White House.

> Publicly, he was careful to preserve his image as a patriotic moral leader eager to preserve traditional standards of decency and common sense even when coping with the most controversial issues. When dealing with his own official family, as well as with Congressmen and Senators, his method was to convince rather than coerce, charm rather than threaten. That attitude of tolerant understanding, of civilized patience, of even his severest critics, carried over into all of his public appearances, particularly during his press conferences.[13]

Eisenhower's refusal to play at negative politics was also a matter of personal preference. He was known as a thoughtful boss, who never undermined or wounded his staff. In speaking of Roosevelt, Eisenhower said, " 'Roosevelt's only idea of humor . . . was a practical joke at some poor fellow's expense.' Then came the shocker: 'Roosevelt was essentially a cruel man.' "[14] The stress on a positive public image was also related to the way Eisenhower understood his office. He was sensitive to what Truman referred to as "the power of the presidency to hurt." In fact, "one of Eisenhower's most rigid rules of life was this: he would never use the prestige of the presidency to promote or tear down another individual publicly by name."[15]

Another part of the positive approach to public speech is Eisenhower's refusal to deal in personalities. This was most dramatically illustrated in his dealings with Senator Joseph McCarthy. When he did criticize McCarthy, it was through vague references, such as in his famous "bookburners" speech at Dartmouth College, or in such a way that the criticism appeared as a defense of something rather than a criticism:

> These characteristics of man that we call ennobling in their effect upon him—courage—imagination—initiative—a sense of decency, of justice, and of right. The faculty of being ready to admit that the limit placed upon our personal rights is that we do not transgress upon similar rights of others. All of which, in a very real sense, is a translation into a political system of a deeply-felt religious faith.[16]

Eisenhower made this rhetorical choice because he felt that the rhetoric of accusation and denial could condemn things he did not approve of but that unless he could replace those things with positive values, he would open the door to nihilism. Thus his rhetoric placed an unusual degree of emphasis on the restoration and promotion of American values as the way to define community and ensure order and stability.

> The purposes of the free world must not be too limited! Our goal is not merely to react against the inroads of Communist lies and attacks. That would be endless and profitless; the tactics of falsehood are limitless. We must join with our friends in a crusade of truth. We must make our aim the building of peace in justice and freedom. That is a worthy objective and a golden reward. Under God, the united energies of a free people can attain it.[17]

This understanding of his personal and political role was reflected in his approach to his political opposition. "President Eisenhower's overt efforts to avoid partisanship or political controversy shielded the intense efforts to effect an internal revolution of political ideology."[18] Although Eisenhower ostensibly got into politics because he disapproved of Truman's approach and policies, and although he was a dedicated middle-of-the-road conservative, he never used strident language or sought to arouse controversy. He believed that "no American—no one group of Americans—can truly prosper unless all Americans prosper.... We must not become a nation divided into factions, or special groups, or hostile cliques."[19] Further, "only in unity can the strength of each of us be multiplied by the total number of all of us."[20]

Given the growing complexity of the postwar United States, this call for unity was problematic at best. Unity could be attained only through the exclusion of certain groups—suspected communists and blacks were most conspicuous among those excluded from the "American consensus" forged under Eisenhower. But there is no doubt that the president gained public support through his appeals to unity, support that Eisenhower apparently valued more than he valued the traditional American commitment to diversity and equality under the law. The point here is not that Eisenhower violated majority beliefs in defining the American polity in such a way that blacks and communists were excluded. The point is that Eisenhower had a choice—as president, he also had a responsibility—to make use of his office to represent all of the people. He decided that "some were more equal than others." Instead of advancing the causes of minorities, defending their rights as Americans, he chose to elide their problems and concerns.

These appeals were possible because the demands of the television media were fairly limited. The president chose when and which speeches were to be telecast and could thus present one image to the television audience while reserving other images, other appeals, for smaller, more narrow audiences. Television did not have as strong a grip on the American political scene as it has today; Eisenhower did not have to worry about the need for conflict and drama that play such a large role in modern political reporting. The president controlled television. Television had little or no control or influence over the president.

Eisenhower's rhetorical choices were not accidental. Throughout his public life, Eisenhower displayed a fondness for and sensitivity to the nuances of language. Although Eisenhower was not known for the facility with words that Adlai Stevenson, for example, possessed, he had something more important: the ability to communicate with common people. He understood that Stevenson was remarkably adept in his use of language, "but said that if that were a qualification for the presidency, 'we ought to elect Ernest Hemingway.'"[21] While intellectuals never warmed up to Eisenhower, and thought his language reflected a lack of sophistication or intelligence or both,[22] the average person apparently felt that he communicated difficult issues without being patronizing. Fred Greenstein notes Eisenhower's "instrumental use of language," and how he used language deliberately to obscure or evade issues he chose not to discuss.[23]

The key here is that Eisenhower's language choices were just that —choices. He was not a prisoner of his speech writers,[24] and he understood the importance of language. He used that understanding to further his political agenda—for if Eisenhower was not the prisoner of his speech writers, he was limited by his ideology.

For example, Eisenhower saw the cold war as a war for the "minds and souls of men," and the weapons in that war were propaganda and truth. For Eisenhower, "communism ... uses bribery, subversion and sabotage. It uses propaganda.... This last weapon—propaganda—is one which emphatically requires from us new and aggressive countermeasures. ... Nothing is more dangerous to our cause than to expect America's message to be heard if we don't bother to tell it."[25] On the American side was Truth; on the side of the Soviet Union was only propaganda.

In conveying this American truth, Eisenhower looked often to Abraham Lincoln. Lincoln was quoted more often than any other historical figure, and Eisenhower's own language would sometimes contain echoes of Gettysburg:

As we meet today, in the 170th year of the Republic, our Nation must continue to provide—as all other free governments have had to do throughout time—a satisfactory answer to a question as old as history. It is: Can government based on liberty and the God-given rights of man, permanently endure when ceaselessly challenged by a dictatorship hostile to our mode of life and controlling an economic and military power great and growing stronger?[26]

Sometimes, however, the Lincolnesque grandeur would be seriously compromised by Eisenhower's tendency to lapse into the vernacular, as in his address to the United Nations, when he said, "So believing and so motivated, the United States will leave no stone unturned to work for peace."[27] Not even the grandeur of Lincoln's language can survive modern parlance.

This kind of awkwardness, surprising in a president who showed such a fondness for the language, is perhaps attributable partly to political exigency and partly to the inevitable conflicts between a speaker and his writers, a conflict that was generally kept to a minimum during the Eisenhower years. Despite the fact that his aides did not feel comfortable putting the president on live television—his press conferences were not broadcast in full until near the end of his first year in office[28]—Eisenhower performed well in press conferences and on television in general. In eight years of regularly held press conferences, Eisenhower never made a single major mistake. Eisenhower's staff also proved well able to succeed at what has become known as "managing the news": Eisenhower's press secretary, James Hagerty, "held two informal press conferences daily and kept a flow of favorable news going to eager reporters. He was thus able, to a remarkable degree, to transfer the blame for mistakes to other government agencies and to appropriate the maximum credit possible for achievements to the White House. He was especially adept in releasing big, favorable stories to blanket the bad news."[29] To a large degree, this success may have had more to do with the presence of a trusting and relatively naive press corps than with any particular ability on Eisenhower's part. In the pre-Vietnam days, the media were more likely to accept the president's interpretations as givens, making "news management" considerably easier.

Eisenhower was also successful whenever he spoke on television. While he was not as technically adept as one could want, "President Eisenhower had what counted on television. As often as he was exposed to this medium, he never failed to convey an impression of honesty, sincerity, and reliability. Indeed, the fact that his delivery was not very facile, and his style not much endowed with the devices relied upon by orators, added to his wholesome impression."[30]

This style was bolstered by rhetoric that relied on human references and that always emphasized Eisenhower's concern for people. Early in his presidency, for example, he said,

> Every gun that is made, every warship launched, every rocket fired, signifies, in the final sense, a theft from those who hunger and are not fed, those who are cold and are not clothed. This world in arms is not spending money alone. It is spending the sweat of its laborers, the genius of its scientists, the hopes of its children.[31]

Eisenhower also had the ability to make grand gestures in the "cool" manner Marshall McLuhan tells us is the key to success on television. One example is his crisis rhetoric. No one during the 1950s doubted that the world was in danger. Truman whipped up that fear without being able to assuage or channel it successfully. Eisenhower, partly because of his style and partly because of his ethos, was much more successful.

His usual pattern was to define a problem in dramatic terms: "The military threat is but one menace to our freedom and security. We must not only deter aggression; we must also frustrate the effort of Communists to gain their goals by subversion."[32] He then defined precisely the nature of the enemy: "Here, then, is joined no argument between slightly differing philosophies. This conflict strikes directly at the faith of our fathers and the lives of our sons.... Freedom is pitted against slavery; lightness against the dark."[33] Eisenhower follows this with a statement on the task facing Americans and their allies: "The building of such a peace is a bold and solemn purpose. To proclaim it is easy. To serve it will be hard. And to attain it, we must be aware of its full meaning—and ready to pay its full price."[34]

Eisenhower does what Truman was unable to do: He makes the threat and the urgency associated with it very clear, but at the same time he expresses a calm and steadfast belief that we will emerge victorious, combining threat and reassurance in an effective manner. He uses battle language, and he makes it clear that the task is neither easy nor short. But it is winnable. Truman could inspire fear, but not confidence. Eisenhower, like Roosevelt, accomplishes both. His confidence is based on the enduring nature of the values that the United States and its allies represent:

For civilization is a matter of spirit; of conviction and belief; of self-reliance and the acceptance of responsibility; of happiness in constructive work and service; of devotion to valued tradition. It is a religious faith; it is a shared attitude toward people and living which is felt and practiced by a whole people, into which each generation is born—and nurtured through childhood to maturity.[35]

This approach was possible for Eisenhower where it was impossible for others (notably Harry Truman and Adlai Stevenson) because of Eisenhower's unimpeachable reputation as a general and a war hero. This is not surprising, for Aristotle tells us that all other things being equal, arguments based on ethos are the most powerful, the most persuasive. The nature of televised communication, like the newsreels that preceded it, allow for such arguments by highlighting the visual above the argumentative. Audiences saw Eisenhower-as-hero in movie theaters and in their living rooms. If Eisenhower says the military situation should be understood in a certain way, not many people could argue authoritatively. If Eisenhower says it is a battle for men's souls that requires information as well as missiles, most people believed him; the same argument, made by another man, might well have been less credible.

But television was not a source of unlimited and unconditional support for Eisenhower. In addition to giving him a forum, the national media also gave one to his detractors and opponents. It contributed to the McCarthy phenomenon, which was distinctly not to the president's advantage. More than this, the fact of increased presidential speech led to the expectation that the president would speak. Eisenhower was criticized for not speaking out, or for not speaking out strongly enough, on the issue of civil rights. He was also criticized for not responding publicly to McCarthy.

The assumption in both cases was that the president would have been on the side of morality and that his personal involvement would have tipped the balance in favor of the moral choice: integration or the removal of McCarthy. In both cases, emotions ran high, and an argument could easily be made that early and eager presidential intervention was more likely to hurt the president than it was to aid the cause. In addition, in both cases, the primary government body lay outside the president's constitutional province: the state of Arkansas and the U.S. Senate. Given Eisenhower's understanding of the limits of his office, he was unlikely to have willingly interfered in any event.

While it is clear that we would like our presidents always to be spokesmen for the best and noblest aspects of our national character, it is not clear that this is a politically advantageous role for a president to assume. The moral power of the presidency is a potent force indeed. But like most forces, it is lessened by usage. Eisenhower felt that his power should be spent reinvigorating America's moral values in order to fight communism better. Despite his emphasis on positive appeals, Eisenhower defined our national persona as that-which-is-not-communism. The United States did not stand for human rights at home, but for freedom and self-determination abroad. When problems such as McCarthyism or civil rights were relevant to that, he would act. But he confined his activities to areas in which he knew he had influence, and where that influence would not be wasted.

The more presidents talk, the less powerful any of their individual words become. The growth of television has made presidential speech imperative. Eisenhower was affected by the first flush of this phenomenon. Kennedy would be subject to—and would feed upon—a much higher premium of presidential speech.

John F. Kennedy and the Power of Words

Kennedy is a difficult president to approach objectively, for in many ways he has become more of a myth than a historical figure, and as Kennedy himself said, "the great enemy of truth is very often not the lie—deliberate, contrived, and dishonest—but the myth—persistent, persuasive, and unrealistic."[36] Kennedy's mythical status derives from his youth, his promises, his tragic death, and most of all from his position relative to the American people. "Kennedy had made skillful use of the media of mass communication to promote the appearance of intimacy between himself and the public, and his death was felt as a personal loss by millions of Americans."[37] In many ways, this mythic status was the inevitable result of changes in the American polity and political environment that had begun under Eisenhower and had come to fruition under Kennedy.

The single clearest element of that environment is its size. Despite the growth and expansion in almost every aspect of postwar American life, as a result of television and other forms of burgeoning technology the world seemed ever smaller; in Marshall McLuhan's terms, it had become a "global village."[38] This shrinking created in people anxiety as well as the need to feel close to something, part of something. And this was precisely what Kennedy's rhetoric was designed to achieve. He said, "We do not want in the United States a nation of spectators. We want a nation of participants in the vigorous life."[39] (The irony here, of course, is that he made this speech to a television audience—an audience of spectators.) For Kennedy, too many Americans were mere spectators in the national life, and he summoned them to action, to participation. For Kennedy, inclusion in the American polity was to be determined by this participation. During a commencement address at George Washington University, Kennedy said: "I don't think that there has ever been a time when we have had greater need for those qualities which a university produces.... No, quite obviously, the duty of the educated man or woman, the duty of the scholar, is to give his objective sense, his sense of liberty to the maintenance of our society at a critical time."[40]

This notion of participation involves two other elements: the belief that the present involves problems and issues that are new, and more difficult than ever before in history, and the importance of service. For Kennedy, the Eisenhower years had been characterized by lack of motivation, which was created by an overly simplistic, cold-war view of the world. He constantly argued for a more complex understanding of world events than seeing everything in terms of "us" and "them":

> Mr. Khrushchev made one point which I wish to pass on. He said there are many disorders throughout the world, and he should not be blamed for them all. He is quite right. It is easy to dismiss as Communist-inspired every anti-government or anti-American riot, every overthrow of a corrupt regime, or every mass protest against misery and despair. These are not all Communist-inspired. The Communists move in to exploit them, to infiltrate their leadership, to ride their crest to victory. But the Communists did not create the conditions which caused them.[41]

Notice that Kennedy has not backed away from the anti-communist line. He is not arguing that the Soviets pose no threat to the United States. He is arguing for a more complex understanding of the nature of that threat. Kennedy does not confine this argument to our relations with the Soviet Union. The argument that the world and its problems are more complex, more difficult, is extended to domestic affairs as well. After discussing the Great Depression and the Democratic response to it, Kennedy says, "We in our time, in this state and in our country, face problems entirely different, but equally important."[42]

This appeal allows him to capitalize on the memory and traditions associated with Franklin Roosevelt, which he does frequently, especially on the campaign trail,[43] and at the same time gives him a platform to establish his own separate, political identity. He is in the tradition of FDR, but because the problems we face are so much more difficult and complex, he cannot be judged by FDR's standard.[44] He, like FDR, is a strong leader, but he is putting himself in a position where he will not be judged by his results, but by his efforts.

Given that our problems are more complex, it follows that, as a nation, we have ever more need of service from those capable of giving it. This service is a privilege. Kennedy made the country feel as if government service, national service, was a high, even noble calling. He never denigrated politics while acting politically. Instead, he was much more likely to exalt politics, perhaps creating inflated expectations, but assuring that people would have respect for and faith in their national government.

> For you and I are privileged to serve the great Republic in what could be the most decisive decade in its long history. The choices we make, for good or ill, may well shape the state of the Union for generations to come.... I pledged no easy answers. I pledged—and asked—only toil and dedication. These the Congress and the American people have given in good measure.... But we cannot be satisfied to rest here. This is the side of the hill and not the top.
>
> The mere absence of war is not peace. The mere absence of recession is not growth.[45]

In making these appeals, television was an invaluable resource for Kennedy, but not a neutral one or one that gave him no problems. For television has uses beyond politics, and entertainment television colors the way the electorate perceives the world. The political implications are clear, if difficult to analyze precisely. For television conditioned the electorate and mandated certain techniques while disallowing others.

> The ordinary citizen could not understand why tiny Laos, so far away, was important. He had been conditioned by the films and television to understand the difference between the good guy and the bad guy. He felt secure in the single knowledge that Communism was the bad guy, Uncle Sam was the good guy. As for the rest, it was up to the man who was President.[46]

It was precisely this simplistic attitude that Kennedy was trying to fight, precisely this sense that the government does all the work, that he argued against: echoing Lincoln, he said, "In your hands, my fellow citizens, more than in mine, will rest the final success or failure of our course."[47] Yet he tried to conduct this argument and conduct this fight via a medium that is understood to demand simplicity and clear choices. This created some tension in Kennedy's communication strategy:

> Kennedy and his advisors were continually torn between urges to arouse and to educate. There was, on the one hand, the belief that Eisenhower had not made the nation face up to the threats confronting it . . . on the other hand, there was a comparable sense of obligation to persuade the public to take a calmer and more rational view of the Cold War, to abandon the passions and the oversimplifications characteristic of the early years of the conflict.[48]

This tension was exacerbated by the fact that Kennedy was sounding challenges and arguing for citizens' active involvement through a medium that encourages its audience's passivity. Television viewers are spectators, not participants. Kennedy was asking the audience to become part of the performance.

His facility with television began before Kennedy was elected, and indeed may have been one of the most important elements of that election. "Without television, Kennedy could not have won the election. . . . 'We wouldn't have had a prayer without that gadget,' the candidate told me one night after watching a replay of one of the TV debates."[49]

To mention the 1960 election is inevitably to discuss the impact of the "Great Debates." Not only did the debates increase the available audience for each candidate,[50] and not only did they indicate the degree to which politics was being tuned to "democratic mass behavior,"[51] they also represented an apparent triumph of style over substance:

> The first debate was relatively bland, which encouraged the electronic audience to respond almost exclusively to cosmetics and style—Kennedy's self-confidence and good looks, his crisp, authoritative, fact-filled delivery made him seem knowledgeable; Nixon's evident discomfort as rivulets of sweat smudged his makeup, and his vagueness and efforts to be agreeable, created a figure uncomfortably incongruous for one who was to be preferred for his "experience."[52]

Kennedy's facility with television has led to charges that the Kennedy administration—including Kennedy himself—was more symbol than substance, committed only to commitment, and that, as Victor Lasky, a vehement critic of the Kennedy administration, says,

> Rarely has there been a candidate in American history who said so much that meant so little. . . . History may well record that the most serious thing that could be said about Kennedy is that he is the product of an age in which men felt they could achieve special distinction by the techniques of super-press-agentry rather than the espousal of serious ideas. . . . He is probably the only candidate who ever sought the Presidency of the United States—the world's highest elective office—not primarily as a political thinker or doer, but as a glamorous celebrity.[53]

Whether he was "merely style" or whether he used the style as a means of promoting policy, Kennedy was adept at his media usage and became one of the most accessible presidents of the modern era. That accessibility, however, was not without its price for the White House media corps. This was particularly evident in press conferences, which, for the first time, were televised live. This not only allowed the president to go over the heads of Congress and the print media and straight to the mass public, it also led to a loss of information. In the days of off-the-record and background news conferences, a president like Roosevelt could be—and was—very candid with the press. The press had much more information than they printed, and that information colored and informed their writing. With the advent of live news conferences, whatever the president wished to keep from the public, he also kept secret from the press. The early system was still open to abuse—and Roosevelt used it to his advantage. But the press also felt like they had some control over the process, that they were, in some sense, "insiders." With the televised news conference, the press were put on the outside, and in some ways became props and scenery for a presidential show. Even Kennedy's press secretary, Pierre Salinger, saw the press conferences "as a powerful propaganda tool the president could use to sell his domestic policies in the face of formidable opposition in both the press and in Congress."[54]

This among other press-related tactics led to cries of "news management" from a media that felt increasingly manipulated and increasingly powerless to do anything about that manipulation. Theodore Sorensen argues that Kennedy "never tried to use his position to intimidate a reporters' thinking, to secure his dismissal, to withhold news privileges from opposition newspapers, to require the publication or suppression of timely stories, to falsify facts deliberately as a means of covering up errors, to blanket as 'secret' or 'private' any matters that deserved to be known or to shift the blame for his errors onto others."[55] Yet, this quote is more interesting for what it evades than for what it says. It does not say, for example, that Kennedy never falsified facts deliberately, only that he never did so to cover up errors. It does not say that he never "blanketed" matters as secret or private, only that he never did so to ones that "deserved to be known." Yet Kennedy was the one who decided what matters were "deserving."

Kennedy tried other methods of assuring a favorable press as well. He is famous for his personal relationships with reporters, particularly Ben Bradlee of the *Post*. In addition, he often asked the advice and assistance of specific members of the press corps. "By asking them for assistance, he in effect was working to keep his Republican opponents from obtaining favorable press coverage."[56]

The most uproar, however, was caused by a speech he gave to the American Newspaper Publishers Association following the Bay of Pigs.[57] After saying that "I want to talk about our common responsibilities in the face of a common danger," Kennedy went on to stress the responsibilities of the press:

> But I do ask every publisher, every editor, and every newsman in the nation to reexamine his own standards, and to recognize the nature of our country's peril.... Our way of life is under attack.... Every newspaper now asks itself, with respect to every story: "Is it news?" All I suggest is that you add the question: "Is it in the interest of national security?"

The press responded immediately and angrily that they were not responsible for the failure of the Bay of Pigs and that Kennedy was equating "the interest of national security" with the interest of the national president. Kennedy denied that he was advocating censorship, but he was probably frustrated by the knowledge that a press amenable to presidential suggestion is also a press amenable to presidential control.

Kennedy, like Eisenhower before him, naturally tried his hand at news management. He would have been a fool to do otherwise. Operating in an environment where public image may be the crucial determinant of presidential ability to act, Kennedy would naturally have done what he could to affect that public image.[58] Even Kennedy, however, was aware of the ironies and pitfalls inherent in this tactic: "Shortly after the

Cuban mishap, someone remarked that the Gallup poll indicated that his popularity had reached a new peak. 'My God,' he exclaimed, 'It's as bad as Eisenhower. The worse I do, the more popular I get.' "[59]

This combination of style and media usage was remarkably effective, both for Kennedy and for his predecessor, who used many of the same tactics. As Michael Geis says,

> I agree with Edelman that the effect, if not the intent, of Kennedy's address was to create wholly verbally, an image of Kennedy as a Valiant Leader—as someone who has great courage and a potent leader. He achieves this effect by asserting his courage, by placing himself in the same tradition as that of the Valiant Leader's [sic] of the past, by associating himself with God's work, and by making an effort to establish the sort of relationship to the citizenry as is required of any Valiant Leader.[60]

This is all very nice for the Valiant Leader, but given the context of American politics and American political institutions, it is a less than realistic portrayal of an American president. Both Eisenhower and Kennedy used verbal appeals and the visuals of television to portray themselves as representatives of the American polity—as the sole authoritative representatives of that polity.

Like Eisenhower, Kennedy "had a gift for popular leadership; he used the presidency as a platform from which to exercise it; and the people were grateful to be led." But, although a president is justified in using the office as a 'bully pulpit,' popular leadership is not the whole of political leadership. When a president relies too heavily upon understanding leadership as solely mass leadership, his control of the rest of leadership is likely to slip away—congressional relations become a burden, both Congress and the bureaucracy become alien, enemies, for they impede the functioning of the "real" government, the government centered in the White House. Once the understanding of the rest of government as equally legitimate, in some senses, equally representative, is lost or weakened, presidents return to mass leadership, this time because they have no other choice if they are to govern.[61]

This has deleterious effects on the governed as well as the leaders: "The people are encouraged to expect too much of their political institutions and of their political leaders. They cease to inquire what politics may accomplish and what they must do for themselves."[62] This is not an argument for the reduction of government spending or programs. It is an argument against looking to the president as the only real source of national legitimacy and national purpose. (And it is an argument that is made in more detail in later chapters.) This tendency did not begin under Eisenhower or Kennedy, but it was exacerbated and encouraged by them. The consequences of this tendency were not fully felt at Kennedy's death, but at the political failures of his successors, Lyndon Johnson and Richard Nixon.

Conclusions

This period continues the era of the personalized president and the systematized policies of public governing. Eisenhower and Kennedy were acutely conscious of their images and knew how to design appeals that were appropriate to them. Their status was created and assured by their adept use of the infant television technology. Eisenhower and Kennedy attained and maintained their position of power with the aid of television and without the benefit of a strong political party, and by deliberately eschewing partisan rhetoric. This appeal was bolstered by the medium through which it was frequently transmitted.

As talented as Eisenhower undoubtedly was, he was surpassed by the "videogenic" abilities of his successor. Kennedy, in many ways the logical extension of Eisenhower's tactics, brought image politics and the various tactics associated with "news management" to a new level. For both presidents, the requirements of public relations seemed to supersede the requirements of governance. The rhetorical opportunities of the office are becoming constrained by the need for a continual flow of presidential messages as television and the public habituate themselves to an expectation of a continual presidential presence.

This is the legacy that Kennedy and Eisenhower left to their successors: an understanding of the importance of the media, especially television, combined with the knowledge that popularity can become a mighty force, capable of eclipsing political skill and even political wisdom. The search for political popularity through the control of popular perceptions characterizes the performance and public rhetoric of both Johnson and Nixon, and is the subject of the following chapter.

Television and Personality:
Lyndon B. Johnson and
Richard M. Nixon

I learned somewhere that no leader can pursue public tranquility as his first and only goal. For a president to buy public popularity at the sacrifice of his better judgement is too dear a price to pay. This nation cannot afford such a price, and this nation cannot long afford such a leader. — *LBJ*

A President can make a hard decision, but a President is not able to carry out that decision unless, in the final analysis, he has the support of the people. — *RMN*

The Imperial Presidency and Television

The so-called Imperial Presidency[1] begins in this period when Presidents Johnson and Nixon abused their power and systematically lied to the American people. Many scholars have studied these presidents from historical, institutional, and psychological perspectives. This chapter brings a rhetorical perspective to their presidencies and locates the kind of presidency they encountered and encouraged in the high public profile and expectations that had become part of the office they inherited.

During this period, the media and the presidency debated which of them would be accepted as the legitimate voice of the American people. During a time when the presidency seemed to lose so much through Lyndon Johnson's public rejection and Richard Nixon's disgrace and resignation, the presidency as an institution won this debate, and the president became America's virtually uncontested interpreter-in-chief.

No one can adequately succeed a myth. Johnson tried, yet even as he sought to build Kennedy's stature, he also competed with it. Nixon faced a divided country and sought to place himself above the political fray, as a statesmanlike figure of the consensus that had been rhetorically created and destroyed under Johnson. Both men were acutely and painfully aware of their media images. Both grew up in a politics that depended on personal ties and hard work. They encountered a very differently defined presidency. To both men, television seemed more "imperial" than the presidency: They cajoled it, catered to it, and castigated it. More important, they saw themselves as controlled by it and by its imperatives; this is especially true for the imperatives they associated with television. Johnson began by courting the media, attempting to use them for his own ends; Nixon treated the media as alien, enemy, from the beginning of his presidency.

At the heart of the imperial presidency is the equation of the man with the office. Neither Johnson nor Nixon seemed able to separate the person of the president from the office of the presidency. Many of their media difficulties stemmed from their efforts to appear "presidential" in public while behaving in a less than presidential manner in private. Both men had been around Washington long enough to know that presidents often engaged in unpresidential behavior. But until Johnson's administration, the president had always been afforded a degree of protection by the media.

Kennedy reduced some of the barriers between the presidential person and presidential media reportage; his family was often featured, his informal games of touch football used to create and bolster a specific image. Johnson was just too good as copy—too flamboyant, too excessive—for the media to resist. Originally flattered by the attention, and trusting that the media would protect his image, Johnson came later to feel embittered and betrayed by them, a sentiment the media reciprocated. The rules of the developing relationship between the president and the media were unclear, as television mores came to dominate those of the press. Both Johnson and Nixon would try to bend the rules to their will, based on what they understood of the media-presidential relationships enjoyed by their predecessors. Both suffered at the hands of the media for this attempt.

The rhetorical style of both men can best be described as inconsistent and cumbersome. In part, this reflects their use of speechwriters; both men used specific writers to engender specific images. When their image requirements changed, so did the writers. In part, it is also a result of their personal interest in appearing "presidential," which to both men meant formal, statesmanlike, and a bit grand. In both cases, it led to a feeling of artificiality, as they sought to mold themselves to fit their images of the office, instead of molding the image of the office to suit their personal selves, as earlier presidents had often done.

Another sign of the new impact of television and the image politics that accompanied it is changed presidential syntax. Reading presidential speeches becomes more difficult because they are increasingly designed to be heard, rather than read. The grammar becomes significantly less precise, use of pronouns increasingly sloppy, and the overall style resembles conversational syntax, not the formal syntax of less recent presidential discourse. This conversational discourse is clearly at odds with Johnson's and Nixon's understanding of the "presidential" image as a formal image. This contradiction is part of the reason for their credibility problems; their attempts to reconcile it become clear as we observe Johnson and Nixon in action.

Lyndon B. Johnson and the Rhetoric of Consensus

Two main themes run through Lyndon Johnson's administration: the legacy of John F. Kennedy and the need for compassion and programs for the underprivileged. It is impossible to understand Johnson's presidency without reference to these themes. It is also important to remember that these themes were played out under the increasingly divisive fact of the Vietnam war.

Johnson took office under singularly difficult circumstances. Not only had Kennedy been assassinated, but the assassination had occurred in Texas, Johnson's home state. The assassination, aftermath, and funeral were all carried on national television, bringing the entire country together to share the grief and mourning of the immediate family. In addition, feeling against the "old style" politics represented by Johnson ran high, especially among Kennedy's decidedly "new politics" staff. Johnson thus had to provide a feeling of continuity and continuance, and at the same time to establish the legitimacy of his very different style and approach. He accomplished the first task brilliantly; the second eluded him.

By all accounts, Johnson's handling of the transition was remarkable:

There is no word less than superb to describe the performance of Lyndon Baines Johnson as he became President of the United States. All accounts of his behavior through the week of tragedy—his command presence, his doings, his unlimited energies—endow him with superlative grace. Yet such stories limit the tale only to his positive deeds. To measure the true quality of his take-over, one must consider not only these positive acts, but what did not happen. So much might have gone wrong—yet did not.[2]

The culmination of "the week of tragedy" was Johnson's speech to Congress. It was a terribly important speech, for it set the tone of the transition and the administration to come. Johnson was never better. The biblical cadence of the statement "All I have I would have given gladly not to be standing here today"; the pathos of his plea for help, "I am here today to say I need your help; I cannot bear this burden alone"; and the grandeur of his closing, "Today, in this moment of new resolve, I would say to all my fellow Americans, let us continue,"[3] spoke beautifully to the moment and touched all the right emotions.

He continued the transition on the same note, although he increasingly stressed the need to move on, to continue, and subtly decreased the emphasis on loss and sorrow: "A great leader is dead; a great nation must move on. Yesterday is not ours to recover, but tomorrow is ours to win or lose. I am resolved that we shall win the tomorrows before us."[4] While the emphasis was increasingly on "the tomorrows," Johnson did not neglect either Kennedy's memory or the chance to make use of it. He once said, "Everything I had ever learned in the history books taught me that martyrs have to die for causes. John Kennedy had died. But his 'cause' was never really clear. That was my job. I had to take the dead man's program and turn it into a martyr's cause. That way, Kennedy would live forever, and so would I."[5]

Johnson may well have regretted that move, for he would be haunted by the ghost of Kennedy and the "Kennedy style" as long as he remained in office. "Senator Harry F. Byrd of Virginia might confide to friends that Lyndon Johnson was the only man from whom he had never won an argument; other Senators might testify to his legislative skill, personal drive, and political acumen; to most Americans, Johnson remained 'just a politician,' and a Southern politician at that."[6] Whether because of his background, his personality, or his style, Johnson was never able to captivate either the American people or the American media the way that Kennedy had. "It was simply that Johnson and Kennedy were two different kinds of men. JFK used wit, irony, and sardonic thrusts as one uses a rapier to prick the skin, to give spice to otherwise dull recitals. LBJ used mimicry and folksy tales of Texas to score and underpin a crucial issue or to make known a point of view."[7]

Johnson did not lack for media attention. The media's emphasis on the person of the president, begun under Eisenhower and continued under Kennedy, accelerated under the Johnson and Nixon administrations. Johnson, on television, lacked the personal warmth and appeal of Eisenhower or Kennedy. He also lacked the ability to communicate effectively through the television medium. The combination was to prove disastrous.

There are two sides to the presidency: the public side, the appearance presidents construct, and the private side, the "real" president. Most presidential images are a combination of these two sides, since the ideal that the president tries to convey is usually hampered or affected by the encroachment of the private side. Presidents are increasingly losing the protection of the private side, as television portrays both sides as often and as uninhibitedly as possible. This is not the sole responsibility of the media; presidents try to take advantage of exploiting what they consider to be beneficial private qualities (the Kennedy children) while hiding less desirable ones (Kennedy's health).

In this, however, as in many other areas of his presidency, Johnson went too far. According to some observers, LBJ "regarded the political process entirely in terms of popularity."[8] Combined with "his conviction that reporters were merely transmission belts for shrewd public relations men,"[9] the result was a strategy of assiduously courting the media. "Johnson tried too hard to win over press and TV people during his first months in office. He associated with them and tried at first to treat them as friends, even buddies. He tried his usually effective flattery, not quite realizing that what worked on a one-to-one basis sounded peculiar when spoken to a group."[10]

Johnson was the most media-aware president of modern times. "The president surrounded himself with the apparatus of the news. . . . He had teleprinters in his office which made him privy to the news before most Washington journalists were aware of it. He made visible, and audible, his outrage at stories, columns, and leaks. Yet he plainly wanted newsmen's approbation of his goals and plans."[11] His desire for approbation, however, was exceeded only by his willingness to punish those who did not provide it. "Because the presidency is the object of unrelenting attention and mandatory 'coverage,' Johnson was able to use routine procedures as political instruments. Private interviews were no longer given solely because they were thought to be the best and most effective way to communicate the president's news or qualities. They were disposed as rewards or denied as punishment."[12]

Johnson's distrust of the media he was trying to control led him to play other games with the press as well. His "peripatetic press conferences" were well known—and greatly disliked by the Washington media corps. "He would let it be known that he felt like taking a walk and head briskly out of the Oval Office, usually for the driveway circling the South Lawn. The reporters scrambled after him, puffing along and clutching their notebooks, getting down his conversational hints ... with a maximum of confusion and a minimum of benevolence toward Lyndon Johnson."[13]

And, most of all, Johnson's energy was overwhelming:

Never, said some in the media, had a president shown such raw energy in performing his duties of office. *Time* was overwhelmed. In a single week of late April, it noted, the president had made nearly two dozen speeches, traveled 2,983 miles, held three press conferences, been on national TV three times, appeared in person before nearly a quarter of a million people, and made his right hand bleed and puff up from handshaking. It was all "breathtaking, nerveshaking, totally implausible"; a handsome Johnson face would grace the cover of the May 1 issue.[14]

Despite all his finagling, all his scheming, all his effort, Lyndon Johnson never succeeded with either the Washington media or the American public. Partly, this can be traced to the nature of television. "Television, strange instrument, has its favorites, whom it somehow shows at their best, but it also has its stepchildren, and television has certainly done nothing for this man. It caught little of the sheer power emanating from him, the handsomeness, in its own way, of the strong-featured, weathered face, the nuances that came in looks, gestures, and intonations of the drawl."[15]

In addition, much of LBJ's continuing image problems were caused by "the fascination of the press with his personality, his foibles, his sudden excesses, the infinite variety of Johnson stories that made their way out of the White House in a flood."[16] The press found Johnson "unpresidential" and did not hesitate to tell him so.[17] And while no one will ever doubt that Johnson had a penchant for making extravagant statements, "still, one must bear in mind the tone given to the Kennedy-Johnson years from the very outset by the 1961 inaugural address."[18] Kennedy spoke extravagantly; Johnson's whole being was extravagant. And the media found themselves unable to focus consistently on the policies or accomplishments of the man when the man himself kept intruding. Whether you liked Johnson personally or not, you were forced to take notice of him. His charm, his force, his "corn pone" style, his sheer size, all demanded unrelenting attention. But the attention he received made him appear "unpresidential," especially when he was compared to the smooth, effortless elegance of the Kennedys. Unhappily for Johnson, no one compared them in terms of accomplishments or legislative skill. Kennedy had been noted for his "style"; Johnson's very skill was demeaning—he was a politician, not a president.

Any discussion of LBJ or his public speech must include discussion of consensus and the Great Society. Johnson wanted to be "president of all the people," to unify a country increasingly divided over his policies in Southeast Asia, in the name of democratic compromise.[19] At an early press conference he said,

> In some countries the solution is determined by the strongest. Free men, however, must take a very different role. They must realize that they can remain free only when they are ready to give and take, when they are willing to reason together, when they are ready to look for that common ground upon which all groups can stand honorably.[20]

For Johnson, compromise was the heart and soul of democracy. Compromise is not an unprincipled surrendering of principle; it is the recognition that other people have principles as well and that in order to live together, some flexibility is necessary. Given the times during which he governed, this was a difficult stance to maintain; people on both sides of issues took strong and often unyielding positions. Out of this, Johnson tried to carve unity based on the principle of compromise and mutual accommodation. "America's leadership at every level is called now to work for America's unity—and to work against America's division. This is not new work. This is the work we must always put first—if we are to keep faith with those who have come to these shores from across the seas."[21]

There are two other components of Johnson's consensus: the importance of social justice and the need for the rule of law. (This consensus building conveniently left Vietnam out of the discussion; for LBJ, as for most presidents, the president is accorded a special role in foreign affairs, and compromise is not part of the policy equation.) Compromise is really possible only among equals. For Johnson, when some people were systematically shut out of the process, compromise was impossible; those people had no choice but to rebel.

Justice under the law was a keystone of this formula. No president has had the kind of publicly announced sentimental and passionate respect for the lawmaking process and the law that Johnson had. He said,

> One hundred and eighty-eight years ago this week a small band of valiant men began a long struggle for freedom. They pledged their lives, their fortunes, and their sacred honor not only to found a nation, but to forge an ideal of freedom—not only for political independence, but for personal liberty—not only to eliminate foreign rule, but to establish the rule of justice in the affairs of men.[22]

LBJ never really understood the antiwar and civil rights protestors; he felt that they could do more for their cause by lobbying Congress than by rioting. This understanding of the importance of law took on particular pathos after the assassinations of Martin Luther King, Jr., and Robert Kennedy. After Robert Kennedy's death, Johnson said, "But those awful events give us ample warning that in a climate of extremism, of disrespect for the law, of contempt for the rights of others, violence may bring down the very best among us. A Nation that tolerates violence in any form cannot expect to be able to confine it to such minor outbursts."[23] For Johnson, the protestors were just as wrong as the assassins, for the violence of the protests engendered the climate that made the violence of the assassinations possible. Unlike Robert Kennedy, who deplored the violence but understood the frustration and desperation that caused it, Johnson understood neither the violence nor why some felt driven to it. For Johnson, the law was a refuge, never a repressor. The end result of all of this violence—both at home and in Vietnam—was the loss of the Great Society. While Johnson discussed, pushed, and worked for his Great Society programs until the end of his administration, as the protests against Vietnam escalated and his own attention became increasingly fixed upon the war, the Great Society stalled.

Johnson loved the Great Society; it was the one thing in his administration that was his alone; not John Kennedy's, and not passed in John Kennedy's name. For Johnson, the Great Society was intimately connected to both the American Dream and the American mission:

> We built this Nation to serve its people. We want to grow and build and create, but we want progress to be the servant and not the master of man.... The Great Society asks not how much, but how good; not only how to create wealth, but how to use it; not only

how fast we are going, but where we are headed.... It will not be the gift of the government or the creation of presidents. It will require of ever American, for many generations, both faith in the destination and the fortitude to make the journey. And like freedom itself, it will always be challenge, and not fulfillment.[24]

The Great Society was an ambitious goal, and one not likely to be realized. Johnson himself understood this: "I hope it may be said, a hundred years from now, that by working together we helped to make our country more just, more just for all its people, as well as to insure and guarantee the blessings of liberty for all our posterity. That is what I hope. But I believe that at least they will say we tried."[25]

More than just being ambitious, the rhetoric of the Great Society may have been guilty of raising false expectations.[26] Johnson spoke so often and so extravagantly about the goals and hopes of the programs, and so rarely and quietly about the effort it would take to achieve those goals, that blacks, the poor, and the disenfranchised expected rapid change. After all, life happens that way on television. And television was absolutely crucial during the 1960s. Television affected the way people perceived the world and structured their expectations and their understanding of reality, both political and nonpolitical. For example, the problem of race relations was highlighted through television coverage; some believe it was exacerbated by such coverage. " 'You got to understand,' said a thoughtful Mississippi cotton planter, 'that every one of those Negroes on my land has a television set in his shack, and he sits in the evening and watches.' "[27]

Of all the modern presidents, Lyndon Johnson was the most passionate spokesman for equal rights. For Johnson, the role of the government was to ensure the well-being of its citizens. "Unfortunately, many citizens live on the outskirts of hope—some because of their poverty, and some because of their color, and all too many because of both. Out task is to help replace their despair with opportunity."[28] Johnson felt that equality did not mean only equal rights, but also equal opportunity and a high quality of life. "We have increased the wealth of our Nation and the prosperity of our people. Yet we did not do this simply to swell our bank deposits, or to raise our gross national product. The purpose of this Nation cannot be listed in the ledger of accounts. It is to enrich the quality of people's lives—to produce the great men and women which are the measure of a Great Society."[29]

Whatever else may be said of Lyndon Johnson, he did dream in public. But his dream never completely captured the imagination of the American people, fragmented as they were into many separate publics and unable to fathom the logic of a man who could order increased bombing in Southeast Asia and plan a new dam for the Mekong Delta at the same time. Johnson seemed to feel that the destruction would be worth it if he could build at the same time; by giving the Vietnamese technology, he would be replacing all that they lost as a result of the war.

> Now, if we ignore those threats, or if we attempt to meet them only by the rhetoric of visionary intentions instead of good works of determination, I am certain that tyranny and not peace will be our ultimate fate. If the strong and the wealthy turn from the needs of the weak and the poor, frustration is sure to be followed by force. No peace and no power is strong enough to stand for long against the restless discontent of millions of human beings who are without any hope.[30]

Which brings us to the "credibility gap."

While most closely connected to the inconsistencies between his rhetoric and his actions concerning Vietnam,[31] it is also attributable to Johnson's treatment of the media regarding domestic issues. After realizing that his assiduous courting of the media was not producing the results he wanted, Johnson vented his considerable ire upon the White House media corps. Johnson had a passion for secrecy and regarded predictability as a sign of weakness. Because he distrusted the media, he treated them poorly, and they responded with equal distrust. Lyndon Johnson's example shows that "mechanical means of amplifying the the voice and a command over all of the media are to no avail if the audience will not listen."[32] The author of that statement might well have added, or if they do not believe what they hear. Credibility is not a matter of mechanics, of controlling the media. It is not merely a matter of looking convincing on television, although that surely helps. Credibility involves far more; it involves the connection between words and actions, a connection that, if broken, cannot be replaced. During Johnson's administration, that connection was visibly and clearly severed for the first time on the presidential level. At the time, it was thought to be a single instance, curable by the removal of the president. The same thought occurred under the Nixon administration. It is not recognized, at least not on a national level, that the credibility problem is related to the realities of the office and its relationship with the media of mass communication.

Television was a key player during LBJ's administration. In addition to increasing coverage of the president, presidential elections, and the personal side of politics generally, this period also saw the inauguration of one of the most peculiar phenomena in politics: images of the media covering itself. This phenomenon was a prominent part of the national convention,[33] as well as the rest of politics. It had not reached the present stage, where reporters interview one other for information instead of relying on traditional news sources, but it is worth noting. During the Johnson administration, television ceased being a background entity whose role was to inform and enlighten, but not to participate. As one analyst puts it, "here was the first president to realize that big media had come to replace big business as his chief rival in running the nation."[34] The modern media are participatory. They make news as well as cover it. During this period, especially, the media sought to become the authentic and legitimate voice of the American public. This is an increasingly problematic role for the mass media, and one whose origins have been largely ignored.

Johnson himself recognized this role. In a meeting at the National Press Club three days before Nixon's inauguration, Johnson said, "I have never, I must say, doubted your energy or your courage or, for that matter, your patriotism.... [But] I would be less than candid if I failed to say that I am troubled by the difficulties of communicating with and through the press."[35] Lacking trust in the media, seeing them as competitors for his role as the legitimate (or most legitimate) voice of the American people, Johnson could offer no solution for the problem of communicating through a participatory media corps.

In summary, LBJ was the first modern president to be more controlled by the media than controlling it. This was not the result of lack of trying. He tried very hard indeed. But governing as he did, in the way that he did, exacerbated the inevitable conflict between the media and the president. While Johnson must be held responsible for his own errors, he also governed during a difficult time for national leadership. His dilemma is perhaps best summarized thus:

> In 1968, after President Lyndon Johnson's announcement that he would not run again, a Chicago columnist wrote this poignant valedictory: "Goodbye LBJ. You weren't the best President a people ever had. But then, we weren't the best people a President ever had." Perhaps we should have the grace to temper our criticism ... by acknowledging that we are not the best audience a speaker ever had.[36]

Richard M. Nixon and the Rhetoric of Conflict

When Richard Nixon took office in January 1969, some people were pleasantly surprised at the "new Nixon" and his inaugural address. In that address, Nixon spoke to the national problems of the 1960s and promised conciliation and openness as the hallmarks of the new administration. The key problem facing the country, according to Nixon, was that "we find ourselves rich in goods, but ragged in spirit.... We are again caught in war, wanting peace. We are torn by division, wanting unity." The solution to that problem is clear: "To a crisis of the spirit, we need an answer of the spirit." The route to that solution was both concise and eloquent: "To lower our voices would be a simple thing.... We cannot learn from one another until we stop shouting at one another.... For its part, government will listen."[37] In this inaugural, Nixon spoke to the fact of national division and sought to prepare the way for the healing of that division. The cause of division was thought to be the Vietnam war; the solution, therefore, was to end the war. This Nixon promised to do from his campaign on. But as the war dragged on, people began to lose faith in his ability—or his willingness—to extricate the United States from Vietnam, and his presidency's credibility began to be questioned.

In part, his credibility problems began with this inaugural. Nixon orchestrated a tension between the style of the speech (which is clearly reminiscent of the Kennedy inaugural) and its message (which is Republican in nature, and which suggests turning away from existing policies and programs). Nixon's statement that "government will listen" was poor preparation for the realities of the Nixon administration.

Nixon traced his credibility problems, not to Vietnam, and not to the gap between his actions and his words, but to the American media. Nixon's relationship with the media is a long, complex, and often studied one. Highlights include the famous Checkers speech of the 1952 election, the debates of the 1960 election, his outburst after losing the California governor's race in 1962, the "enemies list" as president, and the issues of the Watergate crisis.

The common thread running through all these events is Nixon's distrust of the media—a distrust that is evident even when, as in the Checkers speech, television helped Nixon achieve his goals. LBJ learned to distrust the media after he failed to use them to his satisfaction. Nixon never trusted them or tried to bend them to his will. From the beginning, he felt that "their natural bias has an effect, conscious or unconscious, on how they choose their words to tell their stories,"[38] and that natural bias never included support for one Richard Nixon.

The Checkers speech is probably Nixon's most famous public address. It was given during the 1952 presidential election when Nixon, then Eisenhower's vice-presidential running mate, was accused of financial impropriety. Nixon defended his honor in a speech on national television during which he made references to his wife's "Republican cloth coat" and a dog, Checkers, who had been a gift to his children. Nixon pledged to keep to the dog, "no matter what." The public response was both favorable and overwhelming. Nixon stayed on the ticket and served as Eisenhower's vice-president for eight years. Almost more important than the immediate effect of the Checkers episode, however, was the long-term effect it had on national politics:

> The Checkers Speech was a primitive one, in modern terms—hastily produced, amateurishly assembled—but its success scored the mind of every realistic politician. Television would change the mechanics of all future American campaigning, inviting in the manipulators. The new system would require new professionals, image merchants, market analysts, psephologists, artist-producers in a managerial enterprise divorced from party structure, responsible to one man only —the candidate.[39]

The Checkers speech thus highlighted the real movement of television into politics. What it taught Richard Nixon was that he now had a way to circumvent the party politicians and reporters who were opposing him. He could go straight to the people, with the kinds of appeals the people could understand and support. This was a perfectly accurate analysis, as far as it went. What it did not take into account was the potential television had for bringing out the worst in a candidate as well as the best. Candidates became responsible for their own campaigns; they became atomized and were viewed as individuals rather than as constrained members of their political parties. As they became able plausibly to separate themselves from administrative functions while pursuing representational and legitimating functions, the preoccupation of elected leaders shifted from deliberative to ceremonial duties.

According to popular wisdom, this was Nixon's greatest problem in the 1960 debates with John Kennedy. Whereas Nixon performed well in debating terms, Kennedy and his staff orchestrated his performance for television. And the judgment of television won. Television audiences had become more sophisticated since 1952, but Nixon's approach to the medium had not. While this interpretation is debatable (and debated), the fact that it is widely accepted—and was accepted by Nixon—is what matters for this analysis.

Nixon, like LBJ, was simply not good at television communication as it was understood under the Kennedy administration. He could not envision the individual people who were his audience. The process of television communication was a dehumanizing one for Nixon. Where FDR could speak to each individual as he spoke over the radio, Nixon and Johnson froze; they spoke to the electronic eye, not to the human eyes that would watch them speak. Successful in person, neither president was very successful over television.

> The secret to Nixon's success in a small group was the key to his failure in reaching a more sophisticated audience on television. He was far better at speaking to real people than he was at speaking to "the" people. People in a room react; he could feel it and bounce off it; because he was good on his feet, he put his audience at ease. On television, however, the sense of place was missing, and he froze into what he thought he was supposed to be.[40]

Recognizing this, Nixon's people learned to "package the president," allowing him to do what he did best, and do it on television. This was remarkably successful in the 1968 election,[41] but problems arose when the election was over. Behaviors and approaches that are suitable and successful for candidates are not necessarily suitable and desirable for presidents. Nixon increasingly tried to circumvent the media, and as his presidency continued, his style could best be described as "crude, direct, addressed not to press or commentators, but over their heads to Out There."[42]

His goal was not merely to circumvent the national media but "effectively discredit" it.[43] Nixon believed that "the press is the *enemy*, to be hated and beaten,"[44] and with an attitude like that, good relations with the media were not likely to materialize. What did materialize was an obsession with the power of the media. As a convenient scapegoat, the modern mass media are unparalleled. When the public disapproves of a president's program or policy, the president can avoid the blame by putting it on a biased, lazy, and unprofessional media corps.

In addition to being usefule as a scapegoat, the media function as a conduit for presidential public relations. Since both Johnson and Nixon believed that if the people understood them, they would be supported, and since both presidents believed that a biased media contributed to a lack of understanding, it was a short step to taking the communication process into their own hands. To Johnson, this involved phoning offending reporters. To Nixon, it meant an obsession with public relations. Indeed, as one White House aide put it, "Richard Nixon at times seemed to believe that there was no national issue that was not susceptible to public relations treatment."[45] It is not going too far to suggest that the process of government in the United States has become, with the increasing influence of television, a "public-relations problem" and that presidents who ignore this element of national politics do so at their peril.

This is different from merely paying obeisance to public opinion, for turning government into public relations means that truth and accurate information play a decreasing role. The details of policy become deemphasized. What a president does becomes significantly less important than how he or she does it. This process has been developing over time; during the Nixon and Johnson administrations, it was in its awkward adolescence. Both Nixon and Johnson felt that acting presidential was enough to ensure their survival as presidents. They were wrong.

For Nixon, the key to his presidency was his assumption of the role of national statesman. This role established the belief that Nixon was interested in foreign policy to the exclusion of domestic policy, thus establishing one explanation for Watergate. More important, it has provided the basis for Nixon's latest political reincarnation; he has gone from disgraced and reviled former president to gingerly respected elder statesman, a position made possible by his establishment in the national mind as a younger statesman during his presidency.

Nixon's began assuming the statesman's role during his "Kitchen debate" with Nikita Khrushchev. On a visit to the Soviet Union as vice-president, Nixon met Khrushchev in a model American kitchen on display in Moscow. In the ensuing debate, Nixon appeared "tough" and tenacious. He often recalled this debate as a key point in his developing political career. Nixon expanded on this role as statesman early in his presidency, largely with regard to the Vietnam war. It continued through his amazing frequency of overseas trips and culminated in his excursions to China and the Soviet Union.

This position as statesman has several components. One of the more important is his refusal to bow to public pressure as displayed in the national media. On Vietnam, for instance, he says, "We may not make the headlines of today, but what we are interested in are the results of tomorrow."[46] Another, related aspect is the often-stated refusal to engage in image politics: "I would like to describe those policies today, not with a new slogan, because I have none—none that I think would be appropriate to the challenge that we face."[47]

Both aspects allow Nixon to portray himself as above the partisan battle, as nonpolitical. Statesmen, after all, are not good politicians. They are not, in the accepted sense of the word, politicians at all. They are above politics; they stand for principle. In his rhetorical approach to foreign policy, Richard Nixon stood for principle, for refusing to take the easy way out, for doing what is right and not what is expedient.[48]

The statesmanlike stance is usually connected to patriotic appeals, and, in fact, such appeals make up a large part of the Nixon rhetoric. Nixon often says, "I believe in America, and I think we have to speak up more for America and the strength of America and what it means to the world."[49] As the only person in America who can claim to speak for all Americans, to boost the stature of America is also to boost his own stature as national spokesman. As America's prestige falls, so too does the prestige of American presidents. It is in the self-interest of any and all presidents to improve American prestige, to soothe American tempers, and to promote American unity. To accomplish any of these things is to improve their own status as statesmen. Nixon is credited with doing all three.

Nixon-as-statesman had a domestic component as well, in which he used television and radio speeches to draw attention to specific domestic policy proposals and plans. On the domestic front, at least, Nixon never used the statesman stance unconnected to specific policy issues. Instead, he used the stance to provide credibility for his domestic policies. It was as if he was saying, "Look, you trust me on foreign policy, you can also trust me here." He says, for example, "I want to talk to you tonight about a serious national problem, a problem we must all face together in the months and years ahead."[50] This is a standard approach and would not draw comment except for the frequency with which he used it. There is a limit to serious (or grave, or vital, or important) national problems a president addresses. But when every problem he addresses is so described, response is certainly inhibited. Which, given Nixon's attitudes on federal involvement, may have been exactly what he wanted. In the later days of his presidency, it was also a tactic that illustrated how valuable a president is, and an attempt to bolster his public image through appearances as The President of the United States. It was also a response to the nature of television, which encourages drama. In always asserting the gravity of the problems he is discussing, Nixon provides some drama in what is otherwise a "talking head" performance.

Another important aspect of the television presidency is the tendency to replace formal presidential speech with a more conversational style. The long sentences and heavy cadence of earlier presidents do not occur often on television, which observers and practitioners believe favors relatively quick images. Long sentences and quick images are incongruent, and are unsettling to a television audience. As images get quicker, sentences shorten and become choppy. This is barely perceptible during a television speech, for the concentration is on the visuals. But here is an example of how it reads: "I realize that there is a fashion these days—and I understand this attitude and we must all try to understand it—that says we should not dwell on America's material accomplishments, that what really counts are the problems of people. And they do. And what really counts is the spirit and the idealism and that certainly does count."[51]

It is not clear that this passage would be significantly more intelligible within the context of a spoken speech, but it is clear that this passage was not intended solely, or even predominantly, for a reading audience. A similar style pervades much of Nixon's public speech: "Why have we had success in our new dialogue with the People's Republic of China, in our new relations with the Russians? I will tell you why. It isn't because Chou En-lai liked my handshake. And it isn't because I particularly liked vodka. I don't. I think it is a lousy drink. I don't like champagne either. There are things I do like, but not those."[52]

This style, in addition to conforming with the Nixon administration's understanding of appropriate and appealing television style, may also have been deliberately constructed to maintain compatibility between the extemporaneous Nixon and the scripted Nixon. This compatibility provides an impression of honesty and consistency between the "public" and the "private" Nixon. He and his writers constructed an image that conveys the similarity between the "constructed" and the "real" Nixon.

This quote reveals another characteristic of the television medium and its effect on political life. Television is an intimate medium; it comes into homes, becomes literally part of the family circle, and reshapes its configuration. It therefore encourages an intimate kind of communication. Franklin Roosevelt used the radio to convey the feeling that he was close to the people. Lyndon Jonson and Richard Nixon both used it as a self-revealing, almost confessional tool. They revealed much of their personal sides, and in so doing, reminded us that they were not really our friends, they were our presidents, and their behavior made us uncomfortable. Presidents prior to Johnson would probably not have confessed that they did not like vodka (at least not under these circumstances), and they certainly would not have felt the need to add that "there are things that I do like." Partly, this sort of confessional communication can be attributed to the personalities of the presidents involved, but it is also attributable to their understanding of a medium that emphasized some aspects of personality while minimizing others. Their individual styles occurred within a larger context; eventually, those styles became part of the context that would affect later presidents.

Both Johnson and Nixon appealed to "the people" as common men, distinct from the elite. Part of the way they did this was through their language choices. Nixon, for instance, treated language as if it was cause for suspicion itself. Kennedy's elegance of style became equivocal glibness, not to be trusted, its very elegance the reason for its suspicious character. Nixon, instead of appealing to language, appealed to the "silent majority." Public speech, already the province of the elite, is contested by silence, the province of commoners.

Nixon clearly means this as an appeal to the white working class, those Americans most likely to be dissatisfied by the rhetorical unity-through-tolerance-and-compromise of the Great Society. Through these appeals, Nixon began to forge the Republican dominance of presidential politics that has continued through today and the particular appeals of the Reagan administration.

Nixon's biggest flaw as spokesman for the nation is his apparent unwillingness to humanize abstractions, to personalize his policies. This ability is crucial to effective communication, and it is one that Nixon generally either lacked or refused to accommodate. The exceptions to this rule are worth noting. In the Soviet Union, for instance, Nixon gave an eloquent talk centered on a little girl named Tanya, and how she and her family had suffered during the war:

> The pages of her diary tell the terrible story of war. In the simple words of a child, she wrote of the deaths of the members of her family: Zhenya in December. Grannie in January. Leka then next. Then Uncle Vashya. Then Uncle Lyosha. Then Mama. And then the Savichevs. And then finally, these words, the last words in her diary: "All are dead. Only Tanya is left." As we work toward a more peaceful world, let us think of Tanya and of the other Tanyas and their brothers and sisters everywhere.[53]

It was a moving speech, and did much to dramatize détente and Nixon's foreign policy goals. The Tanya episode, however, is best known, not for its effectiveness, but for its comparative rarity. Nixon could use these simple devices, and use them effectively. Apparently he simply chose not to.

While he did advocate government reorganization, welfare reform, and "new federalism," none of these were capable of grasping the national imagination. Nixon himself says, "My strong point is not rhetoric, it isn't showmanship, it isn't big promises—those things that create the glamor and the excitement that people call charisma and warmth. My strong point, if I have a strong point, is performance."[54] This constructed character is designed to shift attention from Nixon's weaknesses to his strengths; it is also designed to shift attention from the constructed nature of his public character (remember, Nixon isn't good at showmanship; he wouldn't try it). The problem is that politics after the advent of television no longer significantly rewarded the kind of communication that Nixon claimed he was good at. The need for short sentences and the fear of "talking heads" meant that debating skills were increasingly deemphasized. The need to look good on television meant that Nixon's heavy beard and coarse features were perceived as a new liability. And the ability of the new medium to spread news farther than ever, faster than ever meant that slow and careful decision making was declining in favor of rapid position taking and instant analysis. None of these things worked to Nixon's advantage. And all of them were so new, and were changing life and politics so rapidly, that they were, at best, incompletely understood.

Nixon identified himself with the commonsensical approach to the presidential office. This involved facing your problems and dealing with them. He sounds very little like FDR, however. Some of his rhetoric on this subject is painfully revealing. He says, for example, "But I also know that defeat or adversity can react on a person in different ways. He can give up; he can complain about a 'world he never made'; or he can search in the lessons of defeat and find the inspiration for another try, or a new career, or a richer understanding of the world and life itself."[55] What applied to the individual applied to the nation as well: "I believe that at this time instead of talking only about what is wrong with America, it is time to stand up and speak about what is right about the United States of America. Because, you see, what is right about America enables us to correct those things that are wrong about America."[56]

Dealing with problems that Johnson and he faced on a scale unknown to previous presidents did not mean that Nixon approved of social protest or civil disobedience. Nixon says, "First, if we are going to have respect for law in the United States, we have to have law that deserves respect. . . . But we also know that in this country, unless we have not only respect for our laws, but for the men and women who are doing their very best to carry them out fairly and equitably, we are not going to survive as a free country."[57]

His approach to the Watergate crisis in particular revealed much about the Nixon presidency and about the rhetorical preferences of the president. Watergate, of course, is the label given to a series of events surrounding the Nixon presidency and the reelection campaign of 1972. It began with a burglary at the Democratic National Committee headquarters in the Watergate complex of Washington, D.C.; escalated through revelations of other campaign improprieties, including a coverup of White House involvement in the original break-in and other "high crimes and misdemeanors"; and eventually led to Nixon's resignation as president.

The rhetorical progression during the Watergate crisis followed these lines: denial of the charges; admission of the truth of some charges, along with the assertion that they were made for political reasons in an endeavor to discredit him; insistence that it was a matter for the courts and thus outside the realm of legitimate media interest; a refusal to resign on constitutional grounds; an overall identification of himself with the office; and finally, martyrdom in the name of the presidency. Of these, only the last two have not received significant attention elsewhere.

That Nixon identified himself with the office of the presidency is clear. He often referred to himself in the third person, as "The President"—"The President wants" or "The President thinks." But in addition to his personal identification with the office, it served a political function. Persecuting plain old Richard Nixon from Whittier was one thing. Impeaching the president of the United States was quite another. Nixon capitalized on this through his trips abroad, by making statesmanlike speeches on national television, and by referring with greater frequency to past presidents in his public speeches. The vilification of Abraham Lincoln during the Civil War was a favorite topic in this regard.[58]

On one occasion, Nixon followed his reference to Lincoln by stating that "it is that respect for other people, despite differences in political philosophy, that has brought us so far along the road to world understanding and world peace in the last five years."[59] This has the effect of uniting Lincoln, who is famous for advocating "malice toward none," and Nixon. It also has the effect of reminding people just what Richard Nixon, as president, has done for the country. We have made progress "in the last five years," not in the last two hundred. The emphasis must have been intentional.

Nixon also identified with Lincoln in terms of his martyrdom. Lincoln had been maligned and criticized, martyred, and reincarnated as an American hero. Nixon may well have seen the same process operating in regard to his own political career. On departing for his last trip abroad, one month before his resignation, he said, "It will be a difficult trip from the physical standpoint . . . it will also be a difficult trip from the standpoint of the diplomacy involved. . . . But I can assure you that on this long, difficult, and very important journey, that when we sometimes may feel tired, that we will never be discouraged, and we will always be heartened by the memory of this luncheon that we are having today."[60] The theme of martyrdom also appears in his final speeches as president: "I would have preferred to carry through to the finish, whatever the personal agony it would have involved, and my family unanimously urged me to do so. But the interests of the Nation must always come before any personal considerations."[61]

In his efforts to ensure good publicity and sound public relations for himself and his administration, and in the face of what he saw as overwhelming opposition in the media, Nixon took matters into his own hands. This meant that everything became not a question of " 'Was it right?' but 'Will it sell?' "[62] The focus on public relations to the exclusion of specific policy had clear—and clearly negative—consequences. Harry Truman could say, "Make good policies, and good relations with the people will follow." Nixon seemed to believe that if he could "make" good relations with the American people, he would then be free to make good policy. This reverses the previous order of things, and does not make for sound democratic policy making. At its best, public relations-oriented policy can bring us expedient and poorly designed programs. At its worst, it exposes all political actors to what William B. Ewald, Jr., an Eisenhower biographer, came to believe of Richard Nixon: "Nixon doesn't give a damn about the truth."[63]

Conclusions

The overwhelming presence of television during these years had an impact on the public perception and private conduct of the office of the presidency. "What has really happened is that a device universally hailed as a boon to communication has become a one-way street. It is a means by which a man can conduct a monologue in public and convince himself that he is conducting a dialogue with the public."[64] The problem with this is that it becomes increasingly possible for a president to convince himself that he has the support of the majority—no matter how silent—of the American polity. And that polity itself becomes increasingly pacified, increasingly absorbed in the moving pictures on their screens. This leads to a "celebritization" of the presidency, where the president joins the ranks of Elizabeth Taylor and Mick Jagger: Presidents are expected to be human, and to display that human side. They are also expected to be presidential, and therefore to be better, stronger, and smarter than anyone else. Both Johnson and Nixon were caught in this trap.

In addition, television was changing the entire face of American politics, not just the parts of it surrounding the presidency. What happened during the terms of Lyndon Johnson and Richard Nixon is that the presidency, while appearing to lose so much, won the debate with the media over which institution was to represent the authentic and legitimate voice of the American people. This debate was set up by the relationship between the media and the presidency since the days of Theodore Roosevelt and Woodrow Wilson. As Nixon said at the dedication of the Lyndon Baines Johnson Library, "As we look back over all the past presidencies, we also find . . . that each one who has been president has recognized, in his turn, that he is the one who must speak for all the people of America."[65] Despite the failures of Johnson and Nixon as individual presidents, the presidency as an institution won the right to be the agenda setter, to determine the issues of national debate; the American president had won the ability to be "interpreter-in-chief" of the American polity. The next chapters detail how well and in what ways later presidents coped with that new responsibility.

5

The Issue of Control: Gerald R. Ford and Jimmy Carter

The essential task of leadership in the modern age, as in ages past, is to inspire, to teach, to act with courage, to live with honor, and to show the way. — *GRF*

There is only one person in this nation who can speak with a clear voice to the American people. There's only one person who can set a standard of ethics and morality and excellence and greatness and call on the American people to make a sacrifice and explain the purpose of the sacrifice, or answer difficult questions or propose and carry out bold programs, or to provide for defense posture that would make us feel secure, a foreign policy that would make us proud again, and that's the President. — *JEC*

The New Hostility of Television

Gerald Ford and Jimmy Carter attempted to exercise leadership during a politically difficult time. Reaction to Watergate and the Vietnam war made the electorate suspicious of power and those who wielded it; the national media, both print and television, were perceived as powerful and hostile. At the same time, national leadership was expected from the president; its lack was strongly felt and strongly criticized. To exercise leadership without the explicit use of power is difficult. To maintain the low profile seemingly required of these "postimperial" presidents and still to inspire the nation is even more difficult.

Both Ford and Carter tried to design appeals, deal with the media, and tailor their public speeches to accommodate the peculiar difficulties of their situations. Neither was successful; each left office tainted with the image of incompetence, having lost bids for reelection. Yet both were successful to the extent of being considered honest men who did their best for a troubled nation.

In terms of their rhetorical style, both Ford and Carter stressed factual presentations above thematic arguments. Neither relied heavily on providing a context for his claims, arguments, and accomplishments, but instead seemed to feel that if the facts were laid before the American people, those facts would speak for themselves, with political support automatically forthcoming. This dynamic has never been possible, and the more dominant television becomes, the less possible it will be. To communicate effectively over television, ideas must be easily condensed, thematically presented, and able to bear repetition. As the following discussion indicates, this is not a description of the rhetoric of either Gerald Ford or Jimmy Carter. This is an important part of the reason why neither of them enjoyed great success as presidential communicators.

Gerald R. Ford and the Rhetoric of Decency

The combination of Vietnam and Watergate left the United States uncertain of its appropriate role in the world and confused about the role of the president at home. It is difficult to give expression to the national culture when the terms of that culture are under intense debate. This was the problem faced by Ford, and to a lesser extent, by Carter. Gerald Ford, the country's first "accidental president," took office under particularly difficult circumstances. He was not given any of the usual rituals through which presidents and the electorate witness and reaffirm the transfer of power. Ford had no inaugural address, no parade, no ball. As he took office, the presidency seemed much enlarged, and the men who served it seemed correspondingly diminished.

Ford's first speech as president gave expression to the confusion and uncertainty that surrounded his ascension to the presidency. After he took the oath of office, he said, "This is an hour of history that troubles our minds and hurts our hearts."[1] This one sentence served both to acknowledge the national emotions and to make an implicit claim that those emotions were temporary—he spoke of an "hour of history," a brief, almost ephemeral time span. Ford then went on to make explicit claims as to what actions he would take to ensure that the trouble and hurt were short-lived: "Therefore, I feel it is my first duty to make an unprecedented compact with my countrymen." That compact is to be based on his conduct and his honesty. He says, "I believe that truth is the glue that holds government together, not only our government, but civilization itself. That bond, though strained, is unbroken at home and abroad." By the end of the speech, the trouble and hurt are assuaged: "My fellow Americans, our long national nightmare is over."

Ford began well. He acknowledged the emotional context of his presidency, promised to end presidential abuses of power, and put a period on one era of national life. There would surely be a time of healing, but Ford made it clear that with Richard Nixon's departure, a new era of government began.

As part of that new era, Ford took particular care of the news media. He promised them honesty and access, and said, "Let me say again, I do look forward to working with you. We will have, I trust, the kind of rapport and friendship which we had in the past. . . . We will have an open, we will have a candid Administration. I can't change my nature after 61 years."[2] In other words, there would be no "new Ford"; what the nation expected, the nation would receive. It must also have been refreshing for the national media to have heard a president talk about "working with" them, recognizing that they have a legitimate interest and right to be there, and a legitimate job to do.

Not much has been written about Ford's relationship with the media, but their early relationship does seem to have been, if not ideal, at least considerably improved from the Nixon years. Much of the suspicion and adversarial aspects of the relationship remained, but Ford did some things to reduce tensions to a manageable level:

> Jerry terHorst suggested some changes in the format that the Nixon administration had used. One was to move reporters' chairs closer to the podium to reduce the sense of "distance" between the President and the press. Another was to discard the blue curtain that Nixon had always stood in front of—it looked stagy and imperial—and to position me on the other side of the East Room before open doors that led to the red-carpeted Grand Entrance hall. That, terHorst predicted, would create a much friendlier atmosphere.[3]

This quote reveals two things. One, Ford was interested in appearing more open to the press, interested in establishing less hostile relations than the media had enjoyed under Nixon. The second item is perhaps more interesting, for it reveals how sensitive the White House had become to the appearances of things. Ford and his press secretary took the time to think about atmosphere and appearance, something that few presidents before television would have done—or if they had done it, would not have done it so self-consciously. During this period, everything the president did was being examined: Was it "imperial" ? anti-imperial? Was it showing the president as a "common man" ? as a leader?

As Ford tried to move away from Nixon's image, he first had to dissect and understand that image. With the rise and dominance of television, images began to be designed on a conscious, institutional level instead of on a personal and personalistic basis. As television seeps into the culture as a whole, and particularly into the political culture, presidents lose the ability to be unself-conscious. All presidential actions are interpreted as meaning something. Sigmund Freud is often quoted as saying that sometimes a cigar is just a cigar. Presidents would benefit from having that dictum applied to them: Not all presidential actions are necessarily indicative of anything. But in the age of television, they will always be interpreted as being indicative of something. The fact of constant national attention robs the presidency of the ability to act and deliberate in private. As the presidency increasingly loses its access to the private sphere of presidential action, the president's ability to conduct the office becomes increasingly constrained.

Ford's transition continued in a televised address to a joint session of Congress, emphasizing that the time had come to move on. It is similar in tone to the speech made by Lyndon Johnson on the death of John Kennedy, except that Johnson had a stake in investing his predecessor with nobility, and Ford had no desire to attempt the same for Nixon. Where Johnson tied himself to Kennedy with the theme "Let us continue," Ford separated himself from Nixon, saying, "I do not want a honeymoon with you. I want a good marriage."[4] Ford was making it clear that he had no intention of continuing the extreme contention and acrimony that characterized Nixon's relationship with Congress.

Unfortunately, Ford did little to support the implicit promises of the transition. One of his first official acts was to speak before a convention of the Veterans of Foreign Wars and offer an amnesty program. This program had little to do with amnesty and a tremendous amount to do with the political imperatives of the Ford administration. While "throwing the weight of my presidency into the scales of justice on the side of leniency" and saying that "while I reject amnesty, so I reject revenge,"[5] Ford was focusing attention away from Watergate per se and onto the fact of a sitting Ford administration.[6] He was also making an appeal to the public that it should let the bygones of the Nixon administration be bygone. The American people should also "reject revenge" and support policies of leniency toward Nixon.

Ford may have seen this speech as preparing the ground for the pardon of Nixon, but it came as a shock to most observers when, after only thirty days in office, Ford "dynamited his own credibility, his reputation for political sincerity and the hopes of the Republican Party in the 1974 congressional elections."[7] Part of the trouble with the pardon is that Ford sprung it on the nation without any direct preparation, indeed, after making several statements that were widely interpreted as promises that he had no intention of pardoning Nixon.[8] Audiences do not react well to surprises, particularly controversial ones. Ford would have done better had he prepared the way for the pardon or had he given compassionate reasons for it—Nixon was in very poor health at the time, and Ford could have saved himself at least some criticism had he cited that as a reason for the pardon.

Whether or not the pardon was part of a political deal or a noble gesture, it provided a taint from which Ford never escaped. "Ford figured when he pardoned Nixon that the public outrage would 'blow over.' It did, but then it went underground. People can shout for only so long, and politicians often mistake silence for contentment. People don't talk much about Watergate—or Vietnam, either—anymore, but it is commonly accepted that both have deeply affected attitudes toward government and politics."[9]

In underestimating the public reaction to the Nixon pardon, Ford made his first public relations mistake. In his conduct of the Whip Inflation Now (WIN) campaign, he made his second. Together, these two mistakes undermined the confidence and support he had when he entered the presidency. Ford considered the economy the most pressing problem of his administration. The problem with speeches on the economy is that it is a difficult subject, and one that intimidates and/or bores many audiences.

Roosevelt used personification to overcome this communication problem—his speeches on the economy combined fatherly advice with stories of individuals, helping to make the complex subject intelligible and interesting to his audience. He simplified without patronizing, and he never lost sight of his role as president. Ford tried some of the same devices, but without the same success. The difference is that Ford erred on the side of folksiness, and his attempts at personalizing energy concerns ended in trivializing them. He says:

From Hillsboro, Oregon, the Stevens family writes they are fixing up their bikes to do the family errands.... Bob Cantrell, a 14-year-old in Pasadena, California, gave up his stereo to save energy.... Kathy Daly, a student at Sacred Heart High School in Weymouth, Massachusetts, has one formula for shopping wisely and saving energy. Kathy suggests buying warmer clothes this winter.... Sylvia Porter tells me that $10 worth of seeds on a 25'-by-30' plot will grow $290 worth of vegetables.[10]

This attempt to personalize economic matters falls far short. "Suggestions for better management of life's little domestic problems are not representative of the kinds of utterances that inspire the building of presidential legends."[11] This is because these little homey examples do not illustrate a theme. What Roosevelt's personalization did was allow people to feel empathy for the suffering of others; the example served to illustrate commonality. Ford does not provide the central theme through which the commonality becomes clear. He provides little examples and ends by sounding more like a column for "Hints from Heloise" than presidential speech.

In taking a "common man" approach, Ford also hurt his stature as president. Even in anti-imperial days, Americans appreciate and expect a certain level of elegance from presidents. They must appear to be of the mass and, at the same time, above it. Ford concentrated at being "one of us" to the point where we lost respect for him as "one of them." He earned affection at the price of respect. And these household hints are one way in which he did it.

Another way was his use of language. One author writes that

Mr. Ford distrusts the simple and unadorned declarative sentence.... the statement in the advance text that "I commend the American Legion" became "I strongly commend." "I am glad" became "I am very, very, happy." "All Americans are proud" became "all Americans are terribly proud." Typically, "I hope" came out "I honestly and sincerely hope."[12]

This lack of simplicity reveals an inability to distill his vision and beliefs into a simple, readily conveyed form. This will be interpreted as lacking vision and beliefs. Past presidents raised the presidential profile and privileged the presidential voice; their successors have had to adapt to this changed presidential role. When public communication became important to the conduct of the presidency, individual presidents began to be judged as presidents on their ability as communicators. Communicative skill replaced the administrative skills that were once important requisites of the presidential office. Ford's administrative abilities were overshadowed by his communicative disabilities.

Despite Ford's early attempts to establish friendly relations with the media, some problems naturally arose. In part these problems were the inevitable result of the press–presidential relationship, in part they were related to the temper of the times, and in part they were related to Ford's poor judgment (as when terHorst resigned because he felt Ford lied to him about the Nixon pardon). One Ford insider remembers "an article that was published at that time (I think in *The New Republic*) called 'The Flowering of Contempt' about how, as a result of Watergate and Vietnam, we had grown contemptuous of our leaders, and were therefore contemptuous in the way we covered them in the media. Ford was the first victim of that attitude."[13]

In addition to hostility from the press, Ford also had to deal with his image as an incompetent, clumsy stumbler. This image began after he fell from an airplane ramp in Salzburg, Austria, and it became an ongoing image problem for the Ford presidency. In part, this may have been related to a suspicion among the press that Ford was not up to the job. They then looked for ways to convey that suspicion to the television audience. In part, it resulted from the Ford administration's inability to focus the administration in an intelligible way.

Ford failed to understand that his problem was one of image and communication, not necessarily of substance. When asked why his campaign was having difficulty, he replied,

> I can't tell you why. I think we have a good program. I think we have done a fine job on the economy. I believe we have restored integrity to the White House. We have restored confidence of the American people in, I believe, the conduct of the presidency. I believe that we have made success around the world in our day-to-day operations of foreign policy. We have peace: we are going to keep peace.[14]

This inability to control and focus the agenda was particularly important during the 1976 campaign when the bumbling image created by the media undercut the "presidential" pose he was attempting to project. As Ford himself said, "The news coverage was harmful, but even more damaging was the fact that Johnny Carson and Chevy Chase used my 'missteps' for their jokes. Their antics—and I'll admit that I laughed at them myself—helped create the public perception of me as a stumbler. And that wasn't funny."[15]

It is worth noting that the American people were comfortable making jokes about their president, for it is an indication of how far the majesty of the office had fallen.[16] Ford played into this phenomenon by trying to meet the jokers on their own terms. He was a nice guy, able to laugh at himself; he even went so far as to appear on "Saturday Night Live." But the nice-guy image was established and maintained at the expense of the presidential image.

He tried hard to establish himself as "the boy next door" and set himself and his family on terms of apparent intimacy with the electorate, even referring to his wife Betty by her CB "handle," "First Mama."[17] Ford's biggest public relations problem was that he tried to combine two contradictory images: those of the "guy next door" and "Mr. President." The usual way to accomplish a union of these elements is to be "the guy next door" who made good and is now president. In this way, presidents can retain the claim to "the common touch" through their background and the claim to superior position through their accomplishments. Ford tried to stress his accomplishments, but he did so through the lens of his still being "one of us." Thus, no one had reason to view his accomplishments as special, unique, or worth admiration.

Another element of the "nice guy" image that hurt Ford was failure to project the image of someone with enough ruthlessness to be president. Americans like their presidents to be tough; they can be grandfatherly and tough, like Eisenhower, or manly and tough, like Johnson, but they must be seen as having the ability to make hard decisions and control the environment and the events that take place within that environment.[18] Gerald Ford was not perceived as having the necessary toughness. As one of his advisers commented:

> Jerry Ford was a great leader, as the term is used in football, or on board an aircraft carrier, or in the Congress. But command is something else. It requires an element of ruthlessness, the toughness that is required to send thousands of fellow human beings to possible death, the cold-bloodedness that sacrifices old and dear friendships, the iron determination to reach a fixed objective no matter what. Much has been written on presidential leadership, but command is what the Presidency is all about.[19]

And command is precisely what Ford was unable to convey. Partly this reflected his understandable reluctance to do anything reminiscent of the Nixon years. Partly it resulted from the nature of the man. Ford was a conciliator, not a commander. But it is worth noting the one instance when he did command, the *Mayaguez* incident—the U.S.S. *Mayaguez* was fired upon, boarded, and captured by Cambodians on 12 May 1975; the next day, following military action, Ford demanded and attained release of the crew. The effect on his standing in the polls was immediate and dramatic. Ford failed to capitalize on this incident, however, and the *Mayaguez* was notable in its absence from most of Ford's campaign speeches, a fact that is more important and noticeable since campaign speeches were plentiful during the Ford years.

Perhaps too plentiful: "During his brief presidency, Gerald Ford spoke some 2,055,600 words and signed his name to a million more. He delivered 1,142 speeches and remarks, averaging more than one a day and, on many occasions, from six to a dozen. During the Bicentennial and election year of 1976, the President set some kind of record by uttering more than one million words."[20] With all this talking, Ford was hurting himself. He was not a particularly good speaker, nor was he a good campaigner. In the degree of his public exposure, he dissipated the impact of the presidency, and undermined his stature as an incumbent president.[21] In asking for public acceptance of himself in his new role, he crippled his ability to assume that role.

In addition, his frequent public appearances gave the media frequent opportunities to note that he was not an inspirational speaker and that he was failing to ignite the electorate. He says, "If 'vision' is to be defined as inspirational rhetoric describing how this or that new government program will better the human condition in the next sixty days, then I'll have to confess I don't have it."[22]

This is a revealing quote, for it tells us that Ford saw inspiring rhetoric on a par with that of Reagan and Carter, his opponents in 1976, and whom he considered demagogic, offering false programs and unworkable ideas for the sake of votes. Ford was not above engaging in interest-group politics, and he appeared at his share of dam openings and other events signaling federal largesse. But he failed to tie these things to a larger theme, a theme that would make the federal programs intelligible and provide the basis for voter support. As a consequence, his campaign lacked focus and contributed to the image of ineptitude.

Even when Ford did have a theme, he often undercut himself by focusing on the negative aspects of the economy and the state of world affairs. Even when he talked about his accomplishments, it was with a reminder of how bad things were under Nixon. This made it easier for his opponents to focus on the Nixon-Ford administration instead of the Ford administration. On the issue of aid to South Vietnam and Cambodia, for example, Ford said,

> I recall quite vividly the words of President Truman to the Congress when the United States faced a far greater challenge at the end of the Second World War. If I might quote: "If we falter in our leadership, we may endanger the peace of the world, and we shall surely endanger the welfare of this Nation." President Truman's resolution must guide us today.[23]

Unfortunately, reminding people of the Korean war in an attempt to garner some funding for the South Vietnamese was probably not the most astute approach. It is no surprise that Ford's request for aid was denied.

Ford felt that the economic times called for sacrifice, and so he asked for sacrifice. He said, for example, that "not all good men rely on goodness. Not all just men agree on justice. But all free men agree that freedom requires sacrifice. It is costly. We must be willing to pay its full price."[24] Instead of going on to discuss the benefits that accrue from such sacrifice, Ford instead chose to emphasize the sacrifice itself. This may be honest, and it may be important. But it is neither inspiring nor good politics.

In many ways, Ford faced the same difficulties that Harry Truman had: Sacrifice is sometimes necessary, but is rarely greeted with unrestrained enthusiasm. It it not surprising, then, that Ford frequently cited Truman as an example and that he relied on the image of a feisty president, given a difficult succession, in much of his own rhetoric. In his first State of the Union Address, for example, Ford said, "Today, that freshman Member from Michigan stands where Mr. Truman stood, and I must say to you that the State of the Union is not good."[25]

Like Truman, Ford had to impress people with the urgency of a situation that they did not perceive as urgent. He said, "I concede that there will be no sudden Pearl Harbor to shock us into unity and to sacrifice, but I think we have had enough early warnings. The time to intercept is right now. The time to intercept is almost gone."[26] The problem is the same one that Truman faced. Using crisis language and crisis rhetoric when there is no perceived crisis serves to undercut the president rather than galvanize the public. This is particularly true when the crisis rhetoric is overstated, as both Truman's and Ford's often was. Ford said, for example, that "we have got to lick inflation. If we don't, it will tear our Government asunder. It will destroy all the principles we believe in. It will weaken us in our resolution to keep peace abroad."[27] To a nation that had recently survived the Vietnam war and Watergate, this was not an appropriate appeal. If the turmoil of the 1960s and early 1970s had not destroyed the country, inflation hardly seemed likely to. And the American resolution did not seem up to any more challenges.

Another problem with the frequent references to Truman was that Ford was not Truman, and appealing to his shade was not helpful in the long run. For, in putting himself next to Truman, Ford invited a comparison that did Ford no favors. Truman excelled at taking his case to the people, in talking their language, and in taking the fight to Congress. He did not excel at compromise and conciliation, but at aggressive argumentation. For people who doubted Ford's ability in this area, inviting a comparison to Truman only seemed to confirm their worst suspicions about the president and provide further evidence that he was not up to the job.

In sum, Ford seems to have richly deserved his reputation as an honorable man who was well intentioned, but not up to the requirements of the presidency. The substantive side of the task he seems to have handled quite well. But on the equally important symbolic side, made increasingly important by the imperatives of television, he faltered. He did an admirable job of providing a transition away from the Nixon administration, but the issue of the pardon made it impossible for him ever to get completely away. His ties to Richard Nixon probably hurt Ford more than any other element of his presidency, but his inability to "define the goals, the vision and the purposes of his presidency in a way that gives coherence to his administration and his campaign"[28] are also key elements in his failure to win the presidency in his own right.

Jimmy Carter and the Rhetoric of Morality

Jimmy Carter, campaigning for president, promised that he would "never lie, never mislead" the American people. More than any president since Eisenhower, Carter sought to identify his personal morality with the conscience of the nation.[29] He ran on the promise of open and honest government, and his "new populist" approach made him the darling of the media in the early days of his administration. Yet Carter ultimately failed to maintain either his image or his popularity, and lost his bid for reelection by an overwhelming margin.

Partly this is because he first overused and then completely stopped using the symbol-oriented approach to governing, and partly it was caused by the nature of the image itself. "Carter's populism was mostly stylistic—a reliance on the rhetoric of the outsider and the outsiders' resentment of those in power."[30] This was not a stance he could well maintain once he was *in* power. Carter's image as an "outsider" was initially beneficial, for it helped him establish his separation from the discredited and distrusted professional politicians. But it was not just an image—Carter was an outsider, one who did not understand the ways and means of Washington politics, and who held those politics in contempt.[31]

We may like the boy next door, we certainly entertain nostalgic feelings for him. But, as Gerald Ford discovered, we do not want him to be president. After a time, the public simply tired of the same old symbols. The president who carried his own bags, who refused the perquisites of office, also seemed to be a president who did not understand the grandeur and the majesty of the presidency:

> The pomp and ceremony of office does not appeal to me, and I don't believe its a necessary part of the Presidency in a democratic nation like our own. I'm no better than anyone else. . . . I don't think we need to put on the trappings of a monarchy in a nation like our own. I feel uncomfortable with it.[32]

Despite this lack of understanding of the symbolic functions of the president-as-monarch, in terms of legitimating the government, Carter began that legitimating reasonably well, thanking Ford in the opening sentence of his inaugural, "For myself and for our Nation, I want to thank my predecessor for all he has done to heal our land." This set a high tone for the speech[33] and signaled the beginning of an administration that would not concern itself with partisan animosities and personal grudges. Then, however, Carter undermined himself through the first of many conflicting signals. After setting a high tone, Carter brought the level down with a thud: "As my high school teacher, Miss Julia Coleman, used to say . . . ." All of us have heroes, and not all those heroes need to be persons of high status and dignity. But to quote a high school teacher as an ultimate authority during an inaugural sent a signal that maybe Carter was not such a genius with symbols after all. Populism can, after all, be carried too far. As Gerald Ford discovered, overemphasizing the "boy next door" symbols can underemphasize the presidential image. Carter had the same problem, and for the same reasons, with his reference to his daughter Amy's political acumen in the 1980 campaign debate against Reagan.

Underemphasizing the presidential image was the conscious and specific intention of the early days of the Carter administration. He announced with great fanfare that "we decided to forgo the 'Ruffles and Flourishes' and 'Hail to the Chief'" and promised that "there will never be an instance, while I am president, when the members of the White House staff dominate, or act in a superior position to the members of the Cabinet."[34] The problem with this is that as Carter gave up more and more of his presidential prerogatives, as he allowed the Cabinet and other high officials to express themselves on an equal basis with the president, his one real power was dissipated: the power to speak for the nation with a single, united voice.

Usually, the president is in a privileged position, a position made more privileged by the dominance of television, with the tendency of television news to personalize issues and institutions. This gives presidents a special advantage, for they are already a personal embodiment of the nation. As Carter allowed other members of his administration to maintain high public profiles, he gave away that advantage, and the number of competing—and equally authoritative—voices contributed to both the real and perceived confusion of the Carter administration.

Human rights is a case in point. There is no doubt that Carter had strong, personal feelings about the importance of human rights: "The OAS Charter pledges us to individual liberty and social justice. I come here now to restate our own commitment to these goals. The challenge before us today, however, is not just to reaffirm those principles, but to find ways to make them a reality."[35] The problem is that he also espoused "a wider, more flexible approach, worked out in close consultation with you." Again, while this is certainly an approach that won Carter the respect and affection of our Latin American allies, it undermined his own ability to appear in control of events. The more power is shared, the less the president has. In addition to sharing it with his Cabinet and advisers (like Andrew Young), he also shared it with our allies. As policy, perhaps laudable. As public relations, disastrous.

In addition, Carter's refusal to act presidential trivialized much of what he wanted to accomplish. Greeting audiences with an informal "Hi, everybody"[36] undercut his own position. A certain degree of formality is important to maintaining credibility. The more "expert" expert opinion is, the more likely audiences are to respect it. The more like "one of us" the source is, the less likely that source is to receive unqualified respect.

Some degree of identification is important: FDR, for example, gave audiences the feeling that he identified with them, understood them. Increasingly, audiences came to feel that *they* understood Carter, both his strengths and weaknesses. Such familiarity may not necessarily breed contempt, but it does not encourage respect.

This failure to encourage respect is also evident in Carter's very public humility. He was fond of saying that "I don't claim to know all the answers. I need you to help me with your support when you agree, with your advice when we're evolving policy, and with your criticism when you think I've made a mistake. I need all three."[37] Eisenhower could make similar claims to humility with less risk, for he had status as a general and a war hero. Carter lacked such a history, and lacked a widespread national ethos as a leader. The public assumption of humility was thus a dangerous one for him to use often, much less continually. Carter was elected because he claimed to be competent. Once elected, he almost appeared to be claiming to be incompetent. Incompetence was always the easier claim to sustain.

Compounding this confusion was the sense that Carter believed himself to be morally superior to his opponents—and to his allies. When the "boy next door" has the uncomfortable habit of preaching at us, we often wait for him to fail, just to "bring him down a peg." Jimmy Carter appeared to combine sincere humility before God with the knowledge that he was smarter, stronger, more persevering, and harder working than anyone he had ever met.[38] It is an uncomfortable combination at best.

Carter's stress on religious topics also merits consideration. While all presidents use religious themes and "civic religion" to some extent,[39] Carter relied heavily on such appeals, using religion not only to "reaffirm our civic piety" but also to communicate trustworthiness and provide a basis for his claim to administer a "government as good as the American people."[40] As his administration progressed, however, with charges of corruption and a general air of incompetence, the image of trustworthiness degenerated into one of smugness and superiority, and the appeals that during the election had served to unite the electorate behind Carter began to distance him from them.

Carter's speeches were heavily autobiographical, which contributed to this phenomenon. Who Carter is became more important that what policies he espouses or what he actually does. Since the president is, by definition, symbolic of the nation, that is not a problem unless, as with Johnson and Nixon, the president loses sight of the difference between the man and the office. In Carter's case, he separated the man so completely from the office that when he later tried to appear "presidential," he instead appeared "political." Had he begun his tenure by being both Jimmy Carter and Mr. President, he could have continued to combine those personae. But because he separated "Jimmy" from "Mr. President," any move to combine them appeared manipulative.

Autobiography can help a speaker create a sense of identity and empathy with an audience, but it can also undermine that speaker's credibility. Carter used it effectively, but he was limited by his own abilities. For a man so often and so publicly proud of his southern roots, Carter "is no Southern talker, orator, writer. He speaks without embellishment," and his writing seems to be "translated from the German."[41] Carter had none of the southerners' affection for, and ability with, words. He had no sense of their potential power. As one analyst notes, the "banner he held out to a troubled people: 'As President, I want you to help me evolve an efficient, economical, purposeful and manageable government for our nation. I recognize the difficulty, but if I'm elected, it shall be done!'"[42] Such oratory may be accurate; the goals espoused are certainly important. But it is difficult to get the electorate enthusiastic over the issue of government reorganization. Particularly when the dominant communicator is uninterested in thematic presentations.

Carter loved lists. Like Lyndon Johnson, Carter identified himself by listing loyalties: "I am an American, a Southerner. . . ." Also like Johnson, Carter used this listing to create ambiguity. Just what does it mean to be an American, a southerner, a family man? This ambiguity allows audiences to find in the speaker whatever they are looking for. There is a problem with this kind of ambiguity, however. For the longer the list, the less importance the audience will attach to any single item. Undergraduates love lists: Lists help students organize and remember information for examinations. Audiences, especially television audiences, do not love lists. They need their information organized differently, for they are not taking notes, nor do they expect an examination.

In a Memorial Day speech aboard the battleship *Nimitz*, Carter says, for example, that

> history most often records the courage and dedication and sacrifice of those who have been in battle, when wars were won and lost and when heroism was apparent and well-publicized. But all of us know that the sacrifice and the courage and the dedication and the service in times of peace to prevent war are equally gratifying to those whom you have served so well.[43]

Carter interrupts the flow and cadence of his speech through such polysyndeton (repetition of a conjunction, in this case "and"). This technique is useful when the speaker wants to prolong an idea without examining each individual component (MacArthur's "The corps and the corps and the corps" in his speech at West Point, for example). Carter's use of polysyndeton, however, serves to amalgamate elements that could be more effective if separated into short declarative sentences. Its use here undermines the power of the separate elements as well as the occasion's symbolic significance. Even his choice of adjectives—a nation that is "gratified"—minimizes the impact of what he is trying to say. This passage would be much more effective had Carter reduced the number of attributes (dedication and service, for example, are redundant) and increased the emotions the nation is supposed to feel—that he as president is supposed to represent the nation as feeling. If "gratified" is the best he can do, then a nation eager to feel more is going to feel cheated.

With the rise of television and the passive participation that television encourages, the audience is expecting what they normally receive from both entertainment and public affairs television: emotions played out on the screen, emotions that they can share in from the comfort and safety of their couches and living rooms. Carter's factual, deliberately nonemotional approach left the audience feeling that it had not shared in anything.

The early colonists and the Puritans relied primarily on oral communication. For them, such communication functioned to draw together the community, to provide a basis for shared beliefs and shared goals.[44] Televised communication is both oral and visual; the sense of commonality and community derive from the linkages between the visual images and the emotional images conjured up by the speaker. Carter's first Fireside Chat, with its populist themes and pictures of Carter in a comfortable sweater before a homey fire, was a superb example of this dynamic. But when he spoke on the *Nimitz,* his visual pictures did not match his words: standing on a battleship, symbolic of American military power, and all things patriotic and grandiose, and a speaker determined to deemphasize precisely those elements that the audience expects to have emphasized. The emotional response to this is likely to be anger and rejection: Television plots that deny the expectations of their audiences do so at their peril. Carter's presidency shows how grave that peril can be when the ratings dropped, and he failed to be renewed for the next season.

Carter understood governing as something both quantitatively and qualitatively different from campaigning. He seemed to believe "that if a decision were correct, it would sell itself."[45] He also believed that his job was to do what was right, not what was political. "Carter felt political leadership required politicians not to fear failure, which would doom progress. It was a mistake .for leaders to seek universal approval, 'because if you fear making anyone mad, then you ultimately probe for the lowest common denominator of human achievement.'"[46] In maintaining this attitude, Carter avoided the trap that tormented Lyndon Johnson. In so doing, however, he fell into another trap. It is the responsibility of the president not merely to propose good policy but also to propose policy that is politically acceptable. Presidents are, after all, supposed to be accountable. In refusing to "pander to public opinion," Carter was also refusing to be held politically accountable. He was assuming that most undemocratic of postures, someone with a corner on the truth market. Carter did not have to curry public favor because he knew what was right, what was best. And if he explained that to the American people, they would agree with him.

In addition to presenting an unacceptably arrogant view of his own abilities and role, this attitude was inconsistent with his requests to "help him be a good president" and his insistence that listening to the people was beneficial. Now, these two stances are not necessarily irreconcilable; it is perfectly possible that Carter intended to listen and then decide, and expect people to approve of his final decision because they had input into the process. But he never explained his position, or tried to reconcile these two seemingly inconsistent attitudes. He simply kept saying that he would "never lie, never mislead the American people." This claim to superior honesty made even small ambiguities and inconsistencies dangerous for Carter, but secure in the belief of his own rectitude, Carter never fully realized this.

Carter seemed to have no sense of balance—he would either ignore the symbolic side of governance or concentrate on it exclusively. As George F. Will writes, "Being didactic is part of governing. But governments cannot live by gestures alone. Governments must be ready to inflict pain as well as deliver exhortations. Fighting the energy crisis with the White House thermostat is, after a while, a bit like fighting inflation with a WIN button."[47]

Will is right in using WIN as an example, for both Ford and Carter flailed around in the same morass. They or their advisers would come up with a surefire way to market their ideas to the public, but the effort would be so clearly a marketing device that the idea would lose credibility as it appeared increasingly "gimmicky" and political. Presidents are not soap, and they cannot be marketed like soap; more sophisticated sales techniques are required to avoid cheapening the office.[48] Presidents are now in the difficult position of having to plan and contrive to look well on television while avoiding any appearance of planning or contriving.

Contributing to Carter's self-inflicted political problems was the fact that Congress owed Carter nothing. Most representatives had run ahead of Carter in their districts, and the coattails were on Congress, not on the president.[49] Members of Congress thus did not feel indebted to Carter, and his failure to woo them and understand their importance and place in the system infuriated many of them.[50]

Although Carter was capable of using television and the media effectively,[51] he "never seemed at ease around reporters, and he had been unable to conceal his distrust, even disapproval, of the press while campaigning."[52] While he owed his "rise to prominence" to "the exposure he got on national television,"[53] he never seemed fully to accept or appreciate that fact. As one analyst says,

> In 1976, Jimmy Carter had won the Democratic nomination and the Presidency not on a given set of issues but on a general impression of an honest, intelligent man who was going to Washington to take a different approach to the country's problems. His message had been thematic. Once he had been elected and was faced with energy shortages and a sick economy, that thematic approach was more difficult to sustain and often not credible. Increasingly, the president approached his speeches like an engineer; he regarded them as vehicles for making local arguments.[54]

This approach, combined with the open media relations, made it impossible for Carter to control the agenda. And a president who does not control the agenda is at the mercy of others who do. Carter kept his speeches brief, and many of them were followed by question-and-answer opportunities. Often these question-and-answer sessions dominated the speech.[55] The theme or idea Carter was interested in stressing might or might not be the theme or idea that the audience was interested in stressing. In opening up his speeches to the themes and ideas of others, in failing to answer the questions in terms of his own theme, Carter lost control of the agendas at various speaking events. In so doing, he fostered the belief that he was not in control of his presidency.

It is not that Carter did not get his chances. Early in his administration, when he first began to get away from the "governing as campaigning" approach, he was frequently asked about his "vision" or whether he lacked one. More often than not, he would respond to such "vision" questions with an answer detailing his policy approach to the problems facing America. "I am trying to fulfill all my promises. And I think I was quite reticent in making those promises, certainly compared to some of my opponents."[56]

By the time Carter began to connect his "vision" passages with his "policy" passages in a meaningful way, it was too late. Carter failed to remember the lessons of his own campaign until his famous energy speech of 1979, which has become known as the "malaise speech," when Carter admitted that his leadership was failing. He returned to the themes that he had begun with and gotten away from, from realizing "that more than ever as president, I need your help," to the theme of spiritual rejuvenation for America: "The threat is nearly invisible in ordinary ways. It is a crisis of confidence. . . . The erosion of our confidence in the future is threatening to destroy the social and political fabric of America."[57] Although the audience may well have agreed with his diagnosis of the problem—a crisis in confidence—they no longer had faith in Jimmy Carter as the bringer of salvation. He had too thoroughly undercut himself for that.

He did have some successes—most notably the Panama Canal treaty and the Camp David accords. Both allowed him to bounce back to some degree from previous problems. But because they were not supported by either a consistent pattern of success or a consistent theme through which Carter could explain failure, the effect of these successes was minimized. "There was, in each of these events, a recurring strain: it was the little mistakes, the personal misjudgments, the failures to understand how actions might be perceived publicly that bedeviled the Carter administration from the beginning, and they were still being made"[58] at the end.

In addition, these successes were undercut and dominated in the national consciousness by the Soviet intervention in Afghanistan and the hostage crisis. In both instances, Carter was in the difficult position of being, in fact, powerless when he knew that the American people expected action, expected that the most powerful nation on earth could control these events. There was little he could do to rescue the hostages or halt the Soviet incursion into Afghanistan except to talk tough and make symbolic gestures. He could say, for example, that Afghanistan "was a sovereign nation, a non-aligned nation, a deeply religious nation, and the Soviets invaded it brutally,"[59] and acknowledge that "I am committed to solving this crisis. I am committed to the safe return of the American hostages and to the preservation of our national honor,"[60] but there was little he could do beyond that.

Carter's most serious mistake in dealing with the hostage situation was to raise the profile of the hostages. Carter himself made the hostages big news by declining to campaign so that he could monitor the situation:

> Today I announced my candidacy for reelection, and so I speak to you tonight as President of the United States of America and also as a candidate. This is a paid political statement, but is is not a campaign speech. . . . My campaign must be, for a time, postponed. I must remain here, near the White House, because of the situation in Iran. While the crisis continues, I must be present to define and to lead our response to an ever-changing situation of the gravest sensitivity and importance. . . . At the height of the Civil War, President Abraham Lincoln said, "I have but one task, and that is to save the Union." Now I must devote my concerted efforts to resolving the Iranian crisis.[61]

On the face of it, this is an effective stance. Carter elevates himself to the statesmanlike stature of Abraham Lincoln and is acting "presidential" rather than "political." The problem is that he also elevates the hostage crisis to the stature of the Civil War. Lincoln staked his presidency and his place in history on the outcome of the Civil War. Carter was staking his presidency on the outcome of the hostage crisis. This strategy might well have paid off had the crisis come to a quick, decisive, and positive end. But the longer the hostage crisis played out, the more it crippled Carter.[62]

Other problems were generated by Carter's nonpolitical stance on the hostage crisis. For one thing, it meant that he could not do anything that had the appearance of being political. All his actions had to be "presidential," rather than "political," and any imputation of "politics" could seriously hurt his image. And, in fact, "the dominant theme in journalists' assessments in 1980 was that President Carter's actions were motivated by his single-minded desire to be reelected."[63] It is difficult, if not impossible, to maintain an image as the president-above-politics when the media constantly refer to your political motives. It cheapens the office to involve the presidency in mere politics, and in cheapening the office, Carter lessened his one major advantage—incumbency.

Carter's image problems were further exemplified by the "meanness issue." In part this issue was the result of Carter's inability to run on his record. With the hostages and the Soviets in Afghanistan, Carter was on the defensive. Instead of taking control of the agenda, Carter responded to

Reagan's agenda, which effectively kept Carter on the defensive. As a tactic to seize control of the agenda, Carter began to attack Reagan. Some of these attacks were perceived as hitting below the political belt, and Carter was forced to recant, which he did while stressing Reagan's "meanness":

> I do not think he is running a campaign of racism or hatred, and I think my campaign is very moderate in its tone. I did not raise the issue of the Klan, nor did I raise the issue of states' rights [as Reagan did], and I believe that it is best to leave these words, which are code words to many people in our country who've suffered from discrimination in the past, out of the election this year. I do not think that my opponent is a racist in any degree.[64]

In another effort to exonerate himself after being charged with "meanness," Carter responded, "It is my responsibility as a candidate in the give-and-take political world that's part of democracy not only to point out what I have done in the last four years, and not only what I intend to do in the next four years, but to point out in a legitimate and accurate way the differences between me and my major opponents."[65] This is an odd response, for it is an attempt to paint Carter as both presidential (as the participant in and definer of democracy) and engaging in legitimate politics ("legitimate and accurate way"). He is saying, "It's not mean if it contributes to democracy, and if my charges are true." In addition to being somewhat inconsistent, both messages miss the point. The accuracy of his charges was never the issue. The issue was that he was trying to appear presidential and at the same time was attacking the personality and person of his opponent—a distinctly unpresidential thing to do. It was a trap that Eisenhower always avoided—he maintained his nonpolitical, presidential image precisely because he refused to dirty his hands in partisan politics. He used Nixon for that. Carter had no Nixon; he did his own dirty work, and his image correspondingly suffered.

Carter's reelection campaign had a familiar ring—it sounded like Ford's. Both men were searching for ways to appear presidential, and both ended up by presenting a too-self-conscious president who consequently was not convincing in the role. Television is very good at picking up and magnifying small gestures and small inconsistencies. When an actor is uncomfortable in his role, when it does not seem natural, those small gestures and inconsistencies are inevitable. When they are broadcast and magnified over television, it appears as if the actor lacks sincerity or ability. In Carter's case, his sincerity was not doubted; only his ability to perform up to the role's expectations.

In sum, what neither Ford nor Carter could convey was the one thing Americans needed in addition to a restoration of honesty—a sense of control.[66] Carter gave up control of the national agenda when he decided to communicate to the electorate through news conferences and question-and-answer dominated "town meetings." He surrendered control of much of his administration when he attempted to rule through "Cabinet government." He lost control of the larger issues of government when he decided to make the decisions about who was to play tennis on the White House courts. He lost control of foreign policy when he allowed Iran and the USSR to dominate the news. He lost control of the nation's emotions when he refused to satisfy those emotions in his public speech. When he tried to reassert his leadership, he allowed Reagan to interpret it as Carter's loss of faith in the American people. Ultimately, the electorate opted for a candidate who offered both emotional expression and control of events.

Conclusions

Both Ford and Carter did much to heal the nation in the aftermath of Vietnam and Watergate. They both sustained images as honest, decent men. Unfortunately, their presidencies also had people wondering if honest, decent men should be president. There was some feeling that perhaps such men were not brutal enough to lead a world power like the United States.

Much of this can be laid directly at the door of these two presidents. They gave the American people honesty, but failed to give them a sense of control. The problems with the economy, the energy crisis, the Soviet invasion of Afghanistan, and the hostage crisis all contributed to a feeling that, as Carter said in his last State of the Union Address, "it has never been more clear that the state of our Union depends on the state of the world."[67] Ronald Reagan told the American electorate that we could be in control; our leadership was the problem. And, as the 1980 election results showed, the American people did not want to be dependent on the state of the world.

An important element in this appearance of lack of control is the inability of either Ford or Carter to control the national agenda. They were very open; the consequence of that openness is a sacrifice of thematic control. With all the competing agendas in the country, as they increasingly toured the country seeking support, what they found was confusion.

And they surrendered their only means of drawing order out of that confusion.

In addition, both Ford and Carter were self-consciously presidential. It is as if they had an image in their minds of what a president is, and they strove to fit themselves to that image. The result was stilted and uncomfortable. Americans do not seem concerned with whether a president wears a cardigan sweater or a suit; they do want to see a person who is comfortable in the role of president. Being "presidential" simply means to carry an aura of command and security. Kennedy could be "presidential" playing touch football or walking on a beach. Eisenhower was "presidential" on a golf course. Being "presidential" comes down to being whatever the president is at a given moment, and accepting that. Neither Ford nor Carter ever seemed able to see himself in the role. Everything they did seemed contrived, unnatural.

While the electorate may not be politically informed, they are extremely television literate. Today's television audience knows good television from bad television. Ford and Carter, in their roles as president, offered bad television. They knew it, and their audiences knew it. As good television becomes ever more important to—perhaps synonymous with—good governance, successful presidents will be presidents who produce good television. The mechanics of this are beautifully illustrated in the presidencies of Ronald Reagan and George Bush.

6

Mastering Televised Politics: Ronald Wilson Reagan and George Herbert Walker Bush

The power of the presidency is often thought to reside within this Oval Office. Yet it doesn't rest here; it rests with you, the American people, and in your trust. Your trust is what gives a President powers of leadership and his personal strength.
— *RWR*

The most fundamental obligation of the Government is to people's health, the people's safety, and ultimately, our values and our traditions. — *GHWB*

New Television Strategies

Given the country's mood by the end of the Carter administration, Ronald Reagan's main task was to restore in the American people a sense of control over their lives and over the world. He chose to do this through storytelling. The plot was simple: Find the villain, and eliminate him. Reagan played both the hero, who promised to slay the villain, and the narrator, who told us who the real villains were, and whether or not the hero had done his job. These dual roles proved very valuable to Reagan in terms of creating and maintaining public support and defusing criticism.[1] Reagan made Carter the personification of the chief villain—the state. Throughout Reagan's career, he has opposed the state and its encroachment into the lives of ordinary Americans.

Reagan spoke to, and for, these Americans. During his Hollywood career, Reagan was known for his "everyman" roles, for being the "boy next door," one of "us." He used that image to become the "boy next door" who made good. Like Eisenhower, Reagan apparently did not seek power for its own sake, but out of duty and a sense of obligation; like Eisenhower, he did not engage in personalities or mudslinging; like Eisenhower, Reagan was a man of the people who had been elevated above the people. He was comfortable with that elevation, unspoiled by it.

Ronald Reagan was the first American president to have truly mastered television. His rhetoric was short, sharp, and thematic. His delivery was designed specifically for television and was full of word pictures designed to complement the visuals of television. His style is best characterized as conversational, even chatty. In keeping with the apparent intimacy of the television medium, Reagan spoke to the electorate in a friendly, informal fashion, reducing the formal distance between himself and his audience.

George Bush seems to be well on his way to following in his predecessor's footsteps, although with a difference: Ronald Reagan both told and starred in his stories; George Bush seems content to be a character in stories told by others and written by his administration. Bush places less overt emphasis on public communication and gives "remarks," rather than speeches.[2] His informal style and chatty presentation play well on television and help him maintain high popularity levels. Despite this, because of the changed nature of the presidency, downplaying his public persona is risky for Bush; the past conduct of the office imposes constraints and expectations on Bush's behavior that he can slight only at his peril.

Even given the lowered presidential position so far favored by Bush, both Reagan and Bush rely heavily on stressing the moral dimension of their role as president. They are far more concerned with their tasks as legitimators and representers than as administrators and educators. As presidents, Reagan and Bush interpret our moral environment; their presidencies have institutionalized the primacy of the presidential role as interpreter-in-chief.

Ronald Reagan and the Rhetoric of the Revolution

Ronald Reagan, the Great Communicator, the Teflon President, is as well known for his effectiveness as a communicator as for the substance of what he communicated. More than any other modern political actor, Reagan understood the importance of mass-media communication. He understood how media work, how to use that to his advantage, and how to structure his appeals to communicate best through television, the dominant medium. As one analyst notes, "Ronald Reagan is our first true television president. His persona, messages, and behavior fit the medium's requirements in terms of form, content, and and industry demands. Reagan made television the instrument of governing. His presidency provides the blueprint for public esteem and popularity."[3]

Reagan, and his staff, understood that much of politics is theater, and they designed a presidency capable of taking full advantage of that understanding.[4] This involved both relations with the media and appeals designed for the public. In dealing with the media, Reagan and his people understood that the national media corps, despite its reputation for aggression, is in reality "fundamentally passive."[5] Reagan understood that if he timed events in a certain way, then he could force coverage or cripple it, depending on his own agenda. Unlike either Ford or Carter, Reagan did not play into the requirements of the media; he forced the media requirements to play into his agenda, and thus maintained control. This was possible because of the central role the presidency has come to play. Television reporters rely on the president to provide news. The news the president chooses to supply can be, and all too often is, orchestrated with attention to the requirements of television, not the requirements of governance.

Reagan often blamed the media for bad news and publicly styled them as tools of the liberal opposition.[6] In 1985, for example, Reagan said, "I sometimes feel that the journalists who cover our everyday political affairs here in Washington have a tendency to miss the real news,"[7] thus undermining the quality of what the media do report. "I've noticed that there's never a 'good news' economic story on the evening news that was not accompanied by, or buried by, finding some individuals who have not yet benefited by the economic recovery."[8]

The media are "acutely concerned with what *Newsweek* referred to as 'backlash': that they might be accused of inflating their reportage and of feverishly chasing exclusives, propelled by visions of a Pulitzer Prize.... [they] studiously tried to avoid [being] vulnerable to charges of shoddy journalism for the sake of personal and professional acclaim" during the Reagan years.[9] Part of the post-Watergate backlash included the media, and it "cowers in dread of being called 'too powerful.' For the myth of media power, which the media never contested in their salad days, is now being used by the enemies of liberty to incite the people against a free press."[10]

This was a particularly strong dynamic when the media encountered a president as publicly popular and amiable as Ronald Reagan. In challenging him, the media ran the risk of being perceived by the public as hounding the president in an undignified manner, instead of pursuing presidential accountability.[11] This was a problem the Reagan administration did its best to magnify. Reagan was very aware of the importance of staging, and of how to manage it to maximize his interests and minimize those of the press. The press was kept at a distance from the president, forcing them to yell questions as he passed, sometimes over the sound of a helicopter rotor. In addition, news conferences were rare and were used for calculated effect.[12]

The media, which lack the will to set their own agenda in the face of official domination, allowed themselves to be undermined. Partly, this is a function of the way the media understand their role. Reporters are supposed to report; what the president says is news. To quote the president and then appear to argue with him or her would create credibility problems with the audience. To refuse to report what the president said would also endanger credibility. For the press to be free, it must be free of both government restraint and government sources. The first is more easily managed than the second.

"Because the Reagan administration understood [the] pattern of reportorial coverage, they took steps that influenced what appeared as news."[13] They understood the importance of providing good visuals, usable copy, and always remembered that "television thrives on simplicity."[14] The more dominant television becomes, the more important good visuals are. "Good" visuals are not necessarily the most appropriate or the most accurate visuals; they are the ones most likely to capture and keep the audience's attention. In the days of radio, audience attention was maintained through skillful and eloquent rhetoric, which was designed to conjure up vivid word pictures. Today's eloquent rhetoric also has such word pictures, but they must be simpler, cleaner, so as not to interfere with the actual pictures being shown on the screen. Reagan's public rhetoric was a masterful combination of arresting visuals and a narrative line that matched and supported those visuals.

Reagan's narrative line nearly always involved clear choices between two opposite alternatives. "This year, New Jersey is being offered a clear-cut choice between those who think government spending and taxing are the solution to our problems and those, like Tom [Kean, Republican gubernatorial candidate], who understand that government spending and taxation are the problem."[15] These clear choices between a well-defined good and an equally well-defined evil make matters simple, easy to understand, easy to get emotional about, and easy to remember. That reality may not be so clear-cut is not material: Ford and Carter tried to use television to portray a complex reality, with little success. Reagan's speech, however unrealistic, worked well on television.

Reagan's personal style fits in beautifully with the simplicity encouraged by television. His approach to communication has always been through narrative, and his speeches are peppered with anecdotes. Two prominent scholars explain, "As all great communicators have always known, the story is probably the best way to get a point across to a wide audience and to insure that the point then sticks in people's minds."[16] The problem with such almost exclusive reliance on storytelling as a communicative device is that it distorts reality. Real-world events do not always follow a single narrative line. Communication that forces events into such a line, regardless of appropriateness, is, if not a lie, then a distortion of the truth.

Some of Reagan's best-known and remembered speeches are memorable because of the stories they contain. The "boys of Pointe du Hoc," "Ivan and Fred"—these stories and others like them captured audience attention and imagination. Like Roosevelt, Reagan excelled at personification, at bringing abstract ideas down to earth, and making them real and human. One major difference is that when Roosevelt conjured up his examples of the human condition, they remained illusory to some degree; his audience, sitting in their living rooms, could imagine the exact characteristics for themselves. When Reagan spoke in France, the "boys of Pointe du Hoc" were there, in the audience, and on television. There was nothing for the audience to fill in. Their participation has been diminished, made passive, by this use of television.

Reagan's rhetoric was well suited to foster this passive participation. In his first inaugural address, for instance, Reagan talked of sacrifice, but in a different way from Truman, Kennedy, or Carter and Ford. For all these men required that some sacrifice be made, that some, more or less specific, action be taken. For Reagan, "all that is required is belief in ourselves ... in our capacity to perform great deeds."[17] There is no need to perform these great deeds, simply to believe in our capacity to perform them.

This call to nonaction is supported by Reagan's use of heroes. The most well-known examples of the heroes are in his annual State of the Union addresses, when he would have heroic individuals sitting in the balcony and would refer to them in the context of his speech. But it was a frequently used tactic in many of his speeches. Essentially, Reagan would cite some instance of heroism, and the hero would be emblematic of us all, not as an example that should be emulated, but as one that summarized what all Americans are capable of. At a tribute to Andrew Mellon, for example, Reagan noted that Mellon's philanthropy was not exceptional: "It was and is a vital part of the American character."[18] Thus the actual performance of heroism was no more necessary than actual sacrifice. Others could do that for the audience, who cheered them on from the safety of their living rooms.

The role of the writer is thus different in the new era of televised politics. Writing is increasingly more of a technical trade than a creative one: Writers search for the perfect soundbite, the perfect slogan, the perfect snappy remark that will make the nightly news and get the message across. What this misses is that communication in advertising slogans is not informational.

> Great speeches have always had great soundbites. The problem now is that the young technicians who put together speeches are paying attention only to the soundbite, not to the text as a whole, not realizing that all great soundbites happen by accident, which is to say all great soundbites are yielded up inevitably, as part of the natural expression of the text. They are part of the tapestry, they aren't a little flower somebody sewed on.[19]

When a speech becomes nothing more than the hanger for a soundbite, then the bulk of the text is rendered largely irrelevant. The earlier, equally oral colonial period relied on slow, careful construction of an argument, built on explicit historical and philosophical premises. In today's oral and visual culture, assertion replaces argumentation, and the premises are left out entirely.

This is a serious problem. Public speech, in our day as well as in the colonial period, functions to express our commonality; to constitute the community. When arguments are reduced to generalized assertions, when the historical and philosophical postulates are ignored, it is unclear what exactly that sense of commonality and community is based on. Reagan's solution to this problem was to base nearly all his arguments on shared American values.

Reagan used these values as a means of inclusion, rhetorically making the audience part of the shared American value system. His use of values had the added advantage of excluding his opposition. Reagan excelled at using values as a basis for inclusive rhetoric: "No, you represent a cross section of Americans from all backgrounds, different regions across the country. In fact, you remind me very much of that one special interest group that I mentioned on Inauguration Day—the one special interest group that has been neglected and needs help—that is, we the people."[20]

These values have strong optimistic overtones: "Perhaps because we control our own destiny, we believe deep down inside that working together we can make each year better than the old."[21] The optimism is important, for not only does it make for easier listening, it is also better television, which tends to encourage "good, positive, upbeat pictures."[22] Reagan's words reinforced the visual images and strengthened the overall impression of control, comfort, and security.

As far as exclusion goes, Reagan characterized his opposition as politically motivated, selfish, and self-interested, as people who loved obscure, complex theories and programs:

> The plan I outlined will stop runaway inflation and revitalize our economy, and there's nothing but politics-as-usual standing in the way of lower inflation, increased productivity and a return to prosperity. Our program for economic recovery does not rely upon complex theories or elaborate Government programs. Instead it recognizes basic economic facts of life and, as humanely as possible, it will move America back toward economic sanity.[23]

Like television, Reagan thrived on simplicity.

Another result of the television-inspired, technical approach to writing, is "an unending effort to separate the word from the policy."[24] Reagan staffers often treated the policy process as divorced from the writing process, which means that one group designs the product and another group sells it. But the group charged with the selling is denied access to the product and is allowed to focus only on the attributes approved by the product designers, who may or may not have any knowledge of the marketplace. As Peggy Noonan, widely considered to be the best of Reagan's writers, says, "Speeches in the staffing process were always in danger of becoming lowest-common-denominator art. There were so many people with so many questions, so many changes. I sometimes thought it was like sending a newborn fawn into the jagged wilderness where the grosser animals would pierce its tender flesh and render mortal wounds; but perhaps I understate."[25]

The major problem with the "staffing process" is that the voice of the author is lost. And when the voice of the author is supposed to be the voice of the speaker, the degrees of removal become a serious problem. It is not clear, for instance, whether in the future we will be electing presidents, or front people for presidents' staffs. We no longer elect a president. We elect a presidency, a body of people who support the president. This has been increasingly true since the development of the modern presidency began with Franklin Roosevelt. The difference that television makes, however, is that there is no longer any necessary relation between the character and attributes of the person sitting in the Oval Office and the policies of his or her presidency. News anchors have little connection to, or actual knowledge of, the news they report. This is becoming increasingly possible (although certainly not inevitable) for the president as well.

Whether mere fronts or active participants, however, the politicians' essential task remains unchanged. Presidents still must engender in the people a sense of confidence, of trust, of what being American means, for us, right now. Reagan did this beautifully: "The most powerful voice in the world comes not from balance sheets or weapons arsenals, but from the human spirit. It flows like a mighty river in the faith, love, and determination that we share in our common ideals and aspirations. . . . In your beliefs, your efforts, and your accomplishments, you are setting the course to progress and freedom that our nation must follow."[26] This sense of confidence in the inherent rightness of all things American is easily transferred into a sense of being in control: To be morally right is therefore to understand and control events.

The issue of control was most apparent in Reagan's dealings with terrorism and the Soviet Union. His hard-line anti-Soviet rhetoric of the early years and his "get tough on terrorists" stances are well known and need no repetition here. What is important is to note that both his anti-Sovietism and his terrorist talk are important elements in his maintenance of a strong, controlled, "America is back" stance.

This appearance of control broke down as the Iran/*contra* revelations became public. "The result was White House confusion. The President's staff became part of a growing communication problem. The media and the public pressed for details and the communication control that had marked his administration was not there."[27] As a result, the media portrayed the president as inattentive, detached, and tentative. Reagan's competence was frequently called into question.

Reagan's first attempt to deal with the Iran/*contra* allegations was to deny them by discrediting their source:

I know you've been reading, seeing, and hearing a lot of stories the past several days attributed to Danish sailors, unnamed observers at

Italian ports and Spanish harbors, and especially government officials in my administration. Well, now you're going to hear the facts from a White House source, and you know my name.[28]

Having established himself as the most—indeed, the only—credible source, Reagan proceeded to present the facts. The rhetorical strategy of this first speech failed utterly in protecting the president's image of credibility and competence. His refusal to admit to mistakes brought his judgment and political savvy equally into question, and his continued emphasis on the position that no laws were broken and no secrecy intended increased the public perception of a cover-up. The public had, after all, heard similar assurances before.[29]

Reagan continued to have difficulty in locating an appropriate strategy to handle the Iran/*contra* revelations in early 1987. In January of that year he attempted to displace Iran by altering the agenda to issues of unity and cooperation in the face of the Soviet Union[30] and the importance of the defense budget. The Iran affair is in the past, and Reagan seemed to feel that it was time to move on: "But in debating the past, we must not deny ourselves the successes of the future. Let it never be said that this generation of Americans that we became so obsessed with failure that we refused to take risks that could further the cause of peace and freedom in the world."[31]

This serves as both a justification for the Iranian arms deal and a prod to put it all behind us and stop focusing on it to the exclusion of the rest of the Reagan presidency. It might have been an attractive possibility, but it did not work. Presidents can offer an interpretation of an event or situation, but even given their rhetorically privileged position, they cannot guarantee that their interpretation will be a plausible or acceptable one. In this case, the environment was imposing too many constraints on Reagan's choices to make the interpretation he offered in the State of the Union viable.

Reagan did not get out from under the scandal until he refocused the plot onto familiar lines. Reagan made the first tentative steps toward a recovery in a March 4 "Address to the Nation" in which he finally implemented a workable strategy regarding the scandal. First, Reagan recognized that he had made mistakes that affected the entire country: "The power of the presidency is often thought to reside in this Oval Office. Yet it doesn't rest here; it rests with you, the American people, and on your trust."[32] Second, Reagan acknowledged that he had denied that the public understanding of the Iranian scandal was the correct one. He stopped making that denial, and admitted that the scenario was, in fact, an arms-for-hostages deal: "A few months ago, I told the American people that I had not traded arms for hostages. My heart and my best intentions still tell me that's true, but the evidence tells me it's not . . . what began as a strategic opening to Iran deteriorated, in its implementation, into trading arms for hostages."[33]

The strategy of this speech was an effective one because it involved ensuring that communication could occur by validating the fact that the public no longer trusted him as they once had, by agreeing to an interpretation of events that his audience shared, and by admitting to mistakes and promising to correct them. This was an emotionally satisfying as well as intellectually solid speech. And there is a powerful ethic in this country that says it is okay to make mistakes as long as we take responsibility for those mistakes, admit to them, and take steps to ensure that similar mistakes will not happen in the future. This is precisely the approach that Reagan took here.

Reagan's real upsurge in the polls came only after the affair had dragged on throughout a summer of hearings, and attention became focused on the Nicaraguan side of the equation. It is important to recognize that attention turned to the *contras* because the Reagan White House wanted it there. Reagan, after all, was the one who divulged the linkage between the Iranian arms sales and funding the Nicaraguan freedom fighters, and he often reminded his audiences of this fact.[34] And he was insistent upon bringing Nicaragua into the picture. Once there, the White House endeavored to keep Nicaragua very prominent.[35] This is because the Nicaraguan situation involved a clear case of a Reagan theme: On the one side, "the moral equivalent of our founding fathers"; on the other, the embodiment of communist evil. Reagan's actions regarding Nicaragua were clear, consistent, and defensible within his known interpretation of the world. What hurt Reagan with the Iran deal was that he appeared to change sides in mid-movie, and American politics is melodrama, not mystery. Reagan was back on track once he shifted the agenda to melodrama and away from mystery.

In sum, Reagan's public speech and public persona were consciously and ideally suited for television. His language was informal, yet his bearing was unfailingly presidential. Reagan thus avoided the credibility problems that befell his two most recent predecessors. Reagan was comfortable in the role of president, as were Roosevelt, Eisenhower, and Kennedy. If he had doubts, they were kept to himself. His public persona was light, "cool," and well suited to the informality of television.

Because Reagan kept tight control over the media, allowing press conferences as they suited his agenda and limiting question-and-answer periods to suit his convenience, no other authoritative voices competed with Reagan on an equal footing. He maintained a limited repertoire of themes, which he applied to a wide variety of situations. These themes were as safe, familiar, and predictable as a television plot. The only instance when he deviated from one of those plots, Iran/*contra,* hurt him more than any other event during his presidency. His recovery in the polls depended, in large part, on his resumption of a familiar story line.

There is little doubt that Ronald Reagan will have a major influence on the pattern of televised presidential speech. This is evident in the rhetoric of his successor, George Bush.

George Bush and the Rhetoric of Succession[36]

It is always difficult to provide an accurate analysis of a sitting president, both because of historical immediacy and loss of perspective and because of the dearth of available scholarly books and insider accounts. But the difficulty of the task in no way affects its importance. Thus a tentative and preliminary accounting of the rhetoric of George Bush during his first two years in office follows.

George Bush faced the difficult task of filling Reagan's political shoes. Reagan left him a legacy of political achievement and popular success particularly difficult to match for several reasons. Politically, Reagan bequeathed Bush an ideological commitment to a reduced federal role in the affairs of the nation. Financially, Reagan left a deficit that limits government spending. Popularly, Reagan's style of rhetoric and communication, perhaps the harbinger of a new relationship between leaders and followers in the United States,[37] would challenge any successor.

Despite the changing political environment, the biggest political problem Bush faces has not changed: how to present himself as the legitimate heir to Ronald Reagan and simultaneously establish himself as his own man and maintain the Republican coalition. The emphasis on these elements has changed over time, as the Bush presidency has developed. The evidence suggests that Bush seeks to resolve this complex political problem through a rhetoric that includes stylistic tones reminiscent of Ronald Reagan, a stress on substantive issues and symbolic approaches distinct from Reagan's, and an emphasis on inclusive themes.

In the first category, the one most important during the transition and early presidency, Bush resembles Reagan in his reliance on values and in his use of the policies of "Reaganism." As the most important of these tactics, Bush continually refers to American values. Bush defined the entire 1988 presidential election as one in which "two different men ... two very different ideas of the future will be voted on." Bush phrased the difference as between decline and growth, "America as just another nation" or as a "unique nation with a special role in the world," between despair and optimism. In other words, George Bush affirmed his belief in the America of the Reagan years.

Both Reagan and Bush rely on inclusive and exclusive rhetoric: Those included within the community are believers in the American value structure as they understand it. "The American Dream—you epitomize it for me in so many ways.... I think I understand Hispanic America. I've got lots to learn, but I think I understand. The roots run deep. And the aspirations run high, and its people ask not the promise of success, only the opportunity to succeed."[38] Inclusion works beautifully on television, for it suits the superficiality and simplicity the prevailing understanding of the medium stresses. Issues are made simple, often personalized, and dramatized. Clear villains are demarcated, and appropriate action seems to be taken against those villains. The outcome is reassuring, for new facts can be fit snugly into a familiar pattern or plot, and the basic boundaries of the known world are unchanged. This dynamic is clearly illustrated by Bush's rhetorical treatment of both Manuel Noriega and Saddam Hussein (to be discussed later).

Bush seeks to reassure members of the Republican coalition by emphasizing his continuity with the Reagan administration. The theme of continuity is to be expected in a president who succeeds a sitting president of his own party, and it played a prominent role in the rhetoric of both Truman and Johnson. Ford had a slightly different transition, but certain elements of continuity were still important. For George Bush, who presided over the first vice-presidential electoral transition since Martin Van Buren, however, the theme has specific applications. He not only promised to follow in the path of history and tradition,[39] he also made specific statements on specific policies.

"Reaganomics," the most important of these policies, equals "a philosophy of lower taxes, of economic growth and of giving Americans the power to make your own choices about their own lives."[40] This is evident in Bush's appointment of Jack Kemp as secretary of the Department of Housing and Urban Development. In the announcement of that appointment, Bush stresses Kemp's importance during the Reagan years as well as his innovative ideas and capacity to find solutions to problems without government.[41] In addition to his commitment to "keep the expansion growing,"[42] Bush also plans to continue the Reagan line on terrorism,[43] and human rights,[44] and to maintain Reagan's "partnership" between the federal government and the private sector.[45] The theme of continuance also provides a ready, if inadequate, justification for the lack of attention Bush gives to domestic affairs.

Bush's indecisiveness during the budget debates in the fall of 1990 hurt him with Reagan's Republicans, however, when Bush rescinded his "no new taxes" pledge. As "read my lips" became "watch my hips," the Republican right found evidence that Bush was not dedicated to their policy agenda. This weakened Bush's standing and rendered him potentially vulnerable on domestic issues within his own party in 1992.

More interesting than the tactics echoing Reagan's are those that depart from the Reagan legacy. These tactics enable Bush to "make himself his own man," and largely replace themes related to continuity during and after the inaugural. Under this heading we can find the best information as to the rhetorical possibilities of the Bush administration.

When Bush mentions change, he links it to images from nature, emphasizing the natural character of change: It is peaceful, not disruptive. He speaks of "new breezes," of "blooming," of a "fresh look."[46] This highlights the idea of change within a stable environment and thus allows the audience to believe in real changes, bringing with them the vigor and rejuvenation of spring.

Bush uses a number of action verbs. His nominees are engaged in "challenging ... leading ... motivating,"[47] in "innovating,"[48] they will be "kept up to speed,"[49] and can "keep the pace."[50] There is relatively little emphasis on passive verbs like "appointing," "listening," advising." All of this implied activity satisfies the desire for a new president to be up and doing. Since Bush succeeded Reagan, this image of action and involvement was particularly important, for Reagan's reputation as a passive leader had been an important part of his final days in office. All this activity gave Bush a way of moving away from identity with that image without having to address i directly or imply criticism of Reagan.

In addition to action verbs, Bush's rhetoric stresses comparative adjectives as a way of implying change without also implying criticism of the Reagan administration. Bush will lead a "kinder and gentler" nation; he wants a "closer relationship with our allies";[51] and talks of education, technology, the environment and military policy in similar terms.[52] This language implies both continuity and change; Bush is going to maintain the best aspects of the Reagan years while building on that legacy to allow for a, well, a more liberal nation, where politicians address problems such as homelessness, poverty, and illiteracy.

This is an important change from the Reagan years, for early in his administration Bush legitimated discussion of these issues. Reagan was not comfortable with these subjects, and he often appeared to be defending himself against charges of "lack of compassion" instead of setting an agenda. When the president voluntarily brings up these problems, they become a valid part of the national agenda. Presidents may increasingly believe that they can substitute speech for action, but speaking on an issue implies that action on it should be forthcoming.

Bush may be digging himself into a hole here—from which he may extricate himself only with difficulty later. One can almost see the protests now—impoverished schoolchildren, the homeless, almost any group, holding signs that ask if this is "kinder and gentler." Bush has himself set the standard by which voters and historians will judge his administration; and when given the opportunity to back away from that standard of "kinder and gentler" in the campaign and during the transition, he refused to do so. "Kinder and gentler" may come back to haunt him. The potential problems with this tactic are becoming clear as the Bush administration progresses. As Bush continued to emphasize foreign affairs and the war in the Persian Gulf, and as the recession at home deepened, his claim to leading a "kinder and gentler" nation was likely to be severely strained if not completely undermined.

The final difference between Reagan and Bush is that Bush consciously strives to reduce the profile of the presidency where Reagan sought the limelight. At the close of his inaugural address, Bush said:

> Some see leadership as high drama and the sound of trumpets calling, and sometimes it is that. But I see history as a book with many pages, and each day we fill a page with hopefulness and meaning. The new breeze blows, a page turns, the story unfolds.[53]

This kind of rhetoric affects our expectations of the president. Bush clearly distinguishes himself from Ronald Reagan, and we cannot expect from Bush Reagan's glamorous leadership. This is effective, for in lowering his profile in general, Bush has potentially given himself more room to maneuver. He does not have to perform up to Reagan's standard, but if he does, it will provide benefits for Bush. In addition, it is a disarming tactic, for it seems to imply that Bush will not attempt the media control of the Reagan years. His control is thus likely to be more subtle, less overtly antagonistic, and less likely to be challenged, for it has become routinized during the Reagan years.

Bush's relationship with the media is apparently open and accessible (holding eleven press conferences during the first hundred days and meeting with the press an additional forty-one times. Ronald Reagan, by contrast, held two press conferences and met only five other times with the national press during his first hundred days), but his style is nonconfrontational and generally low key. Bush provides none of the high-profile personalistic attacks and sharp positions of his predecessor, making it difficult for the media to frame stories about him that center on the drama of conflict. Even during the controversy over the Tower nomination, where Bush's nominee for secretary of defense had his politics, his personal life, and his competence questioned by both the media and the Senate, Bush steadfastly refused to question anyone's motives, accuse anyone of "playing politics," or engage in any sharp rhetoric at all.[54] Conciliation does not make for particularly exciting news stories, and Bush's profile dropped.

This lowered profile did not seem to hurt Bush's presidential persona during his first year. For one thing, political scientists and pundits have been decrying the rise in expectations and focus on the presidency for at least a decade; they seem to feel that one solution is a lessening of the presidential public image. For another, a low profile suits Bush's personal style and is thus preferable to having him force himself to be what he is not, as the Johnson and Carter administrations showed. The potential problem is that it is not clear that Bush can single-handedly alter our national expectations of presidential performance and not be found wanting for his inability to live up to those initial expectations.

In fact, that seems to be happening in his second year in office. The media persistently calls on Bush to provide leadership and bemoans its lack. The budget-deal fiasco and the uncertainty over his position on minority scholarships has many wondering if George Bush is committed to anything beyond his re-election. *Time* magazine named Bush "Men of the Year" because of his strong leadership in the Mideast crisis and apparent lack of it at home.[55]

Bush, like Reagan, has maintained strong control over the national media. His overtures to China, the Panama invasion, and the Malta summit all involved levels of presidential secrecy.[56] He allows access when it suits him, and only when it suits him. Bush is more inclined toward the impromptu press conference than a formal, scheduled, and detailed speech. This level of control may not appear to be a democratic approach to the presidency, but from a communication perspective, Bush's strategy allows him, as it allowed Reagan, to control the agenda, and to increase the president's chances of controlling the national perception of reality. The fewer voices that compete with the president, the better, from the president's point of view.

Early in the Bush administration, enemies were clearly defined as "dishonest federal employees" or "drug dealers," but they remained faceless. We know that these people are bad, but we never need to face them directly. The issues are not personalized, nor are they easily personalizable.[57] This was a potential problem for Bush, for television, as we have seen, is a medium that encourages personalization. Bush solved this particular problem in Panama and later, in the Mideast.

Panama not only provided a clear villain in the drug war but also one who could be easily personalized. The removal of Manuel Noriega from power in Panama was closely tied to Bush's need for a dramatic success in the war on drugs. Even the code name of the invasion, "Operation Just Cause," is related to Bush's drug rhetoric: "Victory, victory over drugs is our cause, a just cause."[58] Noriega, who initially was portrayed by Bush as a "dictator,"[59] later became an "indicted drug trafficker" and a "thug,"[60] as American hostility and the likelihood of intervention increased.

Bush's rhetoric on Noriega and the drug war was well designed for television, right up to providing props for the occasion. In his televised address on the drug problem, Bush held up a bag of white powder, saying, "This is crack cocaine seized a few days ago by Drug Enforcement agents in a park just across the street from the White House."[61] When it later appeared that the drug agents in question had lured the drug dealer to Lafayette Park so that Bush could make that claim, thus making it appear that Bush had manipulated the event, Bush responded,

> I think it was great because it sent a message to the United States that even across from the White House they can sell drugs. And so, I don't know all the details of it, but I think it sends a powerful message to the American people. It was a legitimate drug bust.... Every time that somebody gets caught selling drugs, he pleads that somebody is luring him someplace.... The fact is that the guy was arrested, or busted, in front of the White House. Doesn't matter—I don't care how he got there.[62]

This incident reveals that presidents must be aware of the need for television props to buttress the words of a speech in order to ensure that the message is communicated. It also reveals Bush's vulnerability. He can use the tactics introduced and perfected by Reagan, but he is not Reagan. When Bush even appears to manipulate the communication process, it is immediately pounced upon. It has always been thus: Truman was suspected of manipulation when he attempted to implement Rooseveltian tactics, and Bush faces the same dynamic. Whether this will continue, or whether it will affect Bush's approach to communication, remains to be seen.

The Mideast crisis gave Bush another chance to personalize issues and provide good television. Saddam Hussein is well suited to the role of villain. His attack on Kuwait, seizure of hostages, and vitriolic rhetoric allow Bush to display a tough but calm and determined demeanor. With morality firmly on the American side, Bush rhetorically evokes images of World War II, calling Saddam a "Hitler" and referring to the forces massed against him as "the allies." Clearly Bush is attempting to forestall fears of "another Vietnam" by references to tanks "storming into Kuwait blitzkrieg fashion."[63]

In the early days of the crisis, Bush emphasized his contacts with other world leaders[64] and informed the American public that the U.S. forces were "in a defensive mode right now, and therefore, that is not the mission to drive the Iraqis out of Kuwait. We have economic sanctions that I hope will be effective to that end."[65] Both of these tactics bolstered Bush's image as a calm, forceful, but diplomatic and prudent leader.

When Bush speaks, he does not provide a narrative through which complex and frightening events can be articulated and understood. He avoided a simple, cogent explanation of American involvement in the Persian Gulf until the American attack began. But by neglecting the public aspect of leadership, Bush denied the American people the chance to participate in and approve (or disapprove) of his actions. Lacking argument defending and articulating our policy, the American people had difficulty understanding and integrating unexpected occurrences. The tragedy of the Kurdish refugees illustrates this point. No one expected it, no one knew how to interpret it. The failure regarding the Kurds undermined the military triumph and opened the seemingly invulnerable Bush administration to criticism. His failure to provide a thematic interpretation of events is as important as the events themselves.

In addition to hard-hitting, confrontational rhetoric (primarily in foreign affairs), Bush also used the rhetoric of conciliation (primarily regarding domestic politics). For Bush, governing in the domestic arena seems to mean compromise and allies, and allies are created by healing the wounds made by the election. This is particularly important, for his election campaign left widespread and deep wounds.

It is not surprising that he should have met with Robert Dole and other senators and congressmen immediately after the election, and offered Jack Kemp a plum in the form of a Cabinet appointment. But Bush went the extra mile, holding highly publicized meetings with Michael Dukakis and Jesse Jackson, and making conciliatory statements about Democrats and the USSR,[66] the American media,[67] and making a concerted effort to become "president of all the people."[68]

In Bush's rhetoric, this unity is based in the fact that we all have a "shared interest in a better America."[69] If we are to make progress, it must be as one country. At his inaugural, Bush traced the divisions of the nation to the Vietnam war and suggested that we must put that war and its aftermath behind us and bring back the "old bipartisanship." This sounds very much like George Bush trying to call on Eisenhower's legacy rather than Reagan's, and interestingly he combines the call with nostalgic and sentimental language, not with the ringing patriotism and "feel-good Americanism" that characterized Reagan's inaugurals and public speech.

> A profound cycle of turmoil and great change is sweeping the world from Poland to the Pacific. It is sometimes inspiring, as here in Warsaw, and sometimes it is agonizing, as in China today. But the magnitude of change we sense around the world compels us to look within ourselves and to God to forge a rare alloy of courage and restraint. They future beckons with both hope and uncertainty.[70]

This sense of "prudence" is a new theme, and it is Bush's own. Partly it is a response to the very real constraints placed on the government by the realities of the world situation and the budget deficit. Bush cannot control—and may not even be able to influence—the changes occurring in much of the world. Instead of "talking tough," he is talking prudently. Partly it reflects the fact that while Bush has strong public support, his style is conciliatory, not confrontational; Bush does want to raise the level of conflict.

In some ways, this prudence appears as a refusal to take a strong stand on issues. He has been criticized for waffling on many important issues,[71] and, as David Broder put it, seems "content to nibble."[72] This is not necessarily an inappropriate strategy given Bush's political environment, and it did not seem to be hurting Bush with the American public until his second year in office, when the Gulf crisis abroad and recession at home reduced the euphoria produced by events in Eastern Europe during Bush's first year. While Bush got off to a good start, winning considerable credit for his ability to manipulate symbols,[73] stroke Congress,[74] and separate himself from Ronald Reagan,[75] this start was difficult to maintain as he began moving (or not moving) on domestic policy. By mid-1989 Bush encountered criticism for overemphasizing symbols and for moving too slowly on issues such as foreign policy, the Tower nomination, and the Alaskan oil spill.[76]

Despite this criticism, in terms of his personal popularity, Bush probably would not have done better to take an activist role from the beginning, nor is it clear that his best strategy would have been quick and decisive action on every issue.[77] Instead, Bush's cautious strategy may have let him effectively minimize political damage and maximize potential support in an environment of political and fiscal constraints. That strategy is less viable now than it was during the early days of his presidency, and Bush would do well to adapt his strategy to a changing political climate.

Conclusions

Both Ronald Reagan and George Bush use rhetoric and rhetorical strategies that are well suited to television. They use simple, short words that supplement rather than intrude on television visuals; a conversational, informal style of presentation; and words that convey a sense of familiarity and comfort with the role of president.

While Bush does not use the evocative rhetoric that characterized the Reagan administration, he is clearly capable of using both his speeches and his formal presentation of self to garner and maintain public support. Both Reagan and Bush excel at control of the media, and in understanding media requirements and using those requirements to the president's best advantage. There is nothing inherently wrong with this ability; good communication requires the ability to understand and use the dominant medium of communication. And in today's society, the dominant medium is undoubtedly television.

But there is some doubt whether the television medium is best suited, or even well suited, to the requirements of political communication in a democracy. This issue, made obvious and important by the rhetorical successes of the Reagan and Bush administrations, is the topic of the concluding chapter.

7

(Almost) "Everything Old Is New" Again:
The Consequences of
Televised Politics

THE EVIDENCE presented in the previous chapters indicates that the rhetorical goals of national political actors have not changed substantially over time. All national politicians seek personal and political support from their constituents. Thematic, unified, and integrated communication has always been an important element in that search. This was as true for Cotton Mather, Andrew Jackson, and Abraham Lincoln as it is for George Bush. What has changed is not the goal of political communication, but its context, content, and composition. These changes are related to changes in the political culture as it interacts with the technology of communication. In other words, communication technology affects the communication strategies of all political actors. Because of the president's public dominance, this is most clearly seen in the rhetoric of the modern presidents.[1]

The Political Context of Presidential Speech

As the nation has increased in size and complexity, our notions of who and what constitute the national polity have changed, and as traditional and constitutional linkages between the leaders and led have broken down, the president's role has changed dramatically. During the early days of the Republic, the president's role was more purely administrative. The president was less of an active participant in public debates, but communicated primarily to other elites. This reflected the nature of the presidential selection process; presidents communicated with those by whom they were held accountable.

Even through most of the nineteenth century, the president's voice was rarely heard, except through surrogate speakers or as reported in the partisan press. In enunciating his understanding of the Civil War and the nature of Union, Abraham Lincoln also brought new prominence to the role of the president as a national spokesman. That role continued off and on, depending on the predilections and skills of the specific president and the particular contexts in which they found themselves.

It is important to note that from Lincoln through Franklin Roosevelt, presidents had a choice about the use of public persuasion. Some bit of it was expected, too much would have been dangerous, but the element of choice was there; because of this flexibility, presidential tactics and techniques of persuasion offered more opportunities than constraints to the president. These choices became increasingly circumscribed as the electorate expanded, media technology improved, and the presidential selection process was altered to accommodate primaries.

With the rise of electronic communication media and the simultaneous and drastic weakening of political parties and the increasing role of the United States in the international arena, the presidency assumed a larger, more representational role. By the middle of the twentieth century, the electronic media, interacting with the tremendous political and cultural changes of the post-World War I world, encouraged an increase in presidential speech and an emphasis on the presidential person. These changes were facilitated by the individual presidents themselves, who saw public support as a way to bolster their support in Congress and strengthen the position of the presidency in the government.

Today, as we become a more televised, dramatized society, our politics become more televised, more dramatized as well. The president has become the nation's chief storyteller, its interpreter-in-chief. The president has become the primary focus of national political attention, and the president's talk has become the primary focus of the presidency. This works to the disadvantage of individual presidents, who have become increasingly constrained as television becomes an increasingly important part of the president's political environment.

The Content of Presidential Speech

When presidents spoke rarely, their speech was closely tied to specific issues and concrete concerns. They spoke (or wrote or were reported as speaking or writing) to make specific comments on specific problems. Campaigning rhetoric was nonexistent in the early republic, and the president's role was not one that involved public persuasion.

The first indication that presidents would enlarge their public role came in the nineteenth century when campaigning became partially accepted. Presidents (very occasionally), presidential candidates (more often), and their surrogates (always) hit the campaign trail with gusto, armed with vituperative rhetoric and the odd jug of hard cider.[2] Presidential words were more often quoted than spoken in front of large audiences, and these words were addressed to specific policy concerns and specific partisan political goals.

This is not to suggest that nineteenth-century political rhetoric was somehow more issue oriented, purer, than political speech today. Instead, presidents and other political actors scored their partisan points more frequently through issue-oriented speech. The points were pointed and unambiguous. Andrew Jackson's war on the national bank is the most obvious example of this dynamic; he hated both Nicholas Biddle (the president and chief advocate of the national bank) personally and the bank for what it symbolized politically. Both stances are apparent in his public speech. The Lincoln-Douglas debates also offer examples of the connection between the issues of campaigning and the issues of governance.

With the increase in the size and complexity of the national electorate and the rise of the electronic media, this distinction between campaign rhetoric and governing rhetoric began blurring. FDR had clear notions of electioneering and governing, or things to say in public and those that were more privately understood (his relationship with the national press, for instance, involved public excoriation of editors and publishers and private cooperation with reporters). The presidency was protected; members of the press operated as governmental insiders, and when the president spoke, they listened with both respect and belief. The presidents were aware of this and protected their own credibility by speaking carefully, mindful of the context and implications of their speech.

Presidents like Eisenhower and Kennedy began to show some of the slippage creeping into the presidency as it became a more public—and more constrained—office. There developed a contradiction between the necessity of glib television communication, on the one hand, and the need for measured political action within an ever more complicated political reality, on the other. Words and practices began to require contrary strategies. Both presidents used television and their televised speech to bolster images designed to create and maintain public support for their policies.

The "star quality" of both men helped gloss over inconsistencies between their public positions and their public actions.

These inconsistencies became very clear during the "imperial" presidencies of Johnson and Nixon, whose public speech was often designed to obfuscate their actions, and who sought public support at the cost of public honesty. The slippage between presidential speech and presidential action became both clear and painful. Their successors have learned to present themselves so as to obscure this slippage, but presidents since Johnson seem to be more concerned with their images in the public mind than with the issues those images were thought to be based on. Their rhetoric shifted from emphasizing specific policies to emphasizing the legitimacy of the presidential role and right to take action. This dynamic has become ever more clear, until now the process of governance is wholly intermixed with the processes previously associated with electioneering.

The Composition of Presidential Speech

Presidents now talk to us more than ever before. Even more significantly, the way presidents talk and the medium through which they talk has also changed. The days of impassioned, fiery oratory given to packed auditoriums of live human beings are in abeyance, at least for the moment. This change did not occur overnight. Radio signaled the change from flamboyant oratory to a more conversational style. FDR initiated the Fireside Chats and brought live presidential communication into American living rooms. The inception of radio allowed FDR to establish a feeling of intimacy with an increasingly expanding and complex nation. As the Roosevelt style became institutionalized, and as politicians became accustomed and adapted to the new medium, public address changed. Speeches became conversation. Television, along with the political realities of a changed political culture (in which, for example, assassination is a possibility), furthered this process and encouraged increased intimacy between the president and the electorate. The visuals of television reinforce the casual, intimate exchange between leaders and the citizenry.

The influence of television on presidential politics has also contributed to an understanding of politics that makes presidential image making increasingly immediate and important. Political images have always been significant features of political life, but before the inception of mass-mediated politics, these images could be crafted slowly, carefully, and thoughtfully. The collapse of such images was also a slow process. The images transmitted through television, however, take on an immediacy that print lacks. Reactions to events are speeded up, and public perceptions of issues and political actors can and do change practically overnight.

Because of this rapid transmission of images and reactions, presidents increasingly design appeals intended to increase support for themselves personally, rather than for the policies and programs they espouse. Both Reagan and Bush, for instance, are far more popular personally than are their policies. This divorce of persons from policies has potentially deleterious effects. For one, some very able presidential candidates may become losers early, or may never enter the race at all. Another possibility is that if the electorate votes for "nice" people regardless of their policy positions, and if accountability is divorced from action, then the substance of representational politics is in danger of being lost.

On television, speakers must search for a memorable phrase, what has entered the language as a "soundbite." Kathleen Hall Jamieson points out that "the person who can synopsize an issue in a clear, concise, dramatic statement that takes less than thirty-five seconds to deliver is more likely to be seen and heard on broadcast news than someone who lacks this talent."[3] Thus, speeches can be rendered into synecdoche, and synecdoche distilled into slogan; the whole communication experience becomes compacted. The increased tendency to tell stories, rather than develop arguments, is one aspect of this compaction, which is exacerbated by the visual component of television. Because television requires video as well as sound, synecdoche can be pictorial as well as auditory. Presidents, increasingly sensitive to what appear to them as the needs and requirements of television, allow their communication to be summarized by visual images, rather than elaborated and articulated through argumentation.

We are more careful about written language than spoken. Absurdities that we do not notice slip by us on television. They would be less likely to escape us if the communication was also written and read. The presentation of fast images does not facilitate either reflection or depth of understanding. It encourages rapid emotional responses, as if we were buying another mass-produced product.

Politics is not entirely reducible to marketing. Not even democratic politics, which ultimately depends on the consent of the people. Marketing techniques, when applied to politics, are not inherently evil; after all, speeches that lasted for several days would not draw an audience, and intrinsic merit notwithstanding, if no one listens, it is not good communication. But condensing our politics to narrative lines and soundbites immobilizes the electorate's ability to understand and assimilate political information. This also makes traditional notions of accountability and representation problematic.

Old Politics, New Technologies

Democratic politics is supposed to rely on the active participation of its citizens. The style of politics associated here with television encourages precisely those elements in democratic politics that worried the authors of *The Federalist Papers* and the Constitution. Television provides a new challenge for addressing these old concerns, which involve the respective roles of the citizenry and the executive within the broader political system.

The development of televised politics means that "a device universally hailed as a boon to communication has become a one-way street. It is a means by which a man can conduct a monologue in public and convince himself that he is conducting a dialogue with the public."[4] More important, the public believes that a dialogue is being conducted. Their consent is assumed through assertion, rather than won by argumentation and persuasion. And their allegiance is captured by informal, friendly presidential images. As the presidential role shifts to news reporter at best and game-show emcee at worst, the electorate's role is increasingly that of a consumer of the home shopping network, making instant decisions in response to rapidly changing images and opportunities. This subordinates the role of the public and encourages what the founders would have considered demagoguery. The consent of the governed loses its substantive meaning as the consent is reduced to approving the presidential person rather than presidential, or governmental, policies. We no longer consent to politics, but to images of people, images carefully constructed for their appeal, not their content.

As the electorate becomes increasingly accustomed to the reality presented through television, they are potentially rendered unable to adjust to a more complex, nonthematic reality. Viewing the world in simplified, familiar lines may well be reassuring, but reassurance is not conducive to citizen involvement in democratic politics. As Tom Wicker says, "What the public wants, the public gets, more often than not, and the real problems of American politics are that the public so often wants unworthy things, and is so seldom set straight by anyone who will be listened to."[5] Television is notable for its ability to heighten and exploit the wants of the public, as well as for its tendency to exacerbate the willingness of politicians to go along with public opinion instead of leading it.

The present use of television, with its encouragement of dramatiza-

tion, personification, and simplification, tends to inflate the political expectations of the electorate, who could become accustomed to seeing
complex difficulties easily surmounted and knotty problems resolved at
the end of an hour-long program. People are encouraged by their leaders
to expect the same from these leaders as they receive from their television
programming, and

> the arousal of an elevated sense of national purpose and the activity
> of the presidency which accompanies it create ... the politics of ex-
> pectation. The people are encouraged to expect too much of their
> political institutions and of their political leaders. They cease to in-
> quire what politics may accomplish and what they must do for them-
> selves.[6]

And they increasingly turn to the president.

As presidents reduce the level of formality between the mass public
and themselves, the public could, in turn, come to expect the continuance
of such behavior. The founders designed the presidency to be insulated
from the pressure of public opinion. The distance of formality was intended to protect the president and provide her or him with a certain degree of freedom of action within the constraints of democratic accountability. When presidents act to decrease the distance between themselves
and the mass public, they also decrease the degree of insulation and protection available to them. This in turn increases the fragility of the presidency as an institution.

As presidents become increasingly informal, they also become media
celebrities. They are written about in *People* magazine and other parts of
the popular press. Their families become national icons. Historically,
presidents and their families have attracted national attention. But with
the mass-mediated informality of the present office, we are seeing sides of
them (and insides of them) that would never have been dreamed of as
recently as thirty years ago. As public officials lose the benefits of the distinction between the public and the private, the private becomes increasingly politicized, and as a nation, we endanger our ability to make a
distinction between the public and private spheres. The proper role of
government and of the president within that government becomes blurred
and indistinct. With the increase and compaction of presidential speech,
we are also increasing presidentially dominated politics and the compaction of our politics.

This means it is becoming increasingly difficult to understand and to make moral choices through the vehicle of politics. Assertions supported by appropriate visuals that deemphasize analysis do not help the electorate in understanding the meaning of political choices. Public opinion polls cannot tell politicians which actions are "right," only which actions are popular. Assuming that there is sometimes a difference, and that the difference is an important one, television politics as currently conceived are not designed to facilitate "right" choices but "popular" ones, which can obfuscate the "right" choices. There is a difference, as both Aristotle and James Madison noted, between democratic rhetoric and demagogic rhetoric. Rhetoric that is primarily, or even importantly, deliberative is resistant to demagoguery. Ceremonial rhetoric, in contrast, encourages precisely those elements that nurture demagoguery, and that worried the founders.

This obfuscation does not necessarily mean the end of all thoughtful and meaningful politics and political choices. After all, there was no golden age of political communication when reason ruled and moral choices were made after full debate of the issues, which were fully understood by all. Political communication, like other forms of communication and politics, has always been full of the weak, the shallow, and the superficial. All that television does is to encourage precisely these elements. The question is now whether or not our government, which has come to be based on notions of "of and by the people," can work in the face of the pervasiveness of a technology that reduces the time citizens have for reflection on the public aspects of issues and encourages the privatization of national concerns.

In stressing the public, persuasive understanding of the presidency, presidents have responded to a cultural impetus as well as their own inclination, and the result has been an increasingly constrained office. If presidents want to recover the freedom of action that the presidency has lost by opening the office to public scrutiny, they must find a way to close that office without sacrificing public accountability. This, in turn, requires a shift in our understanding of the presidency, away from the role as interpreter-in-chief as it is currently constituted. We must hold presidents accountable for what they can control, and not expect them merely to present reassuring images in the face of complex and often disturbing social events. Presidents can control only a limited part of the world; to expect them to do more is to create a fiction that contributes little to our communal life and actively detracts from our ability to engage in meaningful politics.

Deliberative rhetoric is at least theoretically possible, even in a television-dominated polity. It is not, however, even remotely likely given the current understanding and practices surrounding televised politics. What we need to do in order to nurture more politically meaningful speech is to reward it. To the extent that we become a better audience, we are likely to get more eloquent, politically vibrant speech, capable of uniting us as a community and providing a substantial basis for moral decisions. Without this, our politics will become steadily more shallow, as we the audience do, and only by deepening the one can we deepen the other.

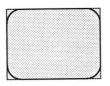

Notes

Introduction: The President as Interpreter-in-Chief

1. Throughout this text, the male pronoun is used when referring to past presidents, and gender-neutral terms are used when referring to the institution or to its future. I do this because it seems to me foolish and unrealistic to speak about past presidents and the historical presidency as if it were not an all-male club. It has been. The language used throughout this text recognizes that fact while aiming our current understanding of the office as non-gender-specific.

2. Karlyn Kohrs Campbell and Kathleen Hall Jamieson, *Deeds Done with Words: Presidential Rhetoric and the Genres of Governance* (Chicago: University of Chicago Press, 1990), 73.

3. See, for example, Robert D. King, "Franklin D. Roosevelt's Second Inaugural Address—A Study in Text Authenticity," *Quarterly Journal of Speech* 23 (October 1937): 439-44; William N. Brigance, ed., *A History and Criticism of American Public Address*, 2 vols. (New York: McGraw Hill, 1943); Lester Thonssen and A. Craig Baird, *Speech Criticism: The Development of Standards for Rhetorical Appraisal* (New York: Ronald Press, 1948).

4. James Ceaser, Glen Thurow, Jeffrey Tulis, and Joseph Bessette, "The Rise of the Rhetorical Presidency," *Presidential Studies Quarterly* 11 (Spring 1981): 233-51.

5. Robert E. Denton, Jr., *The Primetime Presidency of Ronald Reagan: The Era of the Television Presidency* (New York: Praeger, 1988), 6; John Orman, *Comparing Presidential Behavior: Carter, Reagan, and the Macho Presidential Style* (Westport, Conn.: Greenwood Press, 1987), 88.

6. Michael Baruch Grossman and Martha Joynt Kumar, "The Limits of Per-

suasion: Political Communications in the Reagan and Carter Administrations," paper presented at the annual meeting of the American Political Science Association, Chicago, 1987; Theodore Lowi, *The Personal President: Power Invested, Promise Unfulfilled* (Ithaca: Cornell University Press), 20.

7. Richard E. Neustadt, *Presidential Power: The Politics of Leadership from FDR to Carter* (New York: Macmillan, 1980).

8. Jeffrey K. Tulis, *The Rhetorical Presidency* (Princeton: Princeton University Press, 1987); Samuel Kernell, *Going Public: New Strategies of Presidential Leadership* (Washington, D.C.: CQ Press, 1986).

9. Tulis, *Rhetorical Presidency*, 178.

10. Kernell, *Going Public*, 138.

11. Alan O'Connor, ed., *Raymond Williams on Television* (New York: Routledge and Kegan Paul, 1989), 4.

12. Donald N. McCloskey, *If You're So Smart: The Narrative of Economic Experience* (Chicago: University of Chicago Press, 1990), 1-10.

13. Cliff Zukin, "Mass Communication and Public Opinion," in *The Handbook of Political Communication*, ed. Dan D. Nimmo and Keith R. Sanders (Beverly Hills, Calif.: Sage, 1981), 374.

14. Austin Ranney, *Channels of Power: The Impact of Television on American Politics* (New York: Basic Books, 1983), 11.

15. Ibid., 73.

16. Sidney Blumenthal, *The Permanent Campaign* (New York: Touchstone Books, 1980).

17. Ibid., 10.

18. It is important to note, although outside the realm of this book to discuss in depth, the fact that these changes are affecting all politics, not simply presidential politics. Television has altered all the links between elected leaders and the public.

19. David L. Altheide and Robert P. Snow, *Media Logic* (Beverly Hills, Calif.: Sage, 1979).

20. Murray Edelman, "Myths, Metaphors, and Political Conformity," *Psychiatry* 30 (1967): 217-28.

21. Robert E. Denton, Jr., and Gary C. Woodward, *Political Communication in America* (New York: Praeger, 1985), 14.

22. I use the word "rhetoric" in this study in a predominantly instrumental sense. Presidents use words in order to structure reality and persuade others. This is not to indicate that I am blind to, or in disagreement with, other and more all-encompassing uses of the understanding that rhetoric is definitional in a broader sense.

23. Kathleen Hall Jamieson, *Eloquence in an Electronic Age: The Transformation of American Political Speechmaking* (New York: Oxford University Press, 1988), 5.

Chapter 1: *Political Rhetoric in the Pre-Modern United States*

1. Robert E. Denton, Jr., *The Primetime Presidency of Ronald Reagan: The Era of the Television Presidency* (New York: Praeger, 1989), 3.
2. David Potter and Gordon L. Thomas, *The Colonial Idiom* (Carbondale and Edwardsville: Southern Illinois University Press, 1970), xi.
3. Robert T. Oliver, *History of Public Speaking in America* (Boston: Allyn and Bacon, 1965), 9.
4. Ibid.
5. Sacvan Bercovitch, *The American Jeremiad* (Madison: University of Wisconsin Press, 1978), xi.
6. Ibid., 16.
7. Celeste Michelle Condit, "John Cotton: Influential Puritan Minister," in *American Orators Before 1900: Critical Studies and Sources,* ed. Bernard K. Duffy and Halford R. Ryan (Westport, Conn.: Greenwood, 1987), 106-12.
8. Ibid., 106.
9. Bernard L. Brock, "Jonathan Edwards: Eighteenth Century Preacher," in Duffy and Ryan, *American Orators,* 146-53.
10. Eugene E. White, "George Whitefield: Itinerant Evangelist," in Duffy and Ryan, *American Orators,* 427-36.
11. Ibid., 429.
12. Bercovitch, *Jeremiad,* 69.
13. Potter and Thomas, *Colonial Idiom,* xi.
14. Barnet Baskerville, *The People's Voice: The Orator in American Society* (Lexington: University of Kentucky Press, 1979), 10.
15. Ibid., 9.
16. Oliver, *Public Speaking,* 2.
17. See Lawrence W. Hugenberg, "John Adams: Second President of the United States," in Duffy and Ryan, *American Orators,* 1-6.
18. Baskerville, *People's Voice,* 30.
19. Hugenberg, "John Adams," 3.
20. Loch K. Johnson, "Thomas Jefferson: Third President of the United States," in Duffy and Ryan, *American Orators,* 245-50.
21. Ibid., 245.
22. Ibid.
23. Stephen A. Smith, "James Madison: Fourth President of the United States," in Duffy and Ryan, *American Orators,* 278-84.
24. Edward Pessen, *The Log Cabin Myth: The Social Origins of the Presidents* (New Haven: Yale University Press, 1984), 75.
25. Stephen E. Lucas, "George Washington: First President of the United States," in Duffy and Ryan, *American Orators,* 406-15.
26. Ibid., 411.

27. Samuel Kernell, *Going Public: New Strategies of Presidential Leadership* (Washington, D.C.: CQ Press, 1986).

28. James W. Ceaser, *Presidential Selection: Theory and Development* (Princeton: Princeton University Press, 1979), 29.

29. Ibid., 32.

30. Ibid., 29.

31. Robert V. Remini, *The Revolutionary Age of Andrew Jackson* (New York: Harper & Row, 1976), 3.

32. Ceaser, *Presidential Selection*, 30.

33. Remini, *Revolutionary Age*, 53.

34. Carl R. Burgchardt, "Henry Clay: Legislative Leader," in Duffy and Ryan, *American Orators*, 87-97.

35. Craig R. Smith, "Daniel Webster: Defender of the Union," in Duffy and Ryan, *American Orators*, 416-26.

36. Ibid., 421.

37. Remini, *Revolutionary Age*, 168.

38. Oliver, *Public Speaking*, 463.

39. Karen A. Foss, "Sojourner Truth: Anti-Slavery and Women's Rights Lecturer," in Duffy and Ryan, *American Orators*, 385-90.

40. Oliver, *Public Speaking*, 463.

41. Pessen, *Log Cabin Myth*, 16.

42. Hal W. Fulmer, "William Lowndes Yancey: Politician, Diplomat, Secessionist," in Duffy and Ryan, *American Orators*, 437-44.

43. Ibid., 440.

44. Ibid., 440-41.

45. Ronald K. Burke, "Charles Sumner: U.S. Senator," in Duffy and Ryan, *American Orators*, 364-70.

46. Ibid., 367.

47. David Zarefsky, "Stephen A. Douglas," in Duffy and Ryan, *American Orators*, 127-35.

48. Ibid., 128.

49. Ibid., 131.

50. Ibid.

51. Ibid., 135.

52. James M. McPherson, *How Lincoln Won the War with Metaphors* (Fort Wayne, Ind.: Louis A. Warren Lincoln Library and Museum, 1985), 3-6.

53. Denton, *The Primetime Presidency of Ronald Reagan*, 4.

54. Waldo W. Braden, "Abraham Lincoln: Sixteenth President of the United States," in Duffy and Ryan, *American Orators*, 259-70.

55. Ibid., 264.

56. Ibid., 267.

57. Kenneth Cmiel, *Democratic Eloquence: The Fight Over Popular Speech in Nineteenth Century America* (New York: Morrow, 1990).

58. Baskerville, *People's Voice*, 92.

59. Oliver, *Public Speaking*, 320.

60. Ibid., 437.

61. Ibid., 434.

62. Mark R. Winchell, "Ralph Waldo Emerson: Essayist, Philosopher, Poet," in Duffy and Ryan, *American Orators*, 154-61.

63. Ibid., 155.

64. Ibid., 156.

65. Richard J. Calhoun, "Mark Twain: Novelist and Humorist," in Duffy and Ryan, *American Orators*, 391-98.

66. Baskerville, *People's Voice*, 98.

67. Ibid., 133-49.

68. Ibid., 155.

69. William H. Harbaugh, *The Writings of Theodore Roosevelt* (Indianapolis: Bobbs-Merrill, 1967), xx.

70. Jeffrey K. Tulis, *The Rhetorical Presidency* (Princeton: Princeton University Press, 1987), 106.

71. David E. Cronon, ed., *The Political Thought of Woodrow Wilson* (Indianapolis: Bobbs-Merrill, 1965), 102.

72. Neils Aage Thorsen, *The Political Thought of Woodrow Wilson, 1875-1910* (Princeton: Princeton University Press, 1988), 27.

73. Cronon, *Woodrow Wilson*, lxvi.

74. Alexander L. George and Juliette L. George, *Woodrow Wilson and Colonel House: A Personality Study* (New York: Dover, 1964).

75. Leon H. Canfield, *The Political Thought of Woodrow Wilson* (Rutherford, N.J.: Fairleigh Dickinson University Press, 1966), 184, 212.

76. Ibid., 230.

77. Ibid., 207.

78. Tulis, *Rhetorical Presidency*, 133.

79. Ibid., 135.

80. Ibid., 95.

Chapter 2. The Development of Mass-Mediated Politics: Franklin Delano Roosevelt and Harry S. Truman

1. Quoted in Graham J. White, *FDR and the Press* (Chicago: University of Chicago Press, 1979), 7.

2. Samuel I. Rosenman, ed., *The Public Papers and Addresses of Franklin D. Roosevelt*, vols. 1-9 (New York: Random House, 1932-1940); vols. 10-12 (New York: Russell and Russell, 1941-1943). Hereinafter cited as *Public Papers*.

3. Of course, the data used here only capture the formal, public side of presidential communication, and it is to be expected that Roosevelt, like all presidents, participated in informal, private communication with individual members of Congress as well.

4. See, for example, "A Welcome to Rear-Admiral Richard E. Byrd on His Return from the Antarctic," *Public Papers*, 10 May 1935; "Extemporaneous Remarks in San Juan, Puerto Rico," *Public Papers*, 7 July 1934; "A Toast to His Majesty, King George VI, at the White House," *Public Papers*, 8 June 1939.

5. James MacGregor Burns, *Roosevelt: The Lion and the Fox* (New York: Harcourt, Brace, 1956), 176.

6. Ibid., 33.

7. Edgar Eugene Robinson, *The Roosevelt Leadership: 1933-1945* (Philadelphia: Lippincott, 1985), 103.

8. Barnet Baskerville, *The People's Voice: The Orator in American Society* (Lexington: University of Kentucky Press, 1979), 177.

9. Halford R. Ryan, *Franklin D. Roosevelt's Rhetorical Presidency* (Westport, Conn: Greenwood, 1988), 30.

10. Ibid., 34.

11. White, *FDR*, 11.

12. Ryan, *Rhetorical Presidency*, 10.

13. Ithiel de Sola Pool, quoted by Martin Linsky, *Impact: How the Press Affects Federal Policymaking* (New York: Norton, 1986), 17.

14. White, *FDR*, 78.

15. Halford R. Ryan, "Roosevelt's First Inaugural: A Study of Technique," in *American Rhetoric From Roosevelt to Reagan: A Collection of Speeches and Critical Essays*, ed. Halford R. Ryan (Prospect Heights, Ill.: Waveland Press, 1983), 11-13.

16. "Introduction," *Public Papers*, 1934; "Fourth Fireside Chat," *Public Papers*, 22 October 1933; "Address Before the American Retail Federation," *Public Papers*, 22 May 1939.

17. See, for example, "A Special Press Conference with the Members of the American Society of Newspaper Editors," *Public Papers*, 22 April 1938; "The Five Hundred and Fourteenth Press Conference," *Public Papers*, 4 January 1939; "The Eight Hundred and Forty-eighth Press Conference," *Public Papers*, 1 October 1942.

18. See "Radio Address to the Democratic National Convention in Chicago, Ill., from the White House," *Public Papers*, 19 July 1940; "Message to Na-

tional Convention of Young Democrats," *Public Papers,* 21 August 1941; "Fireside Chat Following Declaration of War Against Japan," *Public Paper,* 9 December 1941.

19. "Radio Address Announcing the Proclamation of an Unlimited National Emergency," *Public Papers,* 27 May 1941.

20. "Address Delivered at the Democratic State Convention, Syracuse, New York," *Public Papers,* 29 September 1936.

21. "I Pledge You—I Pledge Myself—to a New Deal for the American People; The Governor Accepts the Nomination for the Presidency," *Public Papers,* 2 July 1932.

22. See "Address at Little Rock, Ark.," *Public Papers,* 10 June 1936; "Address at Grand Forks, N.D.," *Public Papers,* 4 October 1937; and "The Opening of the 1940 Presidential Campaign, Philadelphia, Pa.," *Public Papers,* 23 October 1940.

23. Leonard J. Reinsch, *Getting Elected: From Radio and Roosevelt to Television and Reagan* (New York: Hippocrene Books, 1988), 22.

24. Ibid., xiii. See also, Ryan, *Rhetorical Presidency,* 19.

25. Denis W. Brogan, *The Era of Franklin D. Roosevelt: A Chronicle of the New Deal and Global War* (New Haven: Yale University Press, 1950), 35.

26. Edgar Eugene Robinson, *The Roosevelt Leadership* (Philadelphia: Lippincott, 1955), 66.

27. "Inaugural Address," *Public Papers,* 4 March 1933.

28. See "Campaign Address on Federal Budget," Pittsburgh, Pa., *Public Papers,* 19 October 1932; "Campaign Address at Baltimore, Md.", *Public Papers,* 25 October 1932; and "Campaign Address on a Program for Unemployment and Long-Range Planning," Boston, Mass., *Public Papers,* 31 October 1932.

29. "The Governor Accepts the Nomination for the Presidency," *Public Papers,* 2 July 1932.

30. "Campaign Address on Railroads at Salt Lake City, Utah," *Public Papers,* 17 September 1932.

31. "Address at a Jackson Day Dinner," *Public Papers,* 8 January 1936; "First Fireside Chat of 1934," *Public Papers,* 28 June 1934; "Informal Extemporaneous Remarks at Mt. Marion, N.Y.," *Public Papers,* 5 July 1937.

32. "Fireside Chat on National Defense," *Public Papers,* 11 September 1941; "Interview on Government Reporting Factually to the People," *Public Papers,* 9 May 1939; "Annual Message to Congress," *Public Papers,* 3 January 1940.

33. "Third Fireside Chat," *Public Papers,* 24 July 1933.

34. See "First Fireside Chat of 1935," *Public Papers,* 28 April 1935; "Message to the Extraordinary Session of the Congress Recommending Certain Legislation," *Public Papers,* 15 November 1937; "Four Hundred and Twenty-second Press Conference," *Public Papers,* 4 January 1938.

35. Baskerville, *People's Voice,* 171.

36. "First Fireside Chat of 1934," *Public Papers*, 28 June 1934. See also "Address at Bankers' Convention, Constitution Hall, Washington, D.C.," *Public Papers*, 24 October 1934; and "Address at the Dedication of the Boulder Dam," *Public Papers*, 30 September 1935.

37. "Annual Message to Congress," *Public Papers*, 3 January 1936; see also "Acceptance of the Renomination for the Presidency," *Public Papers*, 27 June 1936; and the "Annual Message to Congress," *Public Papers*, 6 January 1936.

38. See "Annual Message to Congress," *Public Papers*, 3 January 1934; "Introduction," *Public Papers*, 1938; and "Fireside Chat," *Public Papers*, 24 June 1938.

39. Burns, *Roosevelt*, 476.

40. "The Governor Accepts the Nomination for the Presidency," *Public Papers*, 2 July 1932.

41. "Campaign Address on Public Utilities and the Development of Electric Power," *Public Papers*, 21 September 1932.

42. "Graduation Address at the United States Naval Academy," *Public Papers*, 1 June 1933.

43. See "Radio Address on the Occasion of the President's First Birthday Ball in Benefit of Crippled Children," *Public Papers*, 30 January 1933; "Address Before the Code Authorities of Six Hundred Industries," *Public Papers*, 5 March 1933; "A Greeting to the Annual Convention of the American Philatelic Society," *Public Papers*, 17 September 1936.

44. Ryan, *Rhetorical Presidency*, 10.

45. "Address Before the American Legion Convention," *Public Papers*, 2 October 1933.

46. "Graduation Address, United States Military Academy, West Point," *Public Papers*, 12 June 1939.

47. "Address Before the Governor's Conference," *Public Papers*, 6 March 1932.

48. "Address Before the United States Chamber of Commerce," *Public Papers*, 4 May 1933.

49. "Radio Address on Brotherhood Day," *Public Papers*, 23 February 1936.

50. "Second Inaugural Address," *Public Papers*, 20 January 1937.

51. "Address at a Jackson Day Dinner," *Public Papers*, 8 January 1936.

52. "Campaign Address on Public Utilities," *Public Papers*, 21 September 1932; "Campaign Address Before the Republicans-For-Roosevelt League, New York City," *Public Papers*, 3 November 1932; "Second Inaugural," *Public Papers*, 20 January 1937.

53. Reinsch, *Getting Elected*.

54. William E. Pemberton, *Harry S. Truman: Fair Dealer and Cold Warrior* (Boston: Twayne, 1989), 38.

55. Robert Underhill, *The Truman Persuasions* (Ames: Iowa State University Press, 1981), 7.

56. "Address in New York City at the Convention of the Columbia Scholastic Press Association," *Public Papers*, 15 March 1952.

57. Margaret Truman, *Harry S. Truman* (New York: Morrow, 1973), 177.

58. Dean Acheson, quoted in Merle Miller, *Plain Speaking: An Oral Biography of Harry S. Truman* (New York: Berkeley, 1973), 378.

59. Louis William Lebovich, "Failed White House Press Relations in the Early Months of the Truman Administration," *Presidential Studies Quarterly* 19, no. 3 (Summer 1989): 583-91.

60. Reinsch, *Getting Elected*, 12.

61. William E. Leuchtenburg, *In the Shadow of FDR: From Harry Truman to Ronald Reagan* (Ithaca: Cornell University Press, 1983), 4.

62. Robert J. Donovan, *Conflict and Crisis: The Presidency of Harry S. Truman* (New York: Norton, 1977), 19.

63. "Address Before a Joint Session of the Congress," *Public Papers of the Presidents: Harry S. Truman* (Washington, D.C.: U.S. Government Printing Office, 1961-66) 16 April 1945. Hereinafter cited as *Public Papers*.

64. Bert Cochran, *Harry Truman and the Crisis Presidency* (New York: Funk and Wagnalls, 1973), 119.

65. "The President's News Conference," *Public Papers*, 17 April 1945; "Broadcast to the American People on the Surrender of Germany," *Public Papers*, 8 May 1945; "Address at Jackson Day Dinner," *Public Papers*, 23 March 1946.

66. "Address to the United Nations Conference in San Francisco," *Public Papers*, 25 April 1945.

67. "Address in Chicago, Army Day," *Public Papers*, 6 April 1946; "Address in New York City at the Opening of the United Nations General Assembly," *Public Papers*, 23 October 1946; "Address at Jefferson-Jackson Day Dinner," *Public Papers*, 19 February 1948.

68. Robert H. Ferrell, *Harry S. Truman and the Modern American Presidency* (Boston: Little, Brown, 1983), 97.

69. "Address Before the United States Conference of Mayors," *Public Papers*, 29 March 1949.

70. "Commencement Address at Howard University," *Public Papers*, 3 June 1952.

71. "Remarks upon Receiving an Honorary Degree from the University of Kansas City," *Public Papers*, 28 June 1945; "Address in New York City at the Opening Session of the United Nations," *Public Papers*, 23 October 1946; "Annual Message to Congress on the State of the Union," *Public Papers*, 9 January 1952.

72. "Commencement Address at the University of Missouri," *Public Papers*, 9 June 1950.

73. "Radio Address to the American People on the Railroad Strike Emergency," *Public Papers*, 24 May 1946.

74. Cabell Phillips, *The Truman Presidency: The History of a Triumphant Succession* (New York: Macmillan, 1966), 195.

75. Margaret Truman, *Truman*, 26.

76. "Rear Platform and Other Informal Remarks in Pennsylvania and New Jersey," *Public Papers*, 7 October 1948.

77. Robert J. Donovan, *The Tumultuous Years: The Presidency of Harry S. Truman, 1949-1953* (New York: Norton, 1982), 26.

78. Ibid., 27.

79. "Address at a Dinner of the Civil Defense Conference," *Public Papers*, 7 May 1951; "Address at Valley Forge at the Boy Scout Jamboree," *Public Papers*, 30 June 1950; "Address on Foreign Policy at the George Washington National Masonic Memorial," *Public Papers*, 22 February 1950.

80. "Radio Report to the American People on U.S. policy in the Far East," *Public Papers*, 11 April 1951; "Annual Message to Congress on the State of the Union," *Public Papers*, 8 January 1951; "Address in San Francisco at the War Memorial Opera House," *Public Papers*, 17 October 1950.

81. Phillips, *Truman Presidency*, 402-3; see also Cochran, *Crisis Presidency*, 395; Donovan, *Conflict and Crisis*, 118.

82. Miller, *Plain Speaking*, 401.

83. Tris Coffin, *Missouri Compromise* (Boston: Little, Brown, 1947), 21, 29.

84. "Radio and Television Address to the American People on the Situation in Korea," *Public Papers*, 19 July 1950.

85. "Radio and Television Address to the American People on the National Emergency," *Public Papers*, 15 December 1950.

86. "Radio and Television Address to the American People on the Need for Government Operation of the Steel Mills," *Public Papers*, 8 April 1952.

87. Quoted in Donovan, *Tumultuous Years*, 409.

Chapter 3. The Birth of Televised Politics: Dwight D. Eisenhower and John F. Kennedy

1. Blanche Weisen Cook, *The Declassified Eisenhower* (Garden City, N.Y.: Doubleday, 1981), v; Robert L. Branyan and Lawrence L. Larsen, *The Eisenhower Administration: A Documentary History* (New York: Random House, 1971), 7.

2. "Remarks to the Midshipmen at the Naval Academy in Annapolis," *Public Papers of the Presidents: Dwight D. Eisenhower* (Washington, D.C.: Government Printing Office), 17 May 1953. Hereinafter cited as *Public Papers*.

3. "Remarks to the Staff of the United States Information Agency," *Public Papers,* 10 November 1953.

4. "Address at the Dinner of the American Newspaper Publishers Association," *Public Papers,* 22 April 1954. See also "Remarks at the Annual Breakfast of Masonic Leaders," *Public Papers,* 24 February 1955; "Remarks at Fort Benning, Georgia, After Watching a Demonstration of New Army Equipment," *Public Papers,* 3 May 1960.

5. Richard H. Rovere, *Affairs of State: The Eisenhower Years* (New York: Farrar, Straus, and Cudahy, 1956), 112.

6. Arthur Larson, *Eisenhower: The President Nobody Knew* (New York: Scribner's, 1968), 36.

7. Herbert S. Parmet, *Eisenhower and the American Crusades* (New York: Macmillan, 1972), 332.

8. Larson, *Eisenhower,* 12.

9. Fred I. Greenstein, *The Hidden-Hand Presidency: Eisenhower as Leader* (New York: Basic Books, 1983), 19-36.

10. William Bragg Ewald, Jr., *Eisenhower the President: Crucial Days, 1951-1960* (Englewood Cliffs, N.J.: Prentice-Hall, 1981), 146.

11. "Remarks at the United States Military Academy Alumni Luncheon, West Point, N.Y.," *Public Papers,* 6 June 1955.

12. William E. Leuchtenburg, *In the Shadow of FDR: From Harry Truman to Ronald Reagan* (Ithaca: Cornell University Press, 1983), 53.

13. Parmet, *American Crusades,* 175.

14. Quoted in Larson, *Eisenhower,* 8.

15. Ibid., 5.

16. "Address at Transylvania College, Lexington, Ky.," *Public Papers,* 23 April 1954.

17. "Address at the Columbia University National Bicentennial Dinner, New York City," *Public Papers,* 31 May 1954.

18. Parmet, *American Crusades,* 212.

19. "Radio and Television Address to the American People on the Administration's Purposes and Accomplishments," *Public Papers,* 4 January 1954.

20. "Address Recorded for the Republican Lincoln Day Dinners," *Public Papers,* 28 January 1954.

21. Larson, *Eisenhower,* 15.

22. Branyan and Larsen, *Documentary History,* 7.

23. Greenstein, *Hidden-Hand,* 57.

24. Larson, *Eisenhower,* 146-47.

25. "Address at the American Legion Convention," *Public Papers,* 30 August 1954.

26. "Annual Message to Congress on the State of the Union," *Public Papers,* 9 January 1959.

27. "Address at the Tenth Anniversary of the United Nations, San Francisco, Calif.," *Public Papers*, 20 June 1955.

28. Leonard J. Reinsch, *Getting Elected: From Radio and Roosevelt to Television and Reagan* (New York: Hippocrene Books, 1988), 90.

29. Alton R. Lee, *Dwight D. Eisenhower: Soldier and Statesman* (Chicago: Nelson-Hall, 1981), 181.

30. Larson, *Eisenhower*, 165.

31. "Address Delivered Before the American Society of Newspaper Editors," *Public Papers*, 6 April 1953. See also "Radio and Television Address to the American People on the Administration's Purposes and Accomplishments," *Public Papers*, 4 January 1954; "Remarks to the Governors' Conference Dinner," *Public Papers*, 2 May 1955.

32. "Annual Message to Congress on the State of the Union," *Public Papers*, 6 January 1955.

33. "Inaugural Address," *Public Papers*, 20 January 1953.

34. "Second Inaugural Address," *Public Papers*, 21 January 1957.

35. "Address at the Opening Session of the White House Conference on Children and Youth, College Park, Md.," *Public Papers*, 27 March 1960.

36. "Commencement Address at Yale University," *Public Papers of the Presidents of the United States: John F. Kennedy* (Washington, D.C.: Government Printing Office), 11 June 1963. Hereinafter cited as *Public Papers*.

37. Thomas Brown, *JFK: History of an Image* (Bloomington: Indiana University Press, 1988), 3.

38. Marshall McLuhan, *Understanding Media* (New York: New American Library, 1964); and Marshall McLuhan and Quentin Fiore, *The Medium Is the Message* (New York: Bantam Books, 1967). For a specific discussion of the effect of this "shrinking" on the 1960 election, see Theodore H. White, *The Making of the President 1960* (New York: Atheneum, 1961), 177.

39. "Remarks to the Delegates of the Youth Fitness Conference," *Public Papers*, 22 February 1961.

40. "Remarks at George Washington University upon Receiving an Honorary Degree," *Public Papers*, 3 May 1961.

41. "Radio and Television Report to the American People on Returning from Europe," *Public Papers*, 6 June 1961. See also "Radio and Television Report to the American People on the Berlin Crisis," *Public Papers*, 25 July 1961; and "Remarks at the Eighth National Conference on International Economic and Social Development," *Public Papers*, 16 June 1961.

42. "Remarks at a Birthday Dinner for Governor DiSalle," *Public Papers*, 6 January 1962. See also "Remarks at the White House to Members of the American Legion," *Public Papers*, 1 March 1962; and "Address Before the United States Chamber of Commerce on its 50th Anniversary," *Public Papers*, 30 April 1962.

43. "Address in Milwaukee at the Jefferson-Jackson Dinner," *Public Papers*, 12 May 1962; "Remarks at the Dedication of the Oahe Dam, Pierre, S.D.," *Public Papers*, 17 August 1962; "Remarks to the White House Conference on Narcotic and Drug Abuse," *Public Papers*, 27 September 1962.

44. Tom Wicker, *JFK and LBJ: The Influence of Personality upon Politics* (New York: Morrow, 1968), 85; Stan Opotowsky, *The Kennedy Government* (New York: Dutton, 1961), 201; William E. Leuchtenburg, *In the Shadow of FDR: From Harry Truman to Ronald Reagan* (Ithaca: Cornell University Press, 1983), 91-107.

45. "Annual Message to Congress on the State of the Union," *Public Papers*, 14 January 1963.

46. Charles Lam Markham and Mark Sherwin, *John F. Kennedy: Sense of Purpose* (New York: St. Martin's Press, 1961), 273-74.

47. "Inaugural Address," *Public Papers*, 20 January 1961.

48. John Lewis Gaddis, *Strategies of Containment* (New York: Oxford University Press, 1982), 232.

49. Pierre Salinger, *With Kennedy* (Garden City, N.Y.: Doubleday, 1966), 54.

50. White, *Making of the President 1960*, 320.

51. William G. Carleton, "Kennedy in History: An Early Appraisal," in *The Politics of John F. Kennedy*, ed. Edmund S. Ions (New York: Barnes and Noble, 1967), 199-221.

52. Herbert S. Parmet, *JFK: The Presidency of John F. Kennedy* (New York: Dial Press, 1983), 45.

53. Victor Lasky, *JFK: The Man and the Myth* (New York: Arlington House, 1963), 3, 7, 206.

54. Salinger, *With Kennedy*, 143.

55. Theodore C. Sorensen, *Kennedy* (New York: Harper & Row, 1965), 318.

56. Montague Kern, Patricia W. Levering, and Ralph B. Levering, *The Kennedy Crises: The Press, the Presidency, and Foreign Policy* (Chapel Hill: University of North Carolina Press, 1983), 3.

57. "Address on 'The President and the Press,' Delivered Before the American Newspaper Publishers' Association," *Public Papers*, 27 April 1961.

58. Lewis J. Paper, *The Promise and the Performance: The Leadership of JFK* (New York: Crown, 1975), 327.

59. Quoted in Markmann and Sherwin, *Sense of Purpose*, 278.

60. Michael L. Geis, *The Language of Politics* (New York: Springer-Verlag, 1987), 39.

61. Robert H. Ferrell, *Harry S. Truman and the Modern American Presidency* (Boston: Little, Brown, 1983), 176-77.

62. Fairlie, *Kennedy Promise*, 11.

Chapter 4. Television and Personality:
Lyndon B. Johnson and Richard M. Nixon

1. Arthur Schlesinger, *The Imperial Presidency* (New York: Popular Library, 1974).

2. Theodore H. White, *The Making of the President 1964* (New York: Mentor, 1965), 45.

3. "Address Before a Joint Session of Congress," *Public Papers of the Presidents of the United States: Lyndon B. Johnson* (Washington, D.C.: Government Printing Office), 27 November 1963. Hereinafter cited as *Public Papers*.

4. "The President's Thanksgiving Day Address to the Nation," *Public Papers*, 28 November 1963.

5. Quoted in Doris Kearns, *Lyndon Johnson and the American Dream* (New York: Signet, 1970), 185.

6. Tom Wicker, *JFK and LBJ: The Influence of Personality upon Politics* (New York: Morrow, 1968), 155.

7. Jack Valenti, *A Very Human President* (New York: Norton, 1975), 103.

8. George Reedy, *Lyndon B. Johnson: A Political Memoir* (New York: Andrews and McMeel, 1982), 5.

9. Ibid., 67.

10. Vaughn Davis Bornet, *The Presidency of Lyndon Johnson* (Lawrence: University Press of Kansas, 1983), 148.

11. Valenti, *Human President*, 268.

12. Kearns, *American Dream*, 259.

13. Eric F. Goldman, *The Tragedy of Lyndon Johnson* (New York: Knopf, 1969), 202.

14. Bornet, *Presidency*, 106.

15. Goldman, *Tragedy*, 8.

16. Rowland Evans and Robert Novak, *Lyndon B. Johnson: The Exercise of Power* (New York: New American Library, 1966), 508.

17. Bornet, *Presidency*, 160.

18. Ibid., 13.

19. The irony here is that in seeking to be "president of all the people," LBJ pursued policies in Vietnam and civil rights matters that led to the further erosion, if not the destruction, of the majority coalition constructed by FDR.

20. "The President's News Conference," *Public Papers*, 11 April 1964. See also "Remarks at a Democratic Party Dinner in Chicago," *Public Papers*, 17 May 1966; "Recorded Message to the Navajo People on the Occasion of Their Centennial Banquet," *Public Papers*, 24 January 1968.

21. "Remarks to Foreign Language Newspaper Publishers on Their Role in Building American Unity," *Public Papers*, 3 August 1965. See also "Re-

marks to College Students Employed by the Government during the Summer," *Public Papers*, 4 August 1965; "Remarks to Members of the United States Jaycees Governmental Affairs Seminar," *Public Papers*, 31 January 1967.

22. "Radio and Television Remarks upon Signing the Civil Rights Bill," *Public Papers*, 2 July 1964. See also "Remarks to the Lawyer's Conference on Crime Control," *Public Papers*, 13 May 1967; "Remarks upon Signing Order Providing for Coordination by the Attorney General of Federal Law Enforcement and Crime Prevention Programs," *Public Papers*, 7 February 1968.

23. "Address to the Nation Following the Attack on Senator Kennedy," *Public Papers*, 5 June 1968.

24. "Annual Message to Congress on the State of the Union," *Public Papers*, 4 January 1965. See also "Remarks at a Congressional Dinner Held in the National Guard Armory," *Public Papers*, 12 May 1966; "Remarks in Indianapolis at a Luncheon with Indiana Business, Labor, and Professional Leaders," *Public Papers*, 23 July 1966.

25. "Annual Message to Congress on the State of the Union," *Public Papers*, 14 January 1969.

26. Bornet, *Presidency*, 103.

27. White, *Making of the President 1964*, 207.

28. "Annual Message to Congress on the State of the Union," *Public Papers*, 8 January 1964. See also "Remarks to Key Officials of the Internal Revenue Service," *Public Papers*, 30 January 1964; "Remarks Before the National Convention upon Accepting the Nomination," *Public Papers*, 27 August 1964.

29. "Remarks to the Delegates to the White House Conference on Natural Beauty," *Public Papers*, 25 May 1965. See also "Remarks to Members of the Southern Baptist Christian Leadership Conference," *Public Papers*, 25 March 1964; "The President's Remarks at a Reception Given in His Honor by Negro Presidential Appointees," *Public Papers*, 17 December 1968.

30. "'Two Threats to World Peace'—Remarks in Omaha on the Occasion of the Sending of the Five-Millionth Ton of Grain to India," *Public Papers*, 30 June 1966.

31. Larry Berman, *Planning a Tragedy: The Americanization of the War in Vietnam* (New York: Norton, 1982), 57; Walter Bunge, Robert V. Hudson, Chung Woo Suh, "Johnson's Information Strategy for Vietnam: An Evaluation," *Journalism Quarterly* 45 (1968): 419-25; Doris Graber, *Verbal Behavior and Politics* (Urbana: University of Illinois Press, 1976), 176.

32. George Reedy, *The Twilight of the Presidency* (New York: Mentor, 1970), 51.

33. Paul Tillets, "The National Conventions," in *The National Elections of 1964,* ed. Milton C. Cummings (Washington, D.C.: Brookings Institution, 1965), 15-41.

34. Bornet, *Presidency,* 158.

35. "News Conference at the National Press Club," *Public Papers,* 17 January 1968.

36. Barnet Baskerville, *The People's Voice: The Orator in American Society* (Lexington: University of Kentucky Press, 1979), 226.

37. "Inaugural Address," *Public Papers of the Presidents of the United States: Richard Nixon* (Washington, D.C.: Government Printing Office), 20 January 1969. Hereinafter cited as *Public Papers.*

38. Richard M. Nixon, *Six Crises* (New York: Warner, 1962, 1979), 109.

39. Theodore H. White, *Breach of Faith: The Fall of Richard Nixon* (New York: Laurel, 1975), 57.

40. William Safire, *Before the Fall: An Inside View of the Pre-Watergate White House* (Garden City, N.Y.: Doubleday, 1975), 537.

41. Theodore H. White, *The Making of the President 1968* (New York: Pocket Books, 1970), 166.

42. Theodore H. White, *The Making of the President 1972* (New York: Bantam Books, 1973), 304.

43. Safire, *Before the Fall,* 365.

44. Ibid., 343.

45. John Ehrlichman, *Witness to Power: The Nixon Years* (New York: Simon and Schuster, 1982), 275. See also Anthony J. Lukas, *Nightmare: The Underside of the Nixon Years* (New York: Viking Press, 1976), 453.

46. "Remarks at the Convention of the National Association of Broadcasters," *Public Papers,* 25 March 1969.

47. "Remarks to the Assembly of the Organization of American States," *Public Papers,* 14 April 1969.

48. "Address to the Nation on Progress toward Peace in Vietnam," *Public Papers,* 20 April 1970; "Address to the Nation on the State of the Union Before a Joint Session of Congress," *Public Papers,* 20 January 1972; "Radio Address about the Third Annual Foreign Policy Report to Congress," *Public Papers,* 9 February 1972.

49. "Remarks at a 'Briefing for Businessmen' Meeting," *Public Papers,* 21 November 1969; "Remarks at the 50th Anniversary of the United States Jaycees in St. Louis, Mo.," *Public Papers,* 25 June 1970; "Veterans Day Address," *Public Papers,* 24 October 1971.

50. "Address to the Nation about Policies to Deal with the Energy Shortages," *Public Papers,* 7 November 1973. See also "Radio Address About the American Right of Privacy," *Public Papers,* 23 February 1974; "Address to the Nation about Inflation and the Economy," *Public Papers,* 25 July 1974.

51. "Remarks at the 50th Anniversary of the United States Jaycees in St. Louis, Mo.," *Public Papers*, 25 June 1970.

52. "Remarks to State Legislators Attending the National Legislative Conference," *Public Papers*, 30 March 1973.

53. "Radio and Television Address to the People of the Soviet Union," *Public Papers*, 28 May 1972.

54. "'A Conversation with the President,' Interview with Dan Rather of the Columbia Broadcasting System," *Public Papers*, 2 January 1972.

55. "Address in the Alfred M. Landon Lecture Series at Kansas State University," *Public Papers*, 16 September 1970.

56. "Remarks at the 50th Anniversary Convention of the United States Jaycees in St. Louis, Mo.," *Public Papers*, 25 June 1970.

57. "Remarks at the Graduation Exercises of the FBI National Academy," *Public Papers*, 28 May 1969.

58. "Remarks at a Luncheon of the National Citizens' Committee for Fairness to the Presidency," *Public Papers*, 9 June 1974; "Remarks at a National Prayer Breakfast," *Public Papers*, 31 January 1974.

59. "Remarks at a National Prayer Breakfast," *Public Papers*, 3 January 1971.

60. "Remarks at a Luncheon of the National Citizens' Committee for Fairness to the Presidency," *Public Papers*, 9 June 1974.

61. "Address to the Nation Announcing the Decision to Resign the Office of President," *Public Papers*, 8 August 1974.

62. Lukas, *Nightmare*, 453.

63. William Bragg Ewald, Jr., *Eisenhower the President: Crucial Days, 1951-1960* (Englewood Cliffs, N.J.: Prentice-Hall, 1981), 313.

64. Reedy, *Twilight*, 158.

65. "Remarks at the Dedication of the Lyndon Baines Johnson Library, Austin, Texas," *Public Papers*, 22 May 1971.

Chapter 5. The Issue of Control:
Gerald R. Ford and Jimmy Carter

1. "Remarks on Taking the Oath of Office," *Public Papers of the Presidents: Gerald R. Ford* (Washington, D.C.: Government Printing Office), 9 August 1974. Hereinafter cited as *Public Papers*.

2. "Remarks Announcing the Appointment of Jerald F. terHorst as Press Secretary to the President," *Public Papers*, 9 August 1974.

3. Gerald R. Ford, *A Time to Heal: The Autobiography of Gerald R. Ford* (New York: Harper & Row, 1979), 156-57.

4. "Address to a Joint Session of Congress," *Public Papers*, 12 August 1974.

5. "Remarks to Veterans of Foreign Wars Annual Convention, Chicago, Ill.," *Public Papers*, 19 August 1974.

6. W. Lance Bennett, Patricia Dempsey Harris, Janet K. Lasky, Alan H. Levitch, and E. Monrad, "Deep and Surface Images in the Construction of Political Images: The Case of Amnesty," *Quarterly Journal of Speech* 62, no. 2 (April 1976): 109-26.

7. Clark R. Mollenhoff, *The Man Who Pardoned Nixon* (New York: St. Martin's Press, 1976), 93.

8. Elizabeth Drew, *American Journal: The Events of 1976* (New York: Random House, 1977), 235.

9. Ibid., 27.

10. "Remarks to the Annual Convention of the Future Farmers of America, Kansas City, Mo.," *Public Papers*, 15 October 1974.

11. Robert E. Denton, Jr., and Gary C. Woodward, *Political Communication in America* (New York: Praeger, 1985), 7.

12. John Osborne, *White House Watch: The Ford Years* (Washington, D.C.: New Republic Books, 1977), 176.

13. Ron Nessen, "The Ford Presidency and the Press," in *The Ford Presidency: Twenty-Two Intimate Perspectives on Gerald R. Ford*, ed. Kenneth W. Thompson (Lanham, Md.: University Press of America, 1988), 179-208.

14. "Exchange with Reporters Following the Indiana, Georgia, and Florida Primary Election Results," *Public Papers*, 5 May 1976.

15. Ford, *Time to Heal*, 289.

16. John Tebbel and Sarah Miles Watts, *The Press and the Presidency: From George Washington to Ronald Reagan* (New York: Oxford University Press, 1985), 515.

17. "Remarks during a Michigan Whistlestop Tour," *Public Papers*, 15 May 1976.

18. John Orman, *Comparing Presidential Behavior: Carter, Reagan, and the Macho Presidential Style* (Westport, Conn.: Greenwood, 1983), 7-9.

19. Robert T. Hartmann, *Palace Politics: An Inside Account of the Ford Years* (New York: McGraw-Hill, 1980), 424.

20. Ibid., 404.

21. Drew, *American Journal*, 29.

22. Ford, *Time to Heal*, 263.

23. "Address Before a Joint Session of Congress Reporting on United States Foreign Policy," *Public Papers*, 10 April 1975.

24. "Remarks upon Receiving the Man of the Year Award from the Reserve Officers Association of the United States," *Public Papers*, 21 February 1975.

25. "Address Before a Joint Session of Congress on the State of the Union," *Public Papers*, 15 January 1975. See also "Remarks at a News Briefing on

the Fiscal Year 1976 Budget," *Public Papers*, 1 February 1975; "Address at a University of Notre Dame Convocation," *Public Papers*, 17 March 1975.

26. "Address to a Joint Session of Congress on the Economy," *Public Papers*, 8 October 1974.
27. "Remarks at Greensboro, N.C.," *Public Papers*, 19 October 1974.
28. David Broder, quoted in Ford, *Time to Heal*, 384.
29. William Lee Miller, *Yankee from Georgia: The Emergence of Jimmy Carter* (New York: Times Books, 1978), 5.
30. Betty Glad, *Jimmy Carter: In Search of the Great White House* (New York: Norton, 1980), 315.
31. Robert E. Denton, Jr., and Dan F. Hahn, *Presidential Communication: Description and Analysis* (New York: Praeger, 1986), 160–69.
32. "Conversation with the President," *Public Papers of the Presidents of the United States: Jimmy Carter* (Washington, D.C.: Government Printing Office), 28 December 1977. Hereinafter cited as *Public Papers*.
33. "Inaugural Address of President Jimmy Carter," *Public Papers*, 20 January 1977.
34. "Remarks at the Swearing-in Ceremony for Members of the Cabinet," *Public Papers*, 23 January 1977. See also "Question-and-Answer Session with a Group of Publishers, Editors, and Broadcasters," 15 April 1977; "Interview with Members of the Board of Directors of the Radio-Television News Directors Association," *Public Papers*, 29 April 1977.
35. "Address Before the Permanent Council of the Organization of American States," *Public Papers*, 14 April 1977; see also "Remarks at a Working Luncheon for Officials of African Nations," *Public Papers*, 4 October 1977; "Remarks Before the Indian Parliament, New Delhi, India," *Public Papers*, 2 January 1977.
36. "Remarks at a News Briefing on Natural Gas Legislation," *Public Papers*, 26 January 1977; "Remarks and a Question-and-Answer Session with Representatives of the Hispanic Media," *Public Papers*, 12 May 1978; "Remarks and a Question-and-Answer Session with a Group of Editors and News Directors," *Public Papers*, 28 July 1978.
37. "Remarks at a Reception for Members of the National Women's Political Caucus," *Public Papers*, 30 March 1977; see also "ABC News Interview," *Public Papers*, 10 August 1977; "Remarks and a Question-and-Answer Session at the Annual Convention of the Communication Workers of America," *Public Papers*, 16 July 1979.
38. Erwin Hargrove, *Jimmy Carter as President: Leadership and the Politics of the Public Good* (Baton Rouge: Louisiana State University Press, 1988).
39. Roderick P. Hart, *The Political Pulpit* (West Lafayette, Ind.: Purdue University Press, 1977).
40. Keith V. Erickson, "Jimmy Carter: The Rhetoric of Private and Civic Piety," *Western Journal of Speech Communication* 44 (Summer 1980): 221–35.

41. Miller, *Yankee*, 32.

42. Ibid., 69.

43. "Remarks on Board the USS *Nimitz* on the Battle Groups' Return to the United States," *Public Papers*, 26 May 1980; see also "Remarks to the National Education Association, Los Angeles, Calif.," *Public Papers*, 3 July 1980; "Annual Message to Congress on the State of the Union," 16 January 1981.

44. See chapter 1.

45. Frye Gaillard, *The Unfinished Presidency: Essays on Jimmy Carter* (Charlotte, N.C.: Wingate College, 1986), 38.

46. Robert H. Swansborough, "Rhetoric and Reality: The Foreign Policy Beliefs and Political Styles of Presidents Carter and Reagan," paper prepared for the annual meeting of the Southern Political Science Association, Atlanta, Ga., November 1986, 12.

47. Quoted in Mark J. Rozell, *The Press and the Carter Presidency* (Boulder: Westview Press, 1989), 39.

48. In fact, as television audiences become increasingly sophisticated, soap is not even being marketed like soap anymore. Image management has become very important to commercial firms. For a full discussion of this point, see Al Reis and Jack Trout, *Positioning: The Battle for the Mind* (New York: McGraw-Hill, 1981); William Meyers, *The Image-Makers* (New York: Times Books, 1984).

49. Haynes Johnson, *In the Absence of Power: Governing America* (New York: Viking Press, 1980), 25.

50. Thomas P. O'Neill with William Novak, *Man of the House: The Life and Political Memoirs of Speaker Tip O'Neill* (New York: Random House, 1987), 283.

51. Glad, *Carter*, 287.

52. Johnson, *Absence of Power*, 170.

53. John Tebbel and Sarah Miles Watts, *The Press and the Presidency: From George Washington to Ronald Reagan* (New York: Oxford University Press, 1985), 522.

54. Hamilton Jordan, *Crisis: The Last Year of the Carter Presidency* (New York: Putnam, 1982), 331.

55. "Question-and-Answer Session by Telephone with Participants in a Townhall Meeting on the Panama Canal Treaties in Hattiesburg, Miss.," *Public Papers*, 16 January 1978; "Remarks and a Question-and-Answer Session with Thirteen Federal Employees," *Public Papers*, 21 May 1979; "Remarks and a Question-and-Answer Session with Area Residents, Gloucester City, N.J.," *Public Papers*, 24 October 1980.

56. "The President's News Conference," *Public Papers*, 30 November 1977; "Remarks from the White House," *Public Papers*, 2 February 1977; "Address to the Nation on Energy," *Public Papers*, 25 May 1979.

Notes

57. "Address to the Nation on Energy and National Goals," *Public Papers*, 15 July 1979.
58. Johnson, *Absence of Power*, 316.
59. "Remarks at a White House Briefing for Members of Congress on the Situation in Iran and the Soviet Invasion of Afghanistan," *Public Papers*, 8 January 1980.
60. "Remarks Announcing United States Sanctions Against Iran," *Public Papers*, 7 April 1980.
61. "Remarks Concerning Candidacy and Campaign Plans," *Public Papers*, 2 December 1979.
62. For a discussion of the advantages and risks of a "Rose Garden strategy," see Barry Brummett, "Towards a Theory of Silence as a Political Strategy," *Quarterly Journal of Speech* 66 (1980): 289–303; Keith V. Erickson and Wallace V. Schmidt, "Presidential Political Silence: Rhetoric and the Rose Garden Strategy," *Southern Speech Communication Journal* 47 (Summer 1982): 402-21.
63. Rozell, *Press and the Carter Presidency*, 157.
64. "The President's News Conference," *Public Papers*, 18 September 1980.
65. "Remarks and a Question-and-Answer Session with Local Residents, Lansdowne, Pa.," *Public Papers*, 2 October 1980.
66. Gaillard, *Unfinished Presidency*, 38.
67. "Address Delivered Before a Joint Session of the Congress on the State of the Union," *Public Papers*, 23 January 1980.

Chapter 6. Mastering Televised Politics:
Ronald Reagan and George Bush

1. William F. Lewis, "Telling America's Story: Narrative Form and the Reagan Presidency," *Quarterly Journal of Speech* 73 (1987): 280-302.
2. Ann Devroy, "Bush Speeches Lack Reagan's Ideological Passion," Washington Post News Service, 1 February 1990.
3. Robert E. Denton, Jr., *The Primetime Presidency of Ronald Reagan: The Era of the Television Presidency* (New York: Praeger, 1988), xii.
4. Larry Speakes with Robert Pack, *Speaking Out: Inside the Reagan White House* (New York: Scribner's, 1988), 235.
5. Mark Hertsgaard, *On Bended Knee: The Press and the Reagan Presidency* (New York: Schocken Books, 1989), x.
6. For a full discussion of this point, see Mary E. Stuckey, *Playing the Game: The Presidential Rhetoric of Ronald Reagan* (New York: Praeger, 1990), chap. 1.

7. "Remarks at a White House Luncheon for the New Pioneers," *Public Papers of the Presidents: Ronald Reagan* (Washington, D.C.: Government Printing Office), 12 February 1985. Hereinafter cited as *Public Papers.*

8. "Informal Exchange with Reporters on Foreign and Domestic Issues," *Public Papers,* 13 September 1984.

9. Dom Bonafede, "Scandal Time," *National Journal,* 24 January 1987, 199-200, 205-7.

10. Walter Karp, "Liberty under Siege: The Reagan Administration's Taste for Autocracy," *Harper's,* November 1985, 53-67; see also John Tebbel and Sarah Miles Watts, *The Press and the Presidency: From George Washington to Ronald Reagan* (New York: Oxford University Press, 1985), 543.

11. Sam Donaldson, *Hold On, Mr. President!* (New York: Fawcett Crest, 1987), 10.

12. Gregor Goethals, "Religious Communication and Popular Piety," *Journal of Communication* 35, no. 1 (1985): 149-56.

13. Michael Baruch Grossman and Martha Joynt Kumar, "The Limits of Persuasion: Political Communication in the Reagan and Carter Administrations," paper prepared for the annual meeting of the American Political Science Association, Chicago, Ill., November 1987.

14. J. Leonard Reinsch, *Getting Elected: From Roosevelt and Radio to Television and Reagan* (New York: Hippocrene Books, 1988), 277, 310.

15. "Remarks at a Republican Fundraising Reception in Whippany, N.J.," *Public Papers,* 15 October 1981. See also "Remarks on Central America at the Annual Meeting of the National Association of Manufacturers," *Public Papers,* 10 March 1983; "Address to a Special Session of the European Parliament in Strasbourg, France," *Public Papers,* 8 May 1985.

16. B.B. Kymlicka and Jean V. Matthews, "The Ideology of the Reagan Revolution," in *The Reagan Revolution?* ed. B.B. Kymlicka and Jean V. Matthews (Chicago: Dorsey, 1988), 23.

17. "Inaugural Address," *Public Papers,* 20 January 1981.

18. "Remarks at a Tribute to Andrew W. Mellon at the National Gallery of Art," *Public Papers,* 27 January 1983. See also "Address to the Nation on the Observance of Independence Day," *Public Papers,* 3 July 1983; "Remarks at a Luncheon Marking the 40th Anniversary of the Warsaw Uprising," *Public Papers,* 17 August 1984.

19. Peggy Noonan, *What I Saw at the Revolution: A Political Life in the Reagan Era* (New York: Random House, 1990), 70.

20. "Remarks on the Program for Economic Recovery at a White House Reception for Business and Government Leaders," *Public Papers,* 11 June 1981. See also "Remarks at the Annual Convention of the United States Jaycees, San Antonio, Tex.," *Public Papers,* 24 June 1981; "Remarks and a Question-and-Answer Session with Members of the City Club, Cleveland, Ohio," *Public Papers,* 11 January 1988.

21. "Radio Address to the Nation," *Public Papers*, 1 January 1983. See also "Address Before Congress on the State of the Union," *Public Papers*, 25 January 1983; "Remarks of Prime Minister Trudeau and the President Before a Joint Session of the Parliament in Ottawa," *Public Papers*, 11 March 1981.

22. Reinsch, *Getting Elected*, 277.

23. "Message to Congress Transmitting the Fiscal Year 1982 Budget Revisions," *Public Papers*, 10 March 1981. See also "Interview with Burl Osborne and Carl Leubsdorf of the Dallas Morning News," *Public Papers*, 8 January 1985; "Remarks Displaying Weapons Captured in Central America at the State Department," *Public Papers*, 13 March 1986.

24. Noonan, *Revolution*, 71.

25. Ibid., 76.

26. "Remarks at the New York City Partnership Luncheon, New York," *Public Papers*, 14 January 1981.

27. Thomas C. Griscom, "Presidential Communication: An Essential Leadership Tool," in *The Presidency in Transition*, ed. James P. Pfiffner and R. Gordon Hoxie (New York: Center for the Study of the Presidency, 1989), 340.

28. "Address to the Nation on Iran-United States Relations," *Public Papers*, 13 November 1986.

29. Reagan made such assurances in eleven public statements. See "The President's News Conference," *Public Papers*, 19 November 1986; "Address to the Nation on Appointing an Independent Counsel to Investigate Arms Sales to Iran," *Public Papers*, 2 December 1986; "Radio Address to the Nation on Iran Arms and Contra Aid Controversy," *Public Papers*, 6 December 1986.

30. "Address Before a Joint Session of Congress on the State of the Union," *Public Papers*, 27 January 1987.

31. "Address Before a Joint Session of Congress on the State of the Union," *Public Papers*, 27 January 1987.

32. "Address to the Nation on the Iran Arms and Contra Aid Controversy," *Public Papers*, 4 March 1987.

33. Ibid.

34. He stressed this in 80 percent of his Iran/*contra* speeches. See "Address to the Nation on Appointing an Independent Counsel to Investigate Arms Sales to Iran," *Public Papers*, 2 December 1986; "The President's News Conference," *Public Papers*, 19 March 1987; "Statement and a Question-and-Answer Session with Reporters Representing the Regional News Media," *Public Papers*, 15 May 1987; "Interview with Television Journalists Representing Nations Participating in the Venice Economic Summit," *Public Papers*, 27 May 1987.

35. Reagan's rhetoric regarding Nicaragua did not change in substance, with

anticommunist language playing a key role. The amount of such rhetoric did pick up, however. Reagan gave, on average, at least six speeches on Nicaragua every month during the period. See "Remarks at the 100th Annual Convention of the American Newspaper Publishers Association, Ellis Island, N.Y.," *Public Papers*, 3 May 1987; "Radio Address to the Nation," *Public Papers*, 8 July 1987; "Radio Address to the Nation on Philippines-United States Relations/Nicaragua," *Public Papers*, 7 November 1987.

36. The data for Bush include his press conferences and speeches from the period between his election and inauguration, obtained through the Federal Information Systems Corporation (hereinafter cited as Federal Information), as well as his public papers dating since his inauguration, obtained through the *Weekly Compilation of Presidential Documents* (Washington, D.C.: Government Printing Office), hereinafter cited as *Weekly Compilation*.

37. Robert E. Denton, Jr., *Primetime Presidency*, xii.

38. "Remarks at the Annual Convention of the United States Hispanic Chamber of Commerce in New Orleans, La.," *Weekly Compilation*, 8 September 1989. See also "Remarks at the National Hispanic Heritage Presidential Tribute Dinner," *Weekly Compilation*, 12 September 1989; "Remarks to Hispanic and Corporate Leaders," *Weekly Compilation*, 6 December 1989.

39. "President-Elect George Bush Address to the National Republican Governors Conference, Point Clear, Alabama," Federal Information, 22 November 1988.

40. "Press Conference: President-Elect Bush and Representative Jack Kemp, Secretary of Housing and Urban Development Nominee," Federal Information, 19 December 1988.

41. Ibid.

42. "President-Elect Bush Meeting With Hispanic Coalition, EOB," Federal Information, 21 December 1988.

43. "Question-and-Answer with President-Elect Bush, Chase Naval Air Station, Beeville, Tex.," Federal Information, 29 December 1988.

44. "President-Elect George Bush Press Conference to Announce New Cabinet Appointment of Secretary of Labor, Vice Presidential Mansion," Federal Information, 24 December 1988.

45. Ibid.

46. "Inaugural Address," *Weekly Compilation*, 20 January 1989. See also "Remarks at the Alcorn State University Commencement Ceremony, Lorman, Miss.," *Weekly Compilation*, 13 May 1989; "The President's News Conference in San Jose, Costa Rica," *Weekly Compilation*, 28 October 1989.

47. "Press Conference with President-Elect George Bush, Room 450, EOB," Federal Information, 17 November 1988.

48. "President-Elect Bush and Representative Jack Kemp, Secretary of Housing

and Urban Development Nominee," Federal Information, 19 December 1988.

49. "Post-Election Press Conference with Vice-President George Bush, Houston, Tex.," Federal Information, 9 November 1988.

50. "Press Conference, President-Elect George Bush on Cabinet Appointments, Room 450, EOB," Federal Information, 22 December 1988.

51. "President-Elect Bush Meeting With Hispanic Coalition, EOB," Federal Information, 21 December 1988.

52. "Delivery of the Centennial Toast by President-Elect George Bush at a Dinner Celebrating the 100th Anniversary of the National Geographic Society, Sheraton Washington," Federal Information, 17 November 1988.

54. "Inaugural Address," *Weekly Compilation*, 20 January 1989.

55. See "Men of the Year: The Two George Bushes," *Time*, 7 January 1991.

56. Fred Barnes, "Issue Isn't Secrecy, It's Deception," *New Republic*, 12 February 1990.

57. See "Remarks to Members of the Business and Industry Association in Manchester, N.H.," *Weekly Compilation*, 13 February 1989; "Remarks at the Electronic Industries Association's Annual Government-Industry Dinner," *Weekly Compilation*, 15 March 1989; "Remarks at the Junior Achievement National Business Hall of Fame Dinner in Colorado Springs, Colo.," *Weekly Compilation*, 16 March 1989.

58. "Address to the Nation on Drug Control Strategy," *Weekly Compilation*, 5 September 1989.

59. "Remarks to the Council of the Americas," *Weekly Compilation*, 2 May 1989.

60. "Address to the Nation Announcing the United States Military Action in Panama," *Weekly Compilation*, 20 December 1989.

61. "Address to the Nation on National Drug Control Policy," *Weekly Compilation*, 5 September 1989.

62. "Exchange with Reporters on the Drug Purchase in Lafayette Park," *Weekly Compilation*, 22 September 1989.

63. "Address to the Nation Announcing the Deployment of United States Armed Forces to Saudi Arabia," *Weekly Compilation*, 8 August 1990.

64. "Remarks and an Exchange with Reporters on the Iraqi Invasion of Kuwait," *Weekly Compilation*, 3 August 1990; "Remarks and an Exchange with Reporters on the Iraqi Invasion of Kuwait," *Weekly Compilation*, 5 August 1990.

65. "The President's News Conference," *Weekly Compilation*, 8 August 1990.

66. "Remarks of President-Elect George Bush at Arrival Ceremony, Andrews Air Force Base, Maryland," Federal Information, 9 November 1988.

67. "Press Conference with President-Elect George Bush, the Naval Observatory, Washington, D.C.," Federal Information, 15 November 1988.

68. "President-Elect George Bush Address to the National Republican Governors Conference, Point Clear, Ala.," *Federal Information*, 22 November 1988.

69. "Post-Election Press Conference with Vice-President George Bush, Houston, Texas," *Federal Information*, 9 November 1988.

70. "Remarks Before the National Assembly, Warsaw, Poland," *Weekly Compilation*, 10 July 1989.

71. Lester Thurow, "Economically Adrift, the Nation Is Soothed Rather Than Led," Los Angeles Times-Washington Post News Service, 31 January 1990.

72. David Broder, "Bush Content to Nibble," *Washington Post*, 31 January 1990.

73. "Bush, on the Mound, Puts His Spin on Pitch to Press Corps," *New York Times*, 26 January 1989, A10.

74. "Congress Still Purring as Bush Applies the Right Strokes," *New York Times*, 31 January 1989, A10; "Kindness Is Foundation as Bush Builds Bridges," *New York Times*, 6 February 1989, A9.

75. "Bush's Bold Message: Reagan Doesn't Work Here Any More," *New York Times*, 24 January 1989, A9.

76. See "Something Borrowed, Nothing Blue," *New York Times*, 10 February 1989, A8; "Statesman Bush's Debut," *New York Times*, 22 February 1989, A1; "The President's Asian Journey, a Bit of Diplomacy on the Fly," *New York Times*, 28 February 1989, A6; "Bush Disputes 'Drift' Image, Says His Team Is 'On Track,'" *New York Times*, 8 March 1989, A12; "Spill in Alaska, Mark on Washington," *New York Times*, 3 April 1989, A12.

77. For a particularly good discussion of this point, see Robert M. Kaufman, "Agenda '89: Strategies and Constraints in a Consolidative Presidency," paper presented at the annual meeting of the Midwest Political Science Association, Chicago, Ill., 1989.

Chapter 7. (Almost) "Everything Old Is New" Again:
The Consequences of Televised Politics

1. Much of the following discussion is based on arguments found in Robert E. Denton, Jr., and Mary E. Stuckey, "Presidential Communication as Conversation: Media Effects on Presidential Speech," paper presented at the annual meeting of the Midwest Political Science Association, Chicago, Ill., 5–7 April 1990.

2. Frederick J. Antczak, *Thought and Character: The Rhetoric of Democratic Education* (Ames: Iowa State University Press, 1985).

3. Kathleen Hall Jamieson, *Eloquence in an Electronic Age: The Transformation of Political Speechmaking* (New York: Oxford University Press, 1988), 90-91.

4. George Reedy, *The Twilight of the Presidency* (New York: Mentor Books, 1970), 158.

5. Tom Wicker, *JFK and LBJ: The Influence of Personality Upon Politics* (New York: Morrow, 1968), 17.

6. Henry Fairlie, *The Kennedy Promise: The Politics of Expectation* (New York: Doubleday, 1973), 11.

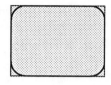

Bibliography

Abramson, Jeffrey B., F. Christopher Arterton, and Gary R. Orren. *The Electronic Commonwealth: The Impact of New Media Technologies on Democratic Politics.* New York: Basic Books, 1988.

Adams, John Quincy. *Lectures on Rhetoric and Oratory.* New York: Russell and Russell, 1962.

Alexander, Charles C. *Holding the Line: The Eisenhower Era, 1952-1961.* Bloomington: Indiana University Press, 1975.

Andrews, James R. *The Practice of Rhetorical Criticism.* New York: Macmillan, 1983.

Arterton, F. Christopher. *Teledemocracy: Can Television Protect Democracy?* Beverly Hills, Calif.: Sage, 1987.

Bailyn, Bernard, and John B. Hench, eds. *The Press and the American Revolution.* Worcester: American Antiquarian Society, 1980.

Baskerville, Barnet. *The People's Voice: The Orator in American Society.* Lexington: University of Kentucky Press, 1979.

Baskerville, Stephen W. *Nothing Else to Fear: New Perspectives on America in the Thirties.* Manchester: Manchester University Press, 1985.

Bell, Daniel. *Power, Influence, and Authority: An Essay in Political Linguistics.* New York: Oxford University Press, 1975.

Benson, Ezra Taft. *Cross Fire: The Eight Years with Eisenhower.* Garden City, N.Y.: Doubleday, 1962.

Berman, Larry. *Planning a Tragedy: The Americanization of the War in Vietnam.* New York: Norton, 1982.

Bernstein, Barton J. *Politics and Policies of the Truman Administration.* Chicago: Quadrangle Books, 1970.

Black, Edwin. *Rhetorical Criticism: A Study in Method.* Madison: University of Wisconsin Press, 1978.

Blair, Joan, and Clay Blair. *The Search for JFK.* New York: Berkeley, 1976.

Bornet, Vaughn Davis. *The Presidency of Lyndon Johnson*. Lawrence: University Press of Kansas, 1983.

Bradlee, Benjamin. *Conversations with Kennedy*. New York: Norton, 1975.

Branyan, Robert L., and Lawrence H. Larsen. *The Eisenhower Administration: A Documentary History*. New York: Random House, 1971.

Brogan, Denis W. *The Era of Franklin D. Roosevelt: A Chronicle of the New Deal and Global War*. New Haven: Yale University Press, 1950.

Brown, Thomas. *JFK: History of an Image*. Bloomington: Indiana University Press, 1988.

Burns, James MacGregor. *Roosevelt: The Lion and the Fox*. New York: Harcourt, Brace, 1956.

Campbell, J. Louis, III. "Jimmy Carter and the Rhetoric of Charisma." *Central States Speech Journal* 30 (Summer 1989): 174-86.

Campbell, Karen Kohrs. *Critiques of Contemporary Rhetoric*. Belmont, Calif.: Wadsworth, 1972.

Canfield, Leon H. *The Presidency of Woodrow Wilson: Prelude to a World in Crisis*. Rutherford, N.J.: Farleigh Dickinson University Press, 1966.

Cannon, Lou. *Reagan*. New York: Putnam, 1982.

Caro, Robert A. *The Years of Lyndon Johnson: The Path to Power*. New York: Vantage, 1983.

Carter, Jimmy, and Rosalynn Carter. *Everything to Gain: Making the Most of the Rest of Your Life*. New York: Random House, 1987.

Chase, Harold W., and Allen H. Lerman, eds. *Kennedy and the Press: The News Conferences*. New York: Crowell, 1965.

Childs, Marquis. *Eisenhower: Captive Hero: A Critical Study of the General and the President*. New York: Harcourt, Brace, 1958.

Cochran, Bert. *Harry Truman and the Crisis Presidency*. New York: Funk and Wagnalls, 1973.

Coffin, Tris. *Missouri Compromise*. Boston: Little, Brown, 1947.

Cook, Blanche Wiesen. *The Declassified Eisenhower: A Divided Legacy*. Garden City, N.Y.: Doubleday, 1981.

Cronon, David E. *The Political Thought of Woodrow Wilson*. Indianapolis: Bobbs-Merrill, 1965.

Cummings, Milton C. *The National Election of 1964*. Washington, D.C.: Brookings Institution, 1966.

Czitrom, Daniel J. *Media and the American Mind: From Morse to McLuhan*. Chapel Hill: University of North Carolina Press, 1982.

Dalleck, Robert. *Ronald Reagan: The Politics of Symbolism*. Cambridge: Harvard University Press, 1984.

Davis, Vincent, ed. *The Post-Imperial Presidency*. New York: Praeger, 1980.

Denton, Robert E., Jr. *The Primetime Presidency of Ronald Reagan: The Era of the Television Presidency*. New York: Praeger, 1989.

——. *The Symbolic Dimensions of the American Presidency*. Prospect Heights, Ill.: Waveland Press, 1981.

Denton, Robert E., Jr., and Dan F. Hahn. *Presidential Communication: Description and Analysis*. New York: Praeger, 1986.

Denton, Robert E., Jr., and Gary C. Woodward. *Political Communication in America*. New York: Praeger, 1985.

Divine, Robert A. *Exploring the Johnson Years*. Austin: University of Texas Press, 1981.

Donovan, Robert J. *Conflict and Crisis: The Presidency of Harry S. Truman, 1945-1948*. New York: Norton, 1977.

——. *Eisenhower: The Inside Story*. New York: Harper & Bros., 1956.

——. *Tumultuous Years: The Presidency of Harry S. Truman, 1949-1953*. New York: Norton, 1982.

Drew, Elizabeth. *American Journal: The Events of 1976*. New York: Random House, 1977.

Duffy, Bernard K., and Halford B. Ryan, eds. *American Orators Before 1900: Critical Studies and Sources*. Westport, Conn.: Greenwood, 1987.

Edwards, George C., III. *The Public Presidency: The Pursuit of Popular Support*. New York: St. Martin's Press, 1983.

Ehrlichman, John. *Witness to Power: The Nixon Years*. New York: Simon and Schuster, 1982.

Elder, Charles D., and Roger W. Cobb. *The Political Uses of Symbols*. New York: Longman, 1983.

Emery, Edwin, and Michael Emery. *The Press and America: An Interpretive History of the Mass Media*. 5th ed. Englewood Cliffs, N.J.: Prentice-Hall, 1984.

Entman, Robert M. *Democracy without Citizens: Media and the Decay of American Politics*. New York: Oxford University Press, 1989.

Erickson, Paul D. *Reagan Speaks: The Making of an American Myth*. New York: New York University Press, 1985.

Eulau, Heinz. *Class and Party in the Eisenhower Years: Class Roles and Perspectives in the 1952 and 1956 Elections*. New York: Free Press, 1962.

Evans, Rowland, and Robert Novak. *Lyndon B. Johnson: The Exercise of Power*. New York: New American Library, 1966.

Ewald, William Bragg, Jr. *Eisenhower the President: Crucial Days, 1951-1960*. Englewood Cliffs, N.J.: Prentice-Hall, 1981.

Fairlie, Henry. *The Kennedy Promise: The Politics of Expectation*. New York: Doubleday, 1973.

Ferrell, Robert H. *Harry S. Truman and the Modern American Presidency*. Boston: Little, Brown, 1983.

Ford, Gerald R. *A Time to Heal: The Autobiography of Gerald R. Ford*. New York: Harper & Row, 1979.

Frankel, Charles. *High on Foggy Bottom: An Outsider's Inside View of Government.* New York: Harper & Row, 1968.

Gaillard, Frye. *The Unfinished Presidency: Essays on Jimmy Carter.* Charlotte, N.C.: Wingate College, 1986.

Geis, Michael L. *The Language of Politics.* New York: Springer-Verlag, 1987.

Glad, Betty. *Jimmy Carter: In Search of the Great White House.* New York: Norton, 1980.

Goldman, Eric F. *The Tragedy of Lyndon Johnson.* New York: Knopf, 1969.

Goodwin, Richard N. *Remembering America: A Voice from the Sixties.* Boston: Little, Brown, 1988.

Gordon, George N. *Persuasion: The Art of Manipulative Communication.* New York: Hastings House, 1971.

Graber, Doris A. *Verbal Behavior and Politics.* Urbana: University of Illinois Press, 1976.

Green, David. *Shaping Political Consciousness: The Language of Politics from McKinley to Reagan.* Ithaca: Cornell University Press, 1987.

Greenstein, Fred I. *The Hidden-Hand Presidency: Eisenhower as Leader.* New York: Basic Books, 1983.

———. *The Reagan Presidency: An Early Assessment.* Baltimore: Johns Hopkins University Press, 1983.

Hadley, Arthur T. *The Invisible Primary.* Englewood Cliffs, N.J.: Prentice-Hall, 1976.

Haldeman, H.R., with Joseph DiMona. *The Ends of Power.* New York: Times Books, 1978.

Hamby, Alonzo L. *Harry S. Truman and the Fair Deal.* Lexington, Mass.: D.C. Heath, 1974.

Harbaugh, William H. *The Writings of Theodore Roosevelt.* Indianapolis: Bobbs-Merrill, 1967.

Hart, Roderick P. *The Sound of Leadership: Presidential Communication in the Modern Age.* Chicago: University of Chicago Press, 1987.

———. *Verbal Style and the Presidency: A Computer-Based Analysis.* Orlando, Fla.: Academic Press, 1984.

Hartman, Susan M. *Truman and the Eightieth Congress.* Columbia: University of Missouri Press, 1971.

Hartmann, Robert T. *Palace Politics: An Inside Account of the Ford Years.* New York: McGraw-Hill, 1980.

Heclo, Hugh, and Lester M. Salamon, eds. *The Illusion of Presidential Government.* Boulder: Westview, 1981.

Hertsgaard, Mark. *On Bended Knee: The Press and the Reagan Presidency.* New York: Schocken Books, 1989.

Holland, DeWitte, ed. *America in Controversy: The History of American Public Address.* Dubuque, Ia.: William C. Brown, 1973.

Hughes, Emmet John. *The Ordeal of Power: A Political Memoir of the Eisenhower Years*. New York: Atheneum, 1963.

Ions, Edmund S., ed. *The Politics of John F. Kennedy*. New York: Barnes and Noble, 1967.

Jamieson, Kathleen Hall. *Eloquence in an Electronic Age: The Transformation of American Political Speechmaking*. New York: Oxford University Press, 1988.

Johnson, Haynes. *In the Absence of Power: Governing America*. New York: Viking Press, 1980.

Jones, Charles O., ed. *The Reagan Legacy: Promise and Performance*. Chatham, N.J.: Chatham House, 1988.

———. *The Trusteeship Presidency: Jimmy Carter and the United States Congress*. Baton Rouge: Louisiana State University Press, 1988.

Jordan, Barbara C., and Elspeth D. Rostow, eds. *The Great Society: A Twenty Year Critique*. Austin: Lyndon Baines Johnson Library, 1986.

Jordan, Hamilton. *Crisis: The Last Year of the Carter Presidency*. New York: Putnam, 1982.

Kantowicz, Edward R. "Reminiscences of a Fated Presidency: Themes from the Carter Memoirs." *Presidential Studies Quarterly* 41, no. 4 (Fall 1988): 651-65.

Kearns, Doris. *Lyndon Johnson and the American Dream*. New York: Signet, 1970.

Kellerman, Barbara. *The Political Presidency: The Practice of Leadership*. New York: Oxford University Press, 1984.

Kerbel, Matthew R. "Against the Odds: Media Access in the Administration of President Gerald Ford." *Presidential Studies Quarterly* 16, no. 1 (Winter 1986): 76-91.

Kern, Montague, Patricia W. Levering, and Ralph B. Levering. *The Kennedy Crises: The Press, the Presidency, and Foreign Policy*. Chapel Hill: University of North Carolina Press, 1983.

Kernell, Samuel. *Going Public: New Strategies of Presidential Leadership*. Washington, D.C.: CQ Press, 1986.

Klapp, Orrin. *Symbolic Leaders*. Chicago: Aldine, 1964.

Klein, Herbert. *Making It Perfectly Clear*. Garden City, N.Y.: Doubleday, 1980.

Kymlicka, B.B., and Jean V. Matthews, eds. *The Reagan Revolution?* Chicago: Dorsey, 1988.

Larson, Arthur. *Eisenhower: The President Nobody Knew*. New York: Scribner's, 1968.

Lasky, Victor. *JFK: The Man and the Myth*. New York: Arlington House, 1963.

Lee, Alton R. *Dwight D. Eisenhower: Soldier and Statesman*. Chicago: Nelson-Hall, 1981.

Leonard, Thomas C. *The Power of the Press: The Birth of American Political Report-ing*. New York: Oxford University Press, 1986.

Leuchtenburg, William E. *Franklin D. Roosevelt: A Profile*. New York: Hill and Wang, 1967.

———. *In the Shadow of FDR: From Harry Truman to Ronald Reagan*. Ithaca: Cornell University Press, 1983.

———. *The New Deal: A Documentary History*. Columbia: University of South Carolina Press, 1968.

Lukas, J. Anthony. *Nightmare: The Underside of the Nixon Years*. New York: Viking Press, 1976.

McPherson, James M. *How Lincoln Won the War with Metaphors*. Fort Wayne, Ind.: Louis A. Warren Memorial Library and Museum, 1985.

McQuaid, Kim. *The Anxious Years: America in the Vietnam-Watergate Era*. New York: Basic Books, 1989.

Magruder, Jeb Stuart. *An American Life: One Man's Road to Watergate*. New York: Atheneum, 1974.

Markmann, Charles Lam, and Mark Sherwin. *John F. Kennedy: Sense of Purpose*. New York: St. Martin's Press, 1961.

Mickelson, Sig. *The Electric Mirror: Politics in the Age of Television*. New York: Dodd, Mead, 1972.

Miller, Merle. *Plain Speaking*. New York: Berkeley, 1973.

Miller, William Lee. *Yankee from Georgia: The Emergence of Jimmy Carter*. New York: Times Books, 1978.

Mollenhoff, Clark R. *The Man Who Pardoned Nixon*. New York: St. Martin's Press, 1976.

Mount, Ferdinand. *The Theatre of Politics*. New York: Schocken Books, 1972.

Nichols, Marie Hochsmith. *Rhetoric and Criticism*. Baton Rouge: Louisiana State University Press, 1963.

Nimmo, Dan, and James E. Combs. *Mediated Political Realities*. 2d ed. New York: Longman, 1990.

———. *Subliminal Politics: Myths and Mythmakers in America*. Englewood Cliffs, N.J.: Prentice-Hall, 1980.

Nimmo, Dan, and Keith R. Sanders, eds. *Handbook of Political Communication*. Beverly Hills, Calif.: Sage, 1981.

Nixon, Richard. *RN: The Memoirs of Richard Nixon*. New York: Grosset and Dunlap, 1978.

———. *Six Crises*. New York: Warner, 1979.

Noonan, Peggy. *What I Saw at the Revolution: A Political Life in the Reagan Era*. New York: Random House, 1990.

Novak, Michael. *Choosing Our King: Powerful Symbols in American Politics*. New York: Macmillan, 1974.

O'Donnell, Kenneth P., and David F. Powers. *Johnny, We Hardly Knew Ye: Memories of John Fitzgerald Kennedy.* Boston: Little, Brown, 1970.

Oliver, Robert T. *History of Public Speaking in America.* Boston: Allyn and Bacon, 1965.

Opotowsky, Stan. *The Kennedy Government.* New York: Dutton, 1961.

Orman, John. *Comparing Presidential Behavior: Carter, Reagan, and the Macho Presidential Style.* Westport, Conn.: Greenwood, 1987.

Osborne, John. *White House Watch: The Ford Years.* Washington, D.C.: New Republic Books, 1977.

Paper, Lewis J. *The Promise and the Performance: The Leadership of JFK.* New York: Crown, 1975.

Parmet, Herbert S. *Eisenhower and the American Crusade.* New York: Macmillan, 1972.

———. *JFK: The Presidency of John F. Kennedy.* New York: Dial Press, 1983.

Pemberton, William E. *Harry S. Truman: Fair Dealer and Cold Warrior.* Boston: Twayne, 1989.

Perrett, Geoffrey. *Days of Sadness, Years of Triumph: The American People, 1939-1945.* Madison: University of Wisconsin Press, 1985.

Pessen, Edward. *The Log Cabin Myth: The Social Backgrounds of the Presidents.* New Haven: Yale University Press, 1984.

Pfiffner, James P., and R. Gordon Hoxie, eds. *The Presidency in Transition.* New York: Center for the Study of the Presidency, 1989.

Phillips, Cabell. *The Truman Presidency: The History of a Triumphant Succession.* New York: Macmillan, 1966.

Potter, David, and Gordon L. Thomas. *The Colonial Idiom.* Carbondale: Southern Illinois University Press, 1970.

Ranney, Austin. *Channels of Power: The Impact of Television on American Politics.* New York: Basic Books, 1983.

Rather, Dan, and Gary Paul Gates. *The Palace Guard.* New York: Harper & Row, 1974.

Reedy, George. *Lyndon B. Johnson: A Memoir.* New York: Andrews and McMeel, 1982.

———. *The Twilight of the Presidency.* New York: Mentor, 1970.

Reinsch, Leonard. *Getting Elected: From Roosevelt and Radio to Television and Reagan.* New York: Hippocrene Books, 1988.

Robinson, Edgar Eugene. *The Roosevelt Leadership: 1933-1945.* Philadelphia: Lippincott, 1955.

Rodgers, Daniel T. *Contested Truths: Keywords in American Politics Since Independence.* New York: Basic Books, 1987.

Roosevelt, Theodore. *An Autobiography.* New York: Macmillan, 1916.

Rovere, Richard H. *Affairs of State: The Eisenhower Years.* New York: Farrar, Straus, and Cudahy, 1956.

Rozell, Mark J. *The Press and the Carter Presidency*. Boulder: Westview, 1989.

Ryan, Halford R. *Franklin D. Roosevelt's Rhetorical Presidency*. Westport, Conn.: Greenwood, 1988.

Safire, William. *Before the Fall: An Inside View of the Pre-Watergate White House*. Garden City, N.Y.: Doubleday, 1975.

Salinger, Pierre. *With Kennedy*. Garden City, N.Y.: Doubleday, 1966.

Schlesinger, Arthur M., Jr. *A Thousand Days: John F. Kennedy in the White House*. Boston: Houghton Mifflin, 1965.

Smith, Gaddis. *Morality, Reason, and Power: American Diplomacy in the Carter Years*. New York: Hill and Wang, 1986.

Smith, Hedrick, et al. *Reagan: The Man, the President*. New York: Macmillan, 1980.

Smith, William Raymond. *The Rhetoric of American Politics: A Study of Documents*. Westport, Conn.: Greenwood, 1969.

Sorensen, Theodore C. *Kennedy*. New York: Harper & Row, 1965.

Speakes, Larry, with Robert Pack. *Speaking Out: Inside the Reagan White House*. New York: Scribner's, 1988.

Spencer, Donald S. *The Carter Implosion: Jimmy Carter and the Amateur Style of Diplomacy*. New York: Praeger, 1988.

Stephens, Mitchell. *A History of News: From the Drum to the Satellite*. New York: Penguin, 1988.

Stockman, David. *The Triumph of Politics: How the Reagan Revolution Failed*. New York: Harper & Row, 1986.

Strong, Robert A. "Recapturing Leadership: The Carter Administration and the Crisis of Confidence." *Presidential Studies Quarterly* 41, no. 4 (Fall 1988): 636-50.

Stroud, Kandy. *How Jimmy Won: The Victory Campaign from Plains to the White House*. New York: Morrow, 1977.

Stuckey, Mary E. *Getting into the Game: The Pre-Presidential Rhetoric of Ronald Reagan*. New York: Praeger, 1989.

———. *Playing the Game: The Presidential Rhetoric of Ronald Reagan*. New York: Praeger, 1990.

Tananbaum, Duane. *The Bricker Amendment Controversy: A Test of Eisenhower's Leadership*. Ithaca: Cornell University Press, 1988.

Tebbel, John, and Sarah Miles Watts. *The Press and the Presidency: From George Washington to Ronald Reagan*. New York: Oxford University Press, 1985.

terHorst, Jerald F. *Gerald Ford and the Future of the Presidency*. New York: Third Press, 1974.

Thompson, Kenneth W., ed. *The Ford Presidency: Twenty-Two Intimate Perspectives of Gerald R. Ford*. Lanham, Md.: University Press of America, 1988.

————. *Ten Presidents and the Press.* Washington, D.C.: University Press of America, 1980.

————. *The White House Press on the Presidency.* Lanham, Md.: University Press of America, 1983.

Thompson, Robert J. "Juggling the President's Time: Constitutional vs. Operational Roles." Paper prepared for delivery at the annual meeting of the Southern Political Science Association, Memphis, Tenn., November 1989.

Thorsen, Neils Aage. *The Political Thought of Woodrow Wilson, 1875-1910.* Princeton: Princeton University Press, 1988.

Truman, Harry S. *Mr. Citizen.* New York: Bernard Geis, 1960.

Truman, Margaret. *Harry S. Truman.* New York: Morrow, 1973.

Tulis, Jeffrey. *The Rhetorical Presidency.* Princeton: Princeton University Press, 1987.

Underhill, Robert. *The Truman Persuasions.* Ames: Iowa State University Press, 1981.

Valenti, Jack. *A Very Human President.* New York: Norton, 1975.

Weaver, David H., Doris A. Graber, Maxwell E. McCombs, and Chaim H. Eyal. *Media Agenda-Setting in a Presidential Election: Issues, Images, and Interest.* New York: Praeger, 1981.

Weinstein, Brian. *The Civic Tongue: Political Consequences of Language Choices.* New York: Longman, 1983.

White, Graham J. *FDR and the Press.* Chicago: University of Chicago Press, 1979.

White, James Boyd. *When Words Lose Their Meaning: Constitutions and Reconstitutions of Language, Character, and Community.* Chicago: University of Chicago Press, 1984.

White, Theodore H. *Breach of Faith: The Fall of Richard Nixon.* New York: Laurel, 1975.

————. *The Making of the President 1960.* New York: Atheneum, 1961.

————. *The Making of the President 1964.* New York: Mentor Books, 1965.

————. *The Making of the President 1968.* New York: Pocket Books, 1970.

————. *The Making of the President 1972.* New York: Bantam Books, 1973.

Wicker, Tom. *JFK and LBJ: The Influence of Personality upon Politics.* New York: Morrow, 1968.

Wills, Garry. *Reagan's America: Innocents at Home.* Garden City, N.Y.: Doubleday, 1985.

Witcover, Jules. *Marathon: The Pursuit of the Presidency 1972-1976.* New York: Viking Press, 1977.

Wooten, James. *Dasher: The Roots and Rising of Jimmy Carter.* New York: Summit Books, 1978.

Wrage, Ernest J., and Barnet Baskerville. *American Forum: Speeches on Historic Issues, 1788-1900.* New York: Harper & Bros., 1960.

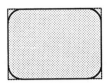

Index